For Judy

Building
Your
Field of Dreams

Blessings & love
Mary
Morrissey

Mary Manin Morrissey

Building
Your
Field of Dreams

BANTAM BOOKS

New York Toronto London Sydney Auckland

BUILDING YOUR FIELD OF DREAMS

A Bantam Book / August 1996

Library of Congress Cataloging-in-Publication Data
Morrissey, Mary Manin.
Building your field of dreams / Mary Manin Morrissey.
p.   cm.
ISBN 0–553–10214–1 (hardcover)
1. Success—Religious aspects—Christianity.   2. Morrissey, Mary Manin.
I. Title.
BV4598.3.M67   1996
248.4—dc20   96–14650
CIP

For information address: Bantam Books.

Published simultaneously in the United States and Canada

Bantam Books are published by Bantam Books, a division of
Bantam Doubleday Dell Publishing Group, Inc. Its trademark, consisting of the words "Bantam Books" and the por-
trayal of a rooster, is Registered in U.S. Patent and
Trademark Office and in other countries. Marca Registrada.
Bantam Books, 1540 Broadway, New York, New York
10036.

PRINTED IN THE UNITED STATES OF AMERICA

MAR   10   9   8   7   6   5   4   3   2

To the Great Spirit,
indwelling all life,
who gives us each the call to build our dreams

A group of young boys knew of a wise man in their village and hatched a plan in order to fool him. They would take a small live bird and stand in front of the wise man. One of them would hold the bird behind his back and say, "Wise man, is this bird alive or is it dead?" If the wise man said the bird was alive, then the boy would quickly squeeze the life out of the bird, responding, "No, the bird is dead." If the wise man said, "The bird is dead," then the boy would present the live bird.

The boys finally received an audience with the wise man. The one holding the bird asked, "Wise man, is the bird in my hand alive or dead?"

The wise man was silent for a moment. Then he bent down until he stood no higher than the boy. "The life you are holding," the wise man told him, "is in your hands."

Contents

AN INVITATION

Whoever you are, whatever your background, wherever you are in your journey of faith, welcome. I invite you to discover a way of living that will make the dreams of your heart come true.

My own greatest dream has been to share the powerful principles in this book with everyone who seeks a greater life experience. After twenty-five years of personal research and application, I know that these spiritual principles can turn your dream into reality. The principles in this book literally saved my life, and over the years I have seen them transform the lives of thousands of people. I know that following the steps detailed in these pages can do the same for you.

This book does not promote any particular religion. The principles contained herein are universal. The foundation of this belief system is "co-creation." God the Creator created creators; therefore, we are all endowed with creative capacities. We cannot help but create, and we can consciously use this inherent gift in partnership with God. This is how co-creation works—it is a melding of human and divine effort toward a shared goal. When you co-create with God, you are guided to the manifestation of a dream beyond anything you could have imagined on your own.

I formed the basis for my ideas about co-creation and dream-building through New Thought, the great spiritual movement that came into being over one hundred years ago with the American transcendentalists, including Emerson and Thoreau, with roots extending to Socrates and Plato. New Thought is the fruiting of the flower found in all the great religions; it differs from more traditional teaching primarily in that it focuses on the message rather than the messenger. New Thought emphasizes increasing awareness in order to produce greater health, better relationships, and an abundance that leads to a deeply fulfilling life.

New Thought portrays Jesus as the great example rather than the great exception. Jesus models for us a life that has no limits and that deems service as the highest activity to which one can aspire. In the course of your dream-building, you will indeed find yourself stretching beyond your present boundaries in pursuit of that which ultimately blesses not only yourself but others as well. For me, the life of Jesus is the one I choose to emulate. For others, Buddha or Mother Mary or Gandhi symbolizes divine wisdom. The particular figure is not as important as your willingness to strive for an amplified way of living.

You will come away from this book identifying yourself in what may be an entirely new way: as a dream-builder. Suppose you have a dream right now, but doubt has rendered you a wishful thinker instead of an active dream-builder. You may possess a vision so magnificent, you fear it can never come true, and so you hesitate to try. I will share with you step-by-step tools for breaking through fear so that you can move forward.

Perhaps you are immobilized by a failed dream. Your broken heart, lost job, bankruptcy—whatever it is—weighs so heavily in your life, there's no room for hope to maneuver. This may surprise you, but all great dream-builders have known failure. What you will discover is how your failures can guide you into a dream greater than the one you lost.

It is entirely possible that you have not yet identified your greatest desire. You simply feel restless. Good. Don't shut off that yearning. That feeling is nudging you toward a more meaningful existence, urging you not to settle for mediocrity.

Deep inside you is a dream for an extraordinary life. You can uncover that extraordinary portion of yourself and bring forth the fulfilling life that is your birthright. By practicing the principles in this book, you will:

- build a base of believing that can support a dream of any magnitude
- learn how to choose a dream and test if it is right for you
- see how to build a dream from idea to reality, one step at a time
- identify and use fear to create positive results
- recognize a way to free yourself from the barriers of your past
- discover how to open the floodgates to untold abundance
- find that your whole life takes on greater meaning and purpose through the very process of building the dream closest to your heart.

Throughout these pages you will meet dreamers like yourself who shrugged off conventional, limited thinking and stepped into a reality others had deemed impossible. Many of the people who have inspired me are or have been members of the ministry I serve. They have been generous in sharing their stories, and their real names have been used whenever possible.

My hope is that you will simply explore these pages and practices with an open mind and a willing heart. Don't take my word that the ideas here will make your dreams come true. I invite you to try them out yourself.

Let us begin. . . .

BUILDING
YOUR
FIELD OF DREAMS

Part One

CLEARING THE FIELD

Chapter One

DIVINE DISCONTENT:
Igniting Your Desire

> If you have faith as a mustard seed, you will say to this mountain, "Move from here to there," and it will move; and nothing will be impossible for you.
>
> —JESUS

- *Honor Your Discontent: Your Longings Call You to a Greater Good*
- *Free Yourself from the Past by Telling Yourself, "Up Until Now . . ."*
- *Become a Conscious Co-creator with God*

Donna Reed was real. I know. I grew up in her neighborhood, in a sprawling split-level smack in the heart of an upper-middle-class suburb called Beaverton, Oregon, complete with doting parents and a shaggy, tail-wagging dog. My life, marked by plenty of friends but few pimples, might have been plucked straight from a 1960s sitcom. My junior year, 1966, promised to be the pinnacle of my high-school career: Within a few short months I had been elected class vice-president, named to the Rhythm B dance team, and been crowned with that most coveted of teen titles, homecoming princess. I wanted to be a schoolteacher when I grew up.

The world had never disappointed me, and I felt invincible, right up until the day I realized I wasn't going to be getting my period after all.

My best friend and I drove my dad's Studebaker to a clinic in downtown Portland, where I'd made an appointment under the name Mrs. Susan Jones. The nurse had me leave my clothing and purse in one room, then sent me to another room for my exam.

Afterward the doctor told me not only that I was pregnant but that he knew my real name. "Mrs. Jones" didn't fool him one bit, and he had taken it upon himself to rifle my purse in search of identification.

"You go home right now and tell your parents," he ordered, "or I will."

It was Mother's Day weekend, and I begged him to give me until Monday, promising my mother would call him to confirm she knew.

Of course, when I got home that afternoon, my mother, who was peeling apples in the kitchen, took one look at my stricken face and asked, "Is something wrong?"

I nodded.

"Did you wreck the car?"

"I wish," I replied, "that I had."

Marriage was the only possible choice. Abortion, unwed motherhood—such concepts did not exist in our household. Although my boyfriend, Haven, and I did what was expected, my parents mourned me as if I had died. All the dreams they had for me—graduation, college, easing into family life at a more mature age—evaporated into nothingness.

Ten days later I became a wife. We didn't have a real wedding. Wearing a hastily purchased blue linen suit one size too large, I sat terrified on a hard courthouse bench with Haven as we waited for our marriage license. My mother sat opposite us on another bench, crying uncontrollably.

Haven had just completed his freshman year of college.

I was sixteen years old.

In those days pregnant girls could not attend regular high schools, but with less than a month to go until the close of the school year, my parents and I decided no one would be the wiser. We were wrong. The news spread with the speed of scandal, and the same students who only months earlier had selected me as one of their leaders now avoided my eyes and cast furtive glances at my waistline instead. "You must be really stupid," a few of my bolder classmates told me. Mothers, including my best friend's mom, cautioned their daughters to keep away. People avoided me as if my condition were contagious.

June couldn't come soon enough. At the end of the year the principal called me into his office and said, "We have a place for people like you."

The "place" was a special school in the inner city for disgraced girls and delinquent boys. The doors didn't open until 7 P.M. Apparently we weren't fit to be seen during the day.

"At least you finished your junior year in high school," my father told me with a sigh.

As my stomach expanded over the summer, I had the prospect of this bleak, nocturnal classroom awaiting me in the fall. Meanwhile, my friends were poring over college catalogues, going to proms, and purchasing college wardrobes. I wore hideous print smocks and checked my profile in the mirror daily, trying to convince myself I didn't "show."

When September rolled around, I went to the segregated evening high school, separated from my friends because I had committed the shameful act of getting pregnant. In my sheltered life, I had never even been to that part of town after dark, but now I walked five blocks alone in a strange part of the city to study geometry with boys who had been arrested. I feared the shadows on those unfamiliar streets. I feared the delinquent boys, most of whom spent class time making paper airplanes and smirking at the girls. Most of all, I feared the future.

My own dreams, however, stubbornly refused to die. Inwardly I said, "I'll show you." I hadn't abandoned my dream of being a teacher. I wrote down the word *teacher* on a scrap of notepaper and jammed it in my coat pocket. Every day I'd reach for that crumpled sheet and gain strength from reading that one word. How I would obtain a high-school diploma, much less a teaching certificate, I had no idea. Intuitively, however, I knew something that my mind could not as yet cognitively process into words. I knew that without dreams, the soul withers and dies.

I believed that something better lay ahead for me, but in the face of so much disappointment, I didn't always believe in my belief. One week before Christmas, our son John was born. I loved him deeply but couldn't help remembering the carefree feeling of past holidays, when the only things that had mattered were getting every present on my list and having a date for the school formal. Now I was listening to carolers with a diaper slung over my shoulder, resenting the effort it took to hang ornaments on the tree. Every time I looked at my husband, I saw his dreams fading, too. He had dreamed of teaching high-school band. Now he had dropped out of college to support us. Every morning he awoke well before dawn, slipped into pressed white trousers and a white shirt, and sped off in a converted white truck to deliver bottles of milk to homes halfway across the county. At night he watched the baby while I went to school.

"Is this all there is?" I asked myself more than once.

Some of the girls I attended class with accepted their lives unquestioningly. They contentedly collected welfare, played with their babies, and boiled macaroni for their husbands. They considered that limited world their lot. I didn't, couldn't, feel superior to them; yet deep down I yearned for a life of greater substance.

"My whole life hasn't been written yet. I'm writing it now. I can be whatever I want to be. The present does not dictate the future." Or so I repeated to myself over and over as I walked the dark, littered streets that led to my school, one hand stuffed in my pocket and touching a crumpled piece of paper with the word *teacher* written on it.

That scrap of paper in my pocket grew worn, the letters on it barely legible. But I clenched my fingers over that paper every day. Maybe I couldn't be a teacher right away, but someday . . . That's how dreams are built. You take a fragment of a possibility and build it thought by thought into an idea. You hold tight and keep believing in the idea.

Mustard seeds come in a little pod which, when opened, reveals thousands of individual seeds. They seem infinitesimally small. If one seed is isolated from the others, an almost impossible task, it appears as a tiny fleck, barely visible on the tip of a finger. Yet the potential for growth in each tiny seed is infinite. This was the message of Jesus: If you possess even a tiny fleck of faith, barely discernible to the eye, it nonetheless is working for you.

Little did I know it at the time, but as a seventeen-year-old teenage mother, I was taking my first steps of what would evolve into an endless adventure in faith. At every turn, even when I've felt most alone, I was not alone. I had a companion who had created me, who had created the universe, and who would not abandon me.

One of my favorite movies is *Field of Dreams*. I love the film because it encourages all of us to take plow in hand and till our own hopes and aspirations into fruition. In the movie, Kevin Costner plays a thirty-six-year-old college-educated Iowa farmer. While out in his cornfield, he begins hearing a voice: "If you build it, he will come." At first Costner's character, Ray Kinsella, thinks he may be going crazy. But as he continues to listen, he begins examining his life more closely. He fears becoming old and ordinary before his time, as his father had after giving up a minor-league baseball career to raise a family and take an ordinary job. Costner's character is guided to create a baseball field from his cornfield, believing that if he does so, his late father's hero—Shoeless Joe Jackson—will return to play. The community thought Kinsella had indeed gone mad when he built a baseball diamond in the middle of nowhere. To make matters worse, his farm was on the verge of bankruptcy. Yet Ray Kinsella's willingness to step out in faith and follow that voice transformed not only his own life but the lives of those around him. The long-dead Jackson did return, bringing with him other ball players. In the end Kinsella's faith was rewarded, and he saved not only his farm but his dream as well.

You can build your own field of dreams. You are the farmer; the field is your life. The earth is available to anyone who is willing to plant. We grow a crop of life through the thoughts we hold. We all have access to an inner voice, but it is not one of reason or logic. Our inner voice is one of guidance. Your inner guidance may not make sense to anyone else in the world, but it can help you recognize and nurture the thoughts that will produce your dream. These thoughts are our seeds, given to us from God in infinite number. We choose which thoughts to plant and how we care for them; we may nourish these seeds with water and delight in their sprouting, or we may neglect them entirely and let the land turn fallow. When you begin to plant, you do not know exactly how your field will look when it is fully grown. Yet when you believe, you continue to nurture the earth even while it remains bare. Faith tells you that something you cannot yet see is growing. As your field begins to materialize out of the dirt, you awaken to the power contained in your very hands by virtue of having planted. And you awaken to the existence of the highest creative power, realizing that when you allow God's will to work through your life, your harvest will be far greater than anything you dared to imagine on your own.

Building your field of dreams changes your life in three essential ways:

First, you come to recognize the deep desires of your heart.

Second, you learn to break through limiting, self-defeating thoughts into a realm where the impossible becomes possible.

And finally, you come to realize that no dream is as great as the person you become for having remained true to it. The crop you harvest may be magnificent. The soul that emerges through the process of your dream-building is more so.

To begin to build your dream, you must first ignite it with an idea. From the void of nothingness, an idea catches spark, setting off the creative process. As creation is described in the Gospel of John: "In the beginning was the word." The word is the idea that you plant in the rich creative soil of your mind, intending to grow it into the life of which you dream. But not just any idea will do. The ideas that can grow great dreams most often come to us from the deep longings stirring in our souls. We are bombarded with so much information that few of us have truly developed the skill of soul sensing. If we long for a more fulfilling life experience, we need to bring the soul's yearnings to the surface and identify them.

♦ Honor Your Discontent

You may not have pinpointed your dream. Or you may have so many hopes and desires that you feel overwhelmed by the idea of selecting the most important. Perhaps you feel bad because you are not content with your life. It doesn't matter. To move into the first phase of dream-building, all your inner rumblings must be brought into the light where you can examine them. For many of us, the moment we feel the stirrings of a restlessness, a yearning, a longing for something better in life, we shut down those feelings. We don't know how to dream, or we dream too small, ask too little. We have so many beliefs that say we can't have, we shouldn't have, we don't deserve. We focus on a lack of education or money, imposing heavy limits on ourselves. The creative power of the universe doesn't have any room to operate and set free that hidden part of ourselves that is chafing at the bit.

God has a wonderful plan for us, but we need to harness all our energy in a positive way if we're to partake in that plan. Discontent without direction breeds nothing but grumbling or numbing. At times, we have all been bitter about a painful void in our lives, but we can't identify the cavity. We complain. We become sour. We settle for a life of mediocrity, living in only a portion of what's possible. We're so quick to listen to others who criticize our yearnings that we shut them off. Many of us who recognize that we're discontented still fall into this trap. Realize that there's a world of difference between whining and wanting. If you shut off your yearning, you grow numb. Many of us have lived lives paralyzed by unexplored yearnings.

In the movie *Good Morning, Vietnam*, Robin Williams's companion, Sergeant Edward Garlick, borrows a bicycle and rides into town. The bike careens out of control and he falls off, his head landing inches away from a moving truck. Later he tells Williams's character: "While I was lying there, my whole life passed before my eyes. And you know what scared me more than anything else? It wasn't even interesting."

If your entire life flashed before you now, would it lull you to sleep?

How alive do you feel in your body, in your relationships, in your work? If you're feeling restless, that feeling could be God's voice speaking to you, saying, "I've got more for you; don't settle. Don't live a little life. There's so much more of you to experience. Don't settle."

Respect the feeling inside you that's nudging you toward a greater experience. This is God's greatest gift—your life—speaking to you. Your inner friction rubs and rubs, creating a divine spark that will ignite your desire into a potent idea.

Today, whenever I feel the urge to shut off my inner yearnings, I think about a friend of mine named Goody Cable. Goody owned a small coffeehouse in Portland, and she worked to make it a place for people who liked to have discussions about literature and truth and making a difference in the world. She enjoyed her business and the friends and authors who would gather at the coffeehouse, but she felt something was missing. She began to feel unsettled, so she went for a long hike one day and asked herself, "What is this restlessness? What is life trying to say to me?" This deep inner restlessness is called *divine discontent*. It is divine because God is sparking those feelings, that restlessness inside you. God's voice is not nagging or tiresome; rather, it is a persistent, loving nudging that guides you to awaken to your own true desires.

"What is my dream?" Goody asked herself as she strode along. "What do I want most?" She began to listen, and she heard, "I want to be able to sit with others and be partners with them in dreaming a new world. I want to be a part of bringing that world forward. What is my role in that?" Then she thought, "Well, some of the best ideas have come forth when people who were really risking to explore new possibilities got together and supported one another and encouraged one another to make a difference. We just need more time." Then the idea came to her to have a hotel—a place where people could gather, stay for a longer period of time, and share their ideas. She wanted a hotel dedicated to authors, with each room decorated in the theme of a different writer.

That dream took Goody through some very difficult waters. She had no money of her own, and nobody wanted to loan her the money to buy a hotel. For two years, bank after bank turned her down. When bank number twenty-nine said no, all her friends told her, "Forget it, Goody. Do something else."

Divine discontent can breathe life into you with a stubborn tenacity, though, and Goody didn't give up. She had created a very clear picture in her mind of one corner of the hotel, the third story, overlooking the ocean. She saw herself there in the library at 1 A.M., with the coffee almost gone, rain pounding the windows, and several people talking and sharing their deepest thoughts.

She had been rejected for two years by more than two dozen banks, but her desire, instead of fading, had only grown stronger. She didn't listen to her friends' advice and decided to try again. When Goody met with bank number thirty, she wanted the loan officer to look beyond the figures on her application and envision the kind of hotel she dreamed of creating. She described in words the hotel her mind had already built. And the officer told her something none of the bank officials had before. He said maybe.

It wasn't easy. Goody had to make three trips to the bank and satisfy a number of legal and financial requirements before convincing the loan officer she was a worthy risk. Then he said yes.

With her loan and renewed energy, she created the now world-renowned Sylvia Beach Hotel on the Oregon coast, named after one of Goody's heroines, the owner of the Shakespeare & Company bookstore in Paris, which was a home away from home to such authors as Ernest Hemingway, Gertrude Stein, and F. Scott Fitzgerald.

To celebrate the completion of her hotel, Goody and her business partner planned an open house at noon on Sylvia Beach's 100th birthday. Rain poured down all morning, so they didn't expect much of a crowd. Yet right at noon, the rain stopped and a triple rainbow shone over the hotel. That day 1,400 people arrived to literally set foot into Goody's dream. They explored the Hemingway room, the Melville room, the Gertrude Stein room, and even the Dr. Seuss room.

Late the following Saturday night, Goody realized how fully she was living her dream. There she was, chatting cozily at one A.M. in the third-floor library overlooking the ocean, rain pouring down outside, the coffee almost gone.

The Talmud says this: "Every blade of grass has its angel that bends over it and whispers, 'Grow, grow.' " You have an angel whispering over you, "Grow, grow. Become, become, become all you can be. Become. There's something wonderful and majestic in you, something beyond your wildest dreams."

You contain much, much more than you know. Your Creator has endowed you with beauty, wonder, and unlimited potential for expression. As you notice your deeper longings, your true desires, you are touching dormant powers. I've learned that one way to bring my greatest longings to the surface is to notice how alive they make me feel. If my desire is sincere—even if I'm worlds away from the reality—just talking about the desire brings forth an energy.

That quality of aliveness was the first thing I noticed about a congregant named Mike after he shared his dream with me. Mike's wife, Colleen, had originally come to me for counseling, distraught that her husband had some "crazy, harebrained idea" to quit his lucrative position as an engineer for a high-tech company near Portland. He craved a simpler life, away from the complexities of city life, away from what he called the rat race. Despite the salary, secure position, and stock options, Mike was discontented. His deepest longing was to move his family 350 miles north to a little spot in the San Juan Islands off the coast of Washington State.

"Impossible," said Colleen. The couple had two young daughters. Wouldn't abandoning his job mean Mike was being irresponsible toward his children? On top of that, Mike and Colleen had purchased a rather splendid house the year before, and the down payment had set them back so far that there hadn't been enough savings left over for a single stick of furniture in the family room. That room had been Colleen's source of discontent. She wanted it filled. Colleen's big plan was to decorate, and suddenly her husband wanted to completely rearrange their lives instead in order to follow some vague longing he felt.

I suggested they come in for counseling together, which they did the following day. As Mike began to describe his longing, an interesting thing happened. There was a brilliance, a sparkle in his eyes I couldn't help but notice. Now that she wasn't preoccupied by her fear, Colleen saw it, too. She watched her husband become alive in a way she hadn't seen in years. She could feel Mike's thrill at the possibility of the life he dreamed of creating with her in his "paradise." Because Colleen deeply loved Mike, she was sensitive to the amplified aliveness, the quickening of enthusiasm and energy Mike expressed as he described his dream. They decided to make a trip to the islands together with open minds.

Mike did not know what work he could find so far away from an urban setting. All he knew was that he was discontented with the couple's present lifestyle and yearned for a greater existence. He had studied engineering in college and had always enjoyed the work. He also enjoyed the salary, if not the long hours and high pressure, yet he felt an emptiness he was no longer willing to deny. Once he allowed the alternative of an is-

land lifestyle to form in his mind, this thought ignited into a flaming desire.

When Colleen and Mike returned, they had made the decision to take steps in the direction of what now had become a shared dream of a new future. Colleen came to realize the real reason her family room felt empty was not the lack of furnishings but the fact that her husband was never there. He worked so much, he barely saw his wife and daughters.

Mike and Colleen honored their discontent by noticing and acknowledging it. They confronted the thoughts that were limiting them, such as the belief they could not live well on anything but a big paycheck and their idea that success could be measured only in terms of acquisition.

Mike and Colleen truly felt more alive as they moved in the direction of the dream. Until that point they had been existing, even prospering, but they were not fully alive because they were occupying only a small portion of themselves; the family room was empty. Mike took a one-year leave of absence from his job so they could explore the new lifestyle. They found an affordable rental on the island and a first job for Mike. Their home sold on the first weekend they had it on the market. They went off to build their new field of dreams, and the postcards and letters I received from them during their early years on the island revealed a vibrantly alive and fulfilled young family.

In your life at this moment, there is something in you that is yearning for a greater expression. If you're not in touch with that yearning, you're not in touch with your true self. If you desire, you have stopped listening to God. Each one of us is greater than our current expression of ourselves. Dreams desires pull at us, tug at us, speak to us, and will not leave us because we came here not to live a cramped, limited life fully and freely express that in ourselves which is divine. desire, not just self-centered interest, comes from God.

The Creator of the universe created you and continues to create through you as you honor your true desires. You discover true desire by first noticing your discontent.

You don't know the great good that God could bring forward through you if you would only listen and follow your deepest, most heartfelt dream. This is the springtime of your mind. Now is the perfect time to plant.

♦ Free Yourself from the Past by Telling Yourself, "Up Until Now . . ."

Many of us define ourselves by our past: Who we are is what has happened to us. "My husband left me, therefore I am not worthy." "I worked years to be an engineer, so I can never leave my job." "I became pregnant at age sixteen, therefore I cannot have a career."

Past and present circumstances influence us—sometimes they may seem almost to crush us—but they do not have to determine our lives. We always have choices, yet we limit ourselves and our life experience by consenting to conditions. We truly have the power within us to say no to past or present particulars and to allow a new life dream to manifest itself in our lives. Your history need not determine your destiny.

We may have been raised with abuse or hardship, and circumstances in our present life may make it easy to stay trapped. Practice telling yourself this: "Yes, bad things happened to me, but I am free to choose again. I am free as soon as I acknowledge that the past does not have to dictate my future. I am free to renew my mind, if I will simply do so."

In the words of Ralph Waldo Emerson, "There is no planet, sun or star that could hold you if you but knew who you are."

Whenever you find a limiting thought interfering with your considering a desire or possible dream, redirect your thinking. When you reach the edge of your knowing and you feel blocked, pause. If you don't pause, you'll repeat your history.

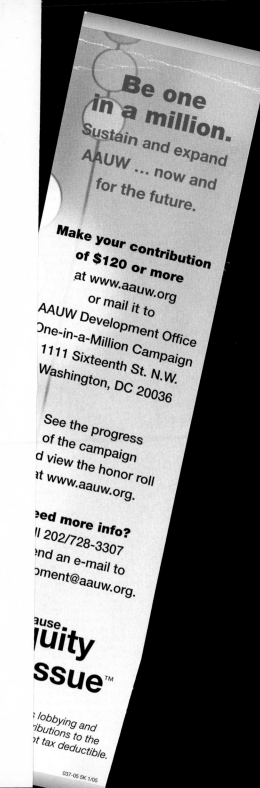

You'll fall back into a familiar pattern. So pause. Then tell yourself, "Up until now . . ."

"Up until now," Goody Cable told herself, "I haven't been able to find financing for my hotel." Up until now. "Up until now, I was only a teenage parent with a limited education. Up until now, I doubted my abilities." *Teen mother, the scandal of Beaverton High School*—those titles belonged to the past; they did not have to ordain the future. And they have not.

Janice, a woman in my congregation, once came to me, desperate over her lack of formal education. "Even though I'd love to, it's too late to go to school now," she told me. "I'm forty-two years old; if I go to school now, I'll be forty-six when I finish my education."

I said, "How old will you be in four years if you don't go to school? The question is, Where do you want to be in your life in four years?"

"I don't know what you mean."

"What is your dream for your life? No limits! If you thought you just might be able to have your dream, and if you were starting fresh with a no-limits attitude, what would you do?"

"Well, I'd . . . I'd begin to look at some colleges."

Janice enrolled in a local community college part-time. She didn't sign up for a full course load; that was too scary for her. But she did sign up for two classes, and she began feeling good about herself. She began to see that her lack of education in the past did not mean she must continue to be uneducated. Janice very deliberately changed the course of her life by telling herself, "Up until now . . ."

"Up until now, I believed school was out of the picture for me. Now I believe . . ."

If you're breathing, God still has plans for you.

A seventy-two-year-old woman graduated from medical school. The woman had been a nun her entire adult life. When asked why she had made the switch, she said the convent mandated retirement at age sixty-five. "I knew God wasn't through with me yet, and it had always been my dream to be a doctor," she said, and so she'd spent the next seven years preparing for the career she would begin in her eighth decade of life.

To open up to dreaming means that we're aware. We can catch ourselves in limited thoughts, such as "What I want cannot happen because I don't have a degree" or "How can I go to medical school? I'm sixty-five, and that's too old." We have all these self-imposed limits. We seduce ourselves into ways of living that appear secure, even if they are ultimately very unhealthy for us. If a part of you is yearning to take up jogging, but you keep yourself home on the couch because you might catch a cold or pull a muscle, you might feel safe—for a time. Eventually your lack of movement causes your muscles to atrophy and your mood to sink. Step outside your safe little world and break through your self-imposed barriers. God is not the one limiting us. We do that ourselves. All we have to do is look carefully at God's creation and we can see abundance everywhere. We are created in the image and likeness of our Creator.

George Bernard Shaw once said, "People are always blaming their circumstances for what they are. I don't believe in circumstances. The people who get on in this world are people who get up and look for the circumstances they want, and, if they can't find them, make them."

I enjoy fables and myths from other cultures, and I often use them as teaching stories on Sunday. One of my favorites is an ancient tale from India that begins as a starving, pregnant tigress comes upon a little flock of goats. She attacks them so desperately that she collapses in exhaustion and dies giving birth to her cub. When the goats return to the field, they find the motherless newborn and adopt him. He grows up bleating and eating grass and believes himself to be a goat. One day a large male tiger pounces on the flock, and the goats scatter. The young cub remains in place, recognizing something dimly familiar about the larger animal. Amazed, the adult tiger asks if the cub actually lives among goats.

"Maaaa," bleats the little tiger.

The adult tiger is mortified at this poor specimen of his species. The little guy, embarrassed, keeps bleating and nibbling grass. So the big tiger brings him to a still pond, where the cub sees his own face for the first time.

"You're no goat," the big tiger tells him. "You're a tiger like me." The little fellow is led to a den, where he's offered the remains of a recently slaughtered gazelle.

"No way," says the little guy. "I'm a vegetarian."

"Nonsense," says the big guy, who shoves a chunk of meat down the small throat. The little tiger gags.

However, when a small piece of meat enters the little tiger's system, he stretches, he bares his teeth, and then he opens his mouth wide and, for the first time, lets out a tiny roar. Then off he goes with his new mentor, into the jungle to hunt.

We are all tigers living as goats. Up until now. That roar, that first roar, is called the roar of awakening.

When we are told, "You are created in the image and likeness of our Creator," the idea is too big, and we gag on it. We can't take it in totally. Take in just a nibble, however, and the idea begins to transform our awareness and, eventually, our lives.

When we still our minds enough, we can begin to sense our divine self, that part in us yearning to roar. Listen to what your heart is longing for. Don't allow fear or "I should have" or the belief that "it can't be" to drive a wedge between you and your desire. Who we have been may have created our limited idea of who we are now and what we can become. But don't let that block you from swallowing the meat of a greater identity. Open your mind and roar triumphantly, celebrating the possibilities that exist inside you. No matter what is happening in your life, it is always too early to abandon hope, too early to relinquish the daily practice of cultivating a faith that can transform your life. You free yourself from being limited by the past when you dare to roar, "Up until now . . ."

♦ Become a Conscious Co-creator with God

Your roar of awakening is only a beginning. As you free yourself from the past, you are confronted by another limitation: your lack of faith in future possibilities. It's not that you cannot create many wonderful things by working hard and using your imagination. You can. But suppose you were not working alone. Suppose that the ultimate Creator was working through you. What then might you create?

Co-creation is at the very heart of my belief system. It has helped me break through barrier after barrier to the realization of each new dream. I define co-creation as partnering with God in order to build the kind of life you want to live. A strong partner guides you through challenges and into excellence, as you no doubt have already discovered. If you play tennis and team up with the club champion for the doubles tournament, your shot at winning greatly increases. Not only do you have the advantage of tremendous skill on your side, but you also possess newfound strength. The sheer knowledge that you'll be playing with the best lifts you to new heights; you stretch for the ball as never before and dare to try shots you once labeled too risky, confident you're backed by a partner whose swing never falters.

Now imagine the most powerful being in the universe as your partner, but instead of playing a game, you're building a dream. With God at your side, encouraging and guiding you through every step of the process, you create a life that is beyond anything your imagination can conjure on its own.

If you believe that God operates through your life, you cannot help but embrace the world as friendly. God's will, God's thinking, and God's power enable you to recognize your discontent as a tremendous dream ready to burst forth. Co-creation means that when you do falter or feel afraid, when your dream seems to be slipping away, you pause and allow God to bolster your spirit again. Co-creation determines how you view the world. If you see the universe as unfriendly, if you see yourself as alone, the universe becomes more daunting and you may cloud your vision with suspicion and doubt. If you believe that God operates through your life, you cannot help but embrace the world as friendly.

There is a beautiful description of co-creation in the words of Henry David Thoreau:

> I learned this, at least, by my experiment; that if one advances confidently in the direction of his dreams, and endeavors to live the life which he has imagined, he will meet with a success unexpected in common hours. He will put some things behind, will pass an invisible boundary; new, universal, and more liberal laws will begin to establish themselves around and within him; or the old laws be expanded, and interpreted in his favor in a more liberal sense, and he will live with the license of a higher order of beings. In proportion as he simplifies his life, the laws of the universe will appear less complex, and solitude will not be solitude, nor poverty poverty, nor weakness weakness. If you have built castles in the air, your work need not be lost: that is where they should be. Now put the foundations under them.

We cannot reach that higher order on our own volition. Even if you believe that you control your own destiny, you remain a finite human being. Your possibilities are limited. When you recognize yourself as a co-creator with God, you have access to unlimited power and an unlimited future. You can ask for help at any time. For a long time I felt limited by my education and diminished by having had my former schoolmates look down on me. I did not believe in the possible. I wanted something more but did not know that my longings were worthy of attention. What about you?

I know it may not be easy to accept this concept. If your life has been stunted by disappointment or embittered by dashed dreams, you may have difficulty envisioning yourself as part of anything remotely divine. You may not believe that a higher power exists that is waiting to guide you toward a greater life. And yet there is evidence of guidance all around us. If we cannot recognize it in our own lives, we can always draw on examples from nature. In Australia there is a very unusual kind of bird called a brush turkey. Once a year the male gathers piles of brush and leaves, and he and his mate build a mound together on the ground. The female lays her eggs in this nest and sits on them; it is the male's job to keep adding and removing leaves every single day, because the eggs will hatch only if the temperature in the nest remains constant. During the day, when the sun is high, he removes leaves from the nest. Then as night falls and the air grows cooler, he adds more leaves to the nest. Scientists have studied this phenomenon and found that the temperature in those nests never varies by more than one degree. How does the male brush turkey know how to regulate the temperature so precisely? How does he know that his vigilance determines the difference between birth and death?

Nature has infused the monarch butterfly with similar direction. In the fall, hundreds of thousands of those beautiful butterflies migrate from our northern meadows as far as two thousand miles to sheltered glens in Florida, Texas, California, and Mexico. They gather on tree trunks and large branches, and there they hibernate. Those butterflies have never been to those glens before. They leave in the spring, never to return. They wing their way north, lay their eggs, and pass on. And yet their offspring are born with inner programming that directs them to show up in the exact same glen every year.

There is the same guidance within us that is in the brush

turkey or the monarch butterfly. That guidance is coded into our true nature. If you plant a corn seed and nurture that seed, it has no choice but to grow into a cornstalk and bear ears of corn. The corn seed will not yield broccoli. Authentic nature always reveals itself. The brush turkey knows how to create and maintain a nest of such delicate balance that its young can safely enter the world. The monarch butterfly knows that its young will find the way to their true destination.

And it is your divine nature, as you are created in the image and likeness of your Creator, to bring forth ideas into form according to your desire. You partner with God to identify the deepest longings of your heart. This is not something you can do on your own. When we separate ourselves from God and attempt to manifest a dream on our own, we are denying our true selves. It would be like the male brush turkey telling his mate, "Honey, the sun's going down and I've had a rough day. Let me just get to those leaves tomorrow, okay?" If he did, nothing would hatch. When we deny our partnership with God, we hatch nothing greater than what our own minds can summon, even though so much more is awaiting us. Deep within you, your life, your divine pattern, is urging you to express yourself. Practice listening. Soul sensing will lead you to your dream.

Begin each day by cultivating your deepest longings, regardless of whether you think they're likely to manifest themselves. As you butter the toast and brew the coffee, listen to your deepest desire. "I may not believe it is probable, but I do believe it is possible that I will . . . own a hotel, even if twenty-nine banks have turned down my loan application . . . teach school, even if I'm a teen parent . . . fall in love, even if I haven't had a decent date in a year."

How can we believe in the possible? I've found a tremendous source of help in the affirmations of Jesus that appear in the

Bible: "For with God, all things are possible." "With men, this is impossible, but with God all things are possible." "All things are possible to him who believes"; "Whatever things you ask when you pray, believe that you receive them and you will have them." "Ask and it will be given to you; seek and you will find; knock and it will be opened to you." "I have come that they may have life, and that they may have it more abundantly."

Every one of these positive statements from Jesus contains within it a qualifier: *with God!* What you desire may not be possible from your human perspective, your limited ideas. It is your willingness to go to a higher level of thinking, a higher level of being that turns the impossible into the possible, the unattainable into reality.

I wish I still had that crumpled piece of paper with the word *teacher* scribbled on it. I'd frame it with the words *If you have faith as a mustard seed . . .*

Growing Your Dream

Your life is a gift from God. You can live only a portion of what's possible in this life, or you can find adventure in building the deep longings of your heart. Take plow in hand and begin to plant your field of dreams.

1. Honor your discontent. Give yourself permission to enter and explore the realm of your deep desires. Harness this discontent by letting the dream begin to live in your mind and heart as a true possibility. Notice your body and your emotions. Does the feeling of desire heighten and your sense of aliveness quicken? If so, keep moving in the direction of your dream. If not, return to the inner chamber and discover a deeper longing.

2. Practice repeating "Up until now . . ." to keep thoughts of your past experience from limiting your possible futures. If you do what you've always done, you'll get the results you've always gotten. Pause for a moment. You'll hear the old chatter that

dictates every reason for not taking a risk. Listen, then pause. All these negative experiences and disappointments may have been true in the past. Now is the time to shrug them off. Your history does not determine your destiny. All your disappointments and regrets belong to a time that is ending at this moment. In the next moment, let out your yearnings in a first roar of awakening. This is a roar of triumph.

3. Consciously co-create with God, and the impossible becomes possible. Co-creation means you partner with God to build the greatest life you can live. When you recognize yourself as a co-creator, you ask for guidance and break through the self-imposed barriers that have stood between yourself and your desires. Begin each new day thanking God and concentrating on a desire of yours that you previously believed was out of reach. Just for that day, act as if what you wanted was possible. Then see what transforms.

Chapter Two

CHOOSING:
Deciding on the Dream

A dream cannot come true unless you dream that dream.
—OSCAR HAMMERSTEIN

♦ *Set Your Intention*
♦ *Test Your Dream with Five Essential Questions*
♦ *Commit to Your Dream*

My son John was just under a year old when I collapsed with a life-threatening kidney disease. The shame and guilt resulting from my unplanned pregnancy had continued to fester to the point that my toxic feelings literally poisoned my body. Tests revealed that my right kidney, ravaged by infection, was sending waste throughout my body, while the left kidney was failing quickly. The doctors gave me six months to live.

The night before I was scheduled to have surgery to remove my right kidney, a minister named Dr. Mila Warn visited me in the hospital. My mother-in-law had heard her preach, and she had asked Dr. Warn to stop by and talk with me.

"Maybe she can help," my mother-in-law told me.

I was doubtful. Even though I'd grown up going to church, I hadn't attended services for the past few years, and I didn't for a minute believe a minister could do anything about malfunctioning internal organs. But if she wanted to pray for me, I wouldn't object. At least, I told myself, a new face would help pass what I anticipated would be a very long evening.

The first thing Dr. Warn did was hand me a pamphlet containing the teachings of Emmet Fox. It was called "The Mental Equivalent." She pointed to a passage that read:

> Whatever enters into your life is but the material expression of some belief in your own mind. The kind of body you have, the kind of home you have, the kind of work you do, the kind of people you meet are all conditioned by and correspond to the deepest mental concepts you hold.

Great, I thought. So my bitter thoughts had killed my kidney, and now they were killing me. It was my fault I was dying. Somehow I didn't feel terribly comforted.

Dr. Warn told me to stop focusing on the past. What I needed to do, she said, was make a decision about my future. Whatever I deeply believed would ultimately greatly influence the outcome of my illness. "Can you believe that you don't need surgery and that both your kidneys are perfect?" she asked.

"No, I can't believe that," I answered truthfully. The tremendous pain in my back could not be denied.

"Then try this," she encouraged. "Think about the right kidney as the repository of all that is presently toxic in your life. Can you do that?"

This I could handle. My insides felt painfully noxious. I told Dr. Warn the story of my disgrace, the feelings of humiliation that still haunted me.

"So imagine," she said, "that when the kidney leaves your body, the toxicity that has been poisoning your life will disappear as well. All your guilt and shame about the pregnancy or anything else can then also be removed. Then, with all the poison gone, your other kidney will no longer be diseased."

While tests had indicated that my left kidney was also badly damaged, it did not hurt as yet, so I figured I had nothing to lose by following Dr. Warn's suggestion. I would try to create a vision of a perfectly healthy organ. And as we continued to talk I made another, deeper decision: I decided that I wanted to live.

It wasn't as if I had consciously wanted to die. Since my diagnosis I had feared death. My heart ached at the thought of leaving behind a baby I loved. I still cherished my dream of teaching. But the dream seemed more elusive than ever, and I didn't feel as if my absence from the world would leave a great void. Life had brought frustration and unhappiness; if I had nothing to look forward to but more of the same, then I wouldn't be missing out on much. In my desolation, I even imagined that my son might be better off raised by someone else.

So while I did not welcome the terrifying experience of dying, I certainly did not object strenuously to my fate. There is a tremendous difference between fearing death and choosing life.

That night I chose life. Dr. Warn remained at my bedside for hours and helped me articulate the new thoughts that would, with God, allow me to build the life I wanted to live. As if a beautiful broom were sweeping away the past, we saw all toxic shame and guilt and unhealthy thoughts being swept into the kidney that would leave my body in the morning. Moment after moment I held fast to the idea of a perfect left kidney. Dr. Warn urged me quietly to focus all my energy on this healthy image.

With God's help, she told me, I would be healed. I wanted very much to believe her.

The next day a baffled team of physicians considered the evidence they found during surgery. Indeed, the right kidney had needed to be removed. The left one, however, contained not a trace of disease. I left the hospital a week later, regaining my strength quickly and feeling alive in a way that went beyond physical health. The scar on my abdomen became an exclamation point marking the precise moment I began my spiritual awakening.

♦ Set Your Intention

My healing experience as a young woman taught me a powerful lesson about intention. I began to learn that I did not have to be a victim of circumstance. With God working through me, I could choose the life I wanted to live and bring my intention to fruition through the thoughts I held.

Have you ever looked in the paper and seen a notice from a bank that is attempting to locate a long-lost client, someone who has money in an account? The person either forgot about that account or never knew it existed, but either way, no one has come forward to claim the money. The funds just sit there, collecting interest, until they're ultimately transferred to the state. The same is true of our lives. Many of us go through life not realizing that we have a key to a rich account, that at any time we can reach in and draw from the currency of life to guide and move us into our dream. Creation's gold mine is in you. The key is deliberate intention. Whatever your dream may be at this moment, identify it. If you cannot define your desire, it can never become a reality.

Setting an intention means declaring a purpose, starting with your thoughts. In Genesis (which means "the beginning of all creation"), we learn that everything originates from thought. In the beginning there was the void. God resolved to fill the emptiness. God had a very specific purpose. God did not begin, "Let there be . . . whatever." God said, "Let there be light." God intended light, and light came into being.

God intended earth. God intended the waters. God intended you and me. We were created in the image and the likeness of God; we are holograms, if you will. So the power, the presence, the energy is within you and me. The energy of God, as life, is within each of us. You have a divine identity as a co-creator with God, the source of all life.

The greatest control you have in your life is the power to direct the thoughts that help your dream take form. We are always constructing the fabric of our lives with our thoughts. If you do not exercise that control, the fabric of your life becomes flimsy. For instance, if you say, "I want something, but I don't know what. I will leave it to God to decide," you are foolish; you are not setting an intention. You must be willing to take responsibility for your wishes and desires if you want to make them real. If you merely wish for a greater life but do not specifically channel your energies into charting that future, the life force moving through you has no definite direction. How can God assist you in a dream that you have not specified?

Identify the life you would like to be living as best you can see from where you're standing. Everything created in the world of form was first identified in mind. Anything you see was first an idea, a blueprint in the mind, and through the power of intention became a pattern. That pattern evolved into something that now we can touch, see, smell, taste, feel, or experience.

You create continually with your thoughts. You can create basically the same life with very little difference over and over again, year after year. You can experience the same life relentlessly, with a little different color to it, a slightly altered texture. Or you can co-create with God, moving confidently in the direction of your dreams. What thoughts are you holding? Do any of these thoughts clutter your mind and prevent you from setting a firm intention for your dream? Clearing your mind isn't always easy. Buddhists call the chattering mind a jumping monkey. You're thinking all the time. At any given time you're running through a myriad of thoughts, perhaps about what happened before, what's going to happen later, whether you're hot, whether you're cold, that awful thing so-and-so said about you. Thoughts may race at a hundred miles an hour, yet you can learn to tether and calm your mind. Just because a thought enters your awareness doesn't mean you have to nourish it with your attention. Direct your attention. The chattering mind undermines your intention by distracting you from your dream.

You can clear your mind much the same way you take a photograph. First you focus, concentrating on the detailed picture of what you want to develop. You can't move toward your dream without knowing what you want to move toward. You take care to use the proper light, so that your final picture is not obscured by shadows. You beam light as energy onto the dream. You direct all your intention toward capturing a fleeting image and turning it into something lasting. Help yourself focus by moving closer to your target; even the best lens can't pinpoint an image a million miles away. Once you learn to focus your mind in this way, what you begin to see through the lens of your life becomes startlingly clear. The mental debris falls away.

When you hold an intention, you direct energy. If you do not consciously intend your dream to become reality, you unconsciously intend that something else will take form. Your very nature directs energy. We make countless choices every single day based on our intentions. Deciding what to eat, what to wear, or whether to pay the electric bill instead of the water bill impacts our lives in ways large and small. Your emotions, relationships, home, career,—every part of your life springs forth from intention.

We will experience all these aspects of our lives, but *how* we experience them is in our hands as a co-creator with God. The only thing we totally control is the thought we think, the thought we nurture. As we nourish that thought and cultivate it through action, we reap a crop called our life.

Setting your intention creates priorities. Your priorities are how you order the decisions you make, the way you decide how to use your resources. If you are going to grow a garden, you design it first in your mind. You don't just toss a bunch of seeds over your shoulder and hope for the best. If you love sweet corn, you space the rows in a manner that allows the stalks to be cross-pollinated. If you intend to make spaghetti sauce, you leave plenty of room for tomatoes and basil.

I learned a long time ago that if I really wanted to bring my ideas into experience, I needed to write down my intentions. When you put pen to paper, you have little choice but to get specific. The actual process of forming your thoughts into words on a page is a creative act, a genesis, moving energy toward the very thing you want to experience. Purchase a small spiral notebook and write on the front "My Dream Journal." Keep in this journal the deepest dreams of your heart. Describe, as specifically as possible, what your life will look like when your dream comes to fruition. Use the power of your imagination to identify a dream that is a deep longing of yours. Do not dismiss your dream as unobtainable. Do not edit your journal by telling yourself, "What I really want is impossible. Maybe I should just settle for . . ." There is no need to render your dreams puny by crossing out what you truly desire. The likelihood of a dream coming true is not based so much on what your logical mind tells you but on your willingness to form an intention, to risk, to step out beyond your current experience.

♦ Test Your Dream with Five Essential Questions

When something as important as your life is at stake, you want to be confident that you have chosen to pursue the dream closest to your heart. You can learn to separate your true desires from your passing fancies, those things that diminish over time. If you have children, you know what I mean about passing fancies. Little ones may whine and plead and beg for some over-priced superhero contraption they saw advertised on television. Even though it goes against your better judgment, you finally relent and buy it. A week later you find the former object of your child's desire broken and buried at the bottom of the toy chest, never to be played with again. As adults, we like to think of ourselves as being somewhat less fickle, yet the truth is that we frequently pursue dreams that have no more substance than a cheap plastic toy. How do you know you have chosen a dream God will join you in manifesting? How can you depend on your dream?

What we're going to do is subject your dream to some rigorous tests, but these tests differ vastly from those you've undertaken before. Just as the FDA does not approve a drug for public consumption until it has been rigorously reviewed and analyzed, so too will your dream be held up to the brightest light and evaluated. The difference between testing a drug and testing a dream is that instead of looking for flaws—does the drug cause side effects such as nausea, dizziness, or vomiting?—you are seeking that which makes your intention pure and honorable: You are testing to confirm the presence of God in your dream.

Ask yourself these five essential questions: *Does this dream enliven me? Does this dream align with my core values? Do I need help from a higher source to make this dream come true? Will this dream require me to grow into more of my true self? Will this dream ultimately bless others?* Let's look at each component of the test in more detail.

1. *Does this dream enliven me?* This is your starting point. Feel your own life energy in regard to the dream. Does the mere thought of your dream quicken your pulse? Is it something you

want passionately? Do you feel an amplified sense of aliveness
as you vividly imagine living the fulfillment of this dream? If
you don't answer yes to these questions, if that dream is just a
big "I should," then you won't harness the energy to bring your
desire into form. When distraction tempts you, when you feel
like turning away, you won't have anyplace in yourself from
which to draw forth the enthusiasm required in order to manifest the dream.

Frank, a member of our congregation, had every reason to be
distracted from his dream, which was to grow an orchid garden
large enough to supply local florists. Frank had AIDS. Yet his
passion for his dream was bigger than his disease, and he decided that illness did not mean he had to forego his dream.
Frank admired in orchids their hidden strength; despite a fragile
appearance, their beautiful blooms can last for months, outliv-
ing far sturdier-looking flowers.

When the dream to grow an orchid garden first came to him,
Frank didn't know much about horticulture, and while his finances were stable, he was by no means wealthy. Orchids are
very expensive, and they mature slowly. Frank checked off his
obstacles one by one: limited knowledge, limited finances,
and—most critical—limited time. Frank knew he would very
likely die before turning thirty-five. And yet every time he
closed his eyes, he saw orchids. He believed that his enthusiasm, combined with God's, would bring forth his garden.

Frank read everything he could on orchids; he visited local
nurseries; and he so infused others with his enthusiasm that
soon friends and acquaintances were working beside him in the
greenhouse. He did not allow himself to be distracted. When
the first buds refused to blossom, when he grew weary in the af-
ternoons, Frank kept going. He held his dream clearly in mind
and took one step after another. As a result, not only did he create an exquisite orchid garden, but he also eventually opened
his own flower shop.

Shortly before he died, Frank and I had a conversation. He smiled, his eyes full of deep knowing, as he told me how grateful he felt to have spent his final years building a dream that would live on beyond him. His happiness and peace taught me a great lesson about being fully alive, even in the face of death.

The root of the word *enthusiasm* is *entheos*, which literally means "God within." In this spiritual test, it is not the obstacles to your dream that count but rather the magnitude of the enthusiasm you bring to it.

2. Does this dream align with my core values? You cannot pursue a dream that forces you to compromise your fundamental sense of integrity. Pursuing your dream will cause you to make many difficult decisions; inevitably you will come across some shortcut to your dream that also cuts deeply into your values. You will be forced to choose one over the other. In this spiritual venture of dream-building, it is critical that at each juncture, each crossroads, you remain true to your self.

When I was a little girl, I used to love the TV show *Leave It to Beaver*. In one episode, Beaver brought home his report card, on which he had received a D. He laid the report card on his father's desk, hoping his dad would sign without really looking so that he could take the card back to school. That afternoon Wally and Eddie Haskell were in the house and happened to see the report card. Eddie noticed that Beaver had a D. After Wally left the room, Eddie very carefully made the D into a B.

Ward signed the card and sent it off with Beaver the next day. That evening, Ward called Beaver into his office and said, "Beaver, I've got to talk to you. Your teacher called today and told me she had given you a D on your report card, but when you returned it with my signature, that D had been made into a B."

Beaver said, "Well, I didn't do it, Dad."

"Beaver, that was very carefully changed from a D to a B."

"But I didn't do it, Dad."

His father said to him, "It's one thing, Beaver, to change a D into a B on your report card. It's quite another thing to lie about it. Are you going to stick with this story?"

Beaver gave this some thought. Then he spoke a great truth about us all: "Gee, Dad, I guess if you have only one story, you have to stick to it."

There is only one true story about you. You are a child of your Creator, endowed with creative abilities. You can be only who you are. You've got only one story, just as the universe has one song: *I'm alive!* You are created in the image and likeness of your Creator and thus endowed with divine creativity. You cannot help but create. When you choose a life-giving dream that adheres to your deepest values, God, the creative power of life itself, will join you.

A man in our congregation, Richard, told me he had spent his entire life building the dreams he believed would make other people happy. He had taken over his father's contracting business to please his parents, although he believed his true vocation to be in architecture. Richard had married a woman he was fond of but didn't try hard to love. He raised his family in an upscale townhouse that his wife had chosen because it gave him the best access to his clients. What he really wanted was to design a Victorian farmhouse and move to the country. Over the years he and his wife, never close to begin with, drifted apart, but none of their friends and business associates ever knew. The couple maintained the appearance of the ideal family, hosting parties and attending all the prominent functions in town hand in hand. Richard knew how important this social position was to his wife. Yet at home he and she rarely spoke to each other.

Finally he awoke to the realization that while consideration of others was one of his essential core values, he had somehow left himself out of the equation. He realized he had been living someone else's dream, not his own. And the truth is that Richard, for all his placating, had not succeeded in making anyone happy. You cannot bring genuine joy into the lives of others when you deny your authentic self.

So Richard reentered his own life. He decided he would find a way to design and move into the house of his dreams. He also set an intention to no longer accept mediocrity in his marriage. He would try to turn it into something meaningful by pouring every ounce of his love into it, and if that didn't work, Richard would free himself and his wife for something better.

One day Richard showed me something he had created to remind him of his intentions. It was a large gilded birdcage. Inside he had placed a Ken doll and a Barbie doll climbing a ladder that led nowhere. Richard called this his "shrine to the gods of other people's approval." This "shrine" helped him bear in mind that in all his choices, he must ultimately be true to himself.

I remember a funeral I performed for the father of a member of our congregation. Vicki's father had died very suddenly at the young age of sixty. She told me about his lifelong dream of adventure. Even as a boy, he had wanted to go deep-sea diving, long before scuba diving equipment became available in Oregon. Later in life, he actually dove all over the world with Jacques Cousteau. He specialized in underwater photography, so that he could share the gift of his undersea treasure with others, and went on to win international photography awards. In his fifties he took up flying, adding the dimension of air to his adventure of sea.

At his funeral Vicki read aloud a message that conveyed her father's deepest values. It was inscribed inside the cover of a book he had given her: "This describes my philosophy of life. The only obligation you have in any lifetime is to be true to yourself. This has been the premise and the power of my life. May you find this for yourself, sweetheart. Love, Dad."

Be true to you! Hold your thoughts to the highest possibility that you can see at any given moment. Once you choose a dream that aligns with your values, the Spirit will guide you into even greater experiences, made available from the vantage point of a higher vision. What you chose five years ago won't be what you choose now, and what you choose at this moment will differ from what you will choose five years in the future; but if you don't make the choice for today, you cut yourself off from options that await you down the road.

Sometimes what we want seems tantalizingly close, with only our integrity separating us from what we deeply desire. To grab hold of our dream, we are tempted to shove that integrity aside momentarily, promising we'll put it back in place at a more convenient time. But true dream-building doesn't work that way. You are required to remain true to your core values at all times, even as you are confronted with questions for which there is no clear, black-and-white answer.

Let's say, for instance, you are a person who has strong feelings of loyalty. Perhaps you've even grown up in a union family. You believe in sticking up for the team and that every individual has an obligation to serve his or her fellow humans.

Let's say further you've identified your desire for a new home for your family. You've collected brochures, reviewed the plan, and budgeted carefully, but your salary just won't allow a costly investment. Suddenly you're offered a promotion at work that comes with a hefty raise. The only catch is that the person you'll be replacing, a person who has mentored you in your position, was fired—unfairly, you believe, because of his age.

Now, remember, *you* didn't fire anyone. You aren't responsible for the discrimination. You've worked hard and deserve a promotion. Taking the job would make your dream of a new home come true. Your family would be ecstatic. You might even vow to fight age discrimination from your new position of higher authority.

What do you do? You are really tempted. Were you to turn

down the job, how could you possibly explain to your family that you let an opportunity for the dream home pass you by? You are tempted, but you must abide by your own moral compass. If you are the person who holds loyalty as a primary value, you recognize that taking the promotion does not feel right to you. Even though you had done nothing to further this person's firing, you would feel that you had unjustly profited from it. This is where your value system comes into play. If you find that obtaining your dream compromises what you believe in, your dream will always feel tainted. You cannot move into that home with a free and open heart. Hard as it is, the person who holds loyalty as a primary value will know, deep inside, that the house must wait a little longer, until the time is right. Being true to yourself is a critical step in testing your dream.

3. *Do I need help from a higher source to make this dream come true?* If you think you alone can accomplish the dream, then your dream is not big enough. If you think you can control every detail, then your scope is restricted. You have no room for God in your dream. To access this higher source, you need to willingly grow, which is impossible to do if you're full of your own ego. The dream must be bigger than you know yourself to be, so that you learn to allow the higher source to do for you what you cannot do for yourself.

In chapter one we talked about co-creating your dream with God, your higher source or power. God can see possibilities that extend well beyond your limited vision. When you allow God to assist, you will be guided into a more fulfilling dream than the one for which you've already mapped out each detail of the journey. God offers guidance that comes to you in the form of inspired insight, and you will be led, step by step, if you listen. If you already think you've got all the answers, then you dismiss inspired ideas as unnecessary or encumbering. Alone on your journey, you may reach a desired goal, but your destination pales in comparison to the place God's guidance would have led you to.

Because the dream is bigger than you, you're going to have to grow and perhaps endure some struggle. Those who recognize and accept struggle manage to make their labor look effortless, yet they are toiling just as the rest of us do, only reaping larger results. Mother Teresa, during an interview with the BBC, was asked, "You know, Mother, it's easy for you to be dedicated to service more so than us ordinary householders. You don't have a house, you don't have possessions, you don't have a car, you don't have insurance, you don't even have a husband."

And Mother Teresa replied: "Wait a minute. I do have a husband." She pointed to the ring on her finger, worn by her order of nuns to symbolize their marriage to Jesus. She said, "I do have a husband, and I want you to know that sometimes He can be very difficult." Sometimes it does feel difficult. The dream that's trying to be dreamed through the lens of our lives does feel big. It should feel bigger than something we think we can accomplish ourselves with our present resources.

Once there was a man who died and found himself in a beautiful place surrounded by every conceivable comfort. A white-jacketed attendant came to him and said, "You may have anything you choose—any food, any pleasure, any kind of entertainment." The man was delighted and sampled all the delicacies he had only dreamed of on earth. Eventually, however, he grew bored. Calling the attendant to him, he said, "I have tried every good thing I could think of, and now I am tired of all of this. I need something to do. What kind of work can you give me?"

The attendant sadly shook his head and said, "Well, I'm sorry, sir, that's the one thing we cannot do for you. There is no work for you here."

To which the man answered, "That's a fine thing. I might as well be in hell."

The attendant asked softly, "Where do you think you are?"

A dream without struggle is a dream without substance. But

we will not be struggling alone. We don't know exactly how our dream will be accomplished. We don't even know if it's probable. But we can believe that with God's help it is possible. That's why we need a higher power. Our job is not to control every last detail, but to let God move through our lives in a more powerful way. You are a single point of awareness in the mind of God, and God's gift of inspiration may reveal itself only one idea at a time. Once you follow that guidance, another idea will present itself to you. Then you take the next idea and the next, and finally you look around and realize you have built a new life. God, the energy of creation, is at the center, urging you along, guiding you to a larger life if you are willing to seek higher help.

4. Will this dream require me to grow into more of my true self? If the dream is bigger than you at the outset, who will you become as you grow into it? Remember, your dream is that part of you longing to express itself. Every choice you make that requires you to grow and stretch moves you closer to your true self. The "you" that has defined the dream is not the "you" that will exist once it has manifested itself. The transition between these two states or expressions requires the lesser you to surrender to the greater you. You're leaving a limited life and moving into a larger one. You are bringing out that part of yourself that's been boxed in, tucked away. As you mold those longings into reality, you are growing and stretching, more accurately expressing your true self.

Others may doubt or attempt to dissuade you. After all, people can look kind of awkward when they stretch. Remember the story of Noah? By building an ark, he became who he was meant to be. At first this was a dream neither his family nor his friends could understand; everyone around him said, "This is crazy. You're building a big boat in the middle of dry land." Yet Noah kept at that ark even as his neighbors ridiculed him. Others may think you're crazy to follow your dream, to risk. You yourself may sometimes feel the same way. Conformity tempts all of us at times; we're all tempted to lower our aims and conform to somebody else's expectations, thus denying our divine nature and deeply held dreams.

A woman who sings at our church, Debbie, told me a story to share with our congregation. She went through a very broken period in her life because she said no to her divine nature. Her greatest joy was singing, yet her song was drowned out by her mother's voice, heard deep in the caverns of her memory. "Singing isn't a real job," Debbie's mother had told her. "To be a success, you have to be in the business world, and if you haven't made it in business, you're nothing. You won't amount to anything if all you do is sing."

She followed that limiting voice instead of her divine nature, and it made her sick. Living in limitation gradually squeezes the life out of you. The way it squeezed the life out of Debbie was through a gradual mental and emotional breakdown. She spent weeks lying on a couch taking drugs and watching television. After fourteen days or so of relentless channel-surfing, she began to turn on the daytime talk shows because, as she put it, they had people even stranger than her on. It began to give her a little hope.

One afternoon she flipped to *Oprah*. On came Dr. Bernie Siegel and the minister Louise Hay. They were very different kinds of guests from those she'd been watching, and she paid more attention. At first it made her angry to hear what they were saying, that you really can heal your life. No matter what's happened to you, no matter how far you've sunk, you can be led into a magnificent life. She thought, "What do they know?" She was angry, yet something in their message resonated in her heart.

The message Noah received never stopped resonating, and thus he kept building his ark. He built one window in the ark, placed directly overhead so that the only way to look out was to look straight up. When you're building the dream of your life, look up. Build yourself an ark, a sacred place in your mind where your dream is safe from the flood of doubt, disapproval, and disbelief that drowns most dreams before they ever have a chance. Just before the floods came, Noah filled his ark with animals. After forty days and forty nights of rain, Noah let a dove out the window. When the dove returned with an olive branch, he knew the flood was over. His dream had saved them all for a new life.

So Debbie began to build herself an ark. She had lain on that couch watching soap operas and feeling sorry for herself for a long time. Then a new dream got through. She got up off the couch. She threw away her bathrobe, got dressed, and bought a book on self-healing. She was building a thought form, a new way of holding herself in a covenant with God. There is a covenant or promise in how the universe works: If we take one step toward a greater life, God takes a hundred steps in helping us. She yearned deeply for a new life. She both saw herself where she began—as a couch potato—and saw the true self that would be revealed as she grew into her dream. "I love singing," she thought. "I will be a singer."

This was a dream bigger than what she alone could accomplish. Debbie sought guidance from within. "Take a pen and paper," her guidance told her, and music began to flow through her. She had never written music before, but now it was all over the page. She recognized that all along life had not been victimizing her. She'd been trapped by old ideas that limited her. Her breakdown, her shattered sense of self, was really the opportunity to break through to her whole self.

If you're feeling broken right now, you will stay broken only to the degree that you don't let God lead you. Noah built an ark. He was willing to move into a new emptiness, into a place he had never been before. Debbie took her whole self into her ark. She asked the higher power, "All right. What would you have me do?" Only this time she really listened. She heard one word: "Sing." Debbie began singing again, and as she did so music began to pour through her. She wrote it down. The next message she heard was: "Create a cassette tape." She took her savings and made a cassette tape that she sent to Louise Hay, thanking the minister for helping to rebuild her life.

A week later Louise called Debbie and said, "Girl, you can sing!" Louise invited her to sing at seminars she was conducting all over the world. Since that time Debbie's whole world has opened up. There is music throughout her life; she has traveled, met the man of her dreams, and married. She continues to sing.

You may tell yourself, "I'm no Noah"; you may tell yourself, "I've got a tin ear." In other words, you don't think you have the talent or ability to create something wondrous. You feel ordinary. This may surprise you, but people who accomplish extraordinary things possess nothing more extraordinary than you do. They just have thought in bigger ways. They know that their thoughts will shape their lives. Extraordinary people are ordinary people who seek to uncover the extraordinary that already exists within them.

To manifest my dream, will I be required to grow into this more extraordinary version of myself? If the answer is yes, proceed.

5. Will this dream ultimately bless others? This is the final test of your dream. Every good and true dream has a seed within it that can bless and benefit others, because in this universe there is no such thing as a private good. We are all connected in the intricate web of life force, and what harms one ultimately harms all, just as what is truly good for one is ultimately good for all.

My first big dream was to be a teacher. Anyone who has ever taught children or dreamed of teaching can see that in education, opportunities to benefit others abound. Your passion for learning infects the youngsters in your classroom, and they double their efforts to master reading and math; your belief in the worthiness of your students bolsters their self-esteem. In some cases, you may be the only person who believes in them. Your caring may make the difference between their dropping out of school and their going on to finish their education.

"That's fine," you may say. "But what if I just love selling real estate? What if I feel tremendous energy for a goal such as selling $5 million worth of property a year?" Benefit to others is fairly simple to test if your dream includes joining a helping profession or is inherently philanthropic. Frequently, however, the benefit to others is less obvious. As a real-estate agent, say, you may find homes for families who didn't think they could afford them and, in doing so, literally help move those people into their own dreams. Furthermore, if your dream has withstood the first four questions, you cannot help but become a real-estate agent who benefits others. Your transactions will be honest, and you will willingly struggle, going the extra mile to find the right home for each client. Your enthusiasm for the profession and your refusal to coerce a sale or compromise your integrity will do more than ensure your own prosperity; your integrity will set standards for others in the profession to follow.

Benefits may abound that are beyond your vision at this moment. Debbie's singing makes her happy, but it also brings joy to everyone who hears her voice. When I chose to live, to visualize my left kidney as healthy, I knew that my son would benefit by virtue of having his mother alive. What I did not know at that time was that I would become mother to three more beautiful children. These children grew up to have an impact on and bring joy into the lives of others. We benefit others by choosing to cherish our own dreams.

Put your dream to the test. Can you answer yes to these five questions? If so, you have passed a spiritual exam more rigorous than any laboratory could administer, and you have confirmed God's presence in your venture. You have established a dream worth spending a portion of your precious life in building.

♦ Commit to Your Dream

Think about all those promises you may have made to your-self over the years only to break them: lose weight, take up jog-ging, make more money, stop smoking, find and maintain a loving relationship. You began with such high hopes. Why did your commitment falter? What stands between us and the deep-est desires of our heart? Commitment is where we begin the work of putting our faith into action. Commitment is required to grow the dream from idea to substance, from little sprout into full blossom.

Primary commitment is an inside job; you invest your mind and your heart. Invest yourself mentally by creating a clear, focused picture of where you're headed so that you can move to-ward it. Mental commitment is an energy dynamic; where you place attention, therein lies your intention. Invest yourself emo-tionally by keeping your passion alive. Unless you are committed to your dream, over time your energy wanes. When the unexpected arises, throwing you off track, you give up. If you can maintain your enthusiasm for the dream, you will draw to it greater inspiration and substance. Doors open in the form of new opportunities and fresh guidance, yet you've got to remain pliable. Your commitment to willingly be molded moves you into the space and shape in which your dream can come true.

As the joke goes: "In a ham-and-egg breakfast, the chicken is involved, but the pig is committed." Whenever you're merely involved, part of you stands outside the experience, deciding whether or not to invest your full energy. You let relationships wane by withholding your full energy. When the relationship disappears entirely, you pat yourself on the back for not having thrown too much away on a losing proposition. The same is true of our dreams. Without full commitment, the moment something goes awry, our dreams slip away, and we tell our-selves, "See, it wouldn't have worked out anyway."

Your commitment is required to build your dream. True commitment is much greater than simply "feeling committed." If you participate in life only to the degree it suits you, you will inevitably come up short. True commitment moves us past our inertia and into a new way of being. If you're a parent or pet owner, you understand this high level of commitment. If the baby cries in the middle of the night, we don't relish leaving our warm beds to change a dirty diaper. If the dog gets out of the house at two in the morning and wanders away, we probably would much rather stay under the covers than get up and search for Fido. But we do these things because our commitment is bigger than the inconvenience.

Are you willing to do whatever it takes to remove the obstacles between yourself and your dream? In the movie *The Empire Strikes Back*, the Jedi master Yoda told Luke Skywalker, "No. Try not. There is no try. Do. Or do not. " When we say, "I'm trying," the truth is that we are participating at less than full commitment. It is the doing—the persistence—that creates dreams from our desires.

Some people may shrug off responsibility and say that whatever happens is God's will, but that's the easy way out; that's not doing. If you want your dreams to become manifest, you must do. A friend told me a story that I've used in sermons to help illustrate this point. An extension agent is going through the countryside and comes upon an absolutely gorgeous farm. He stops to chat with the farmer, who is sitting in a rocking chair on the front porch, chewing on a piece of straw. "You have a magnificent farm, one of the prettiest I've ever seen," the extension agent says. "God has really done a great thing here on this farm."

And the old farmer snorts, "Yeah, I suppose so, but you should have seen it when God had it alone."

The universe can do for you only what it can do through you. You have been given the capacity to grow whatever life you choose. You cannot expect the Almighty to guide you when you're stuck and unwilling. God is great, but even God can't steer a parked car. Commitment builds a path to your dream. Commitment builds upon itself, bringing you little successes along the way. Success breeds success. As you build a history of success, the path toward the dream becomes wider until it broadens into a highway.

The beauty of co-creation is that you need not know all the answers when you set out on your dream, because God reveals the next step as you advance. You are a dream-builder, not a dictionary. Your compendium of knowledge is limited to your experience up until the present moment. You can't plan every inch of your success. Support that you can't create for yourself will come to you through your willingness to be guided by God, to go to the edge of the light you see and take another step.

Imagine if when the Israelites said to Moses, "Take us to the promised land," Moses had responded, "No problem. I've got the map. Now, it looks to me as if there's a big body of water somewhere in the middle and we don't have a boat, but don't you worry. I've got all the answers." In fact, Moses did not have a map; he did not know the way. Initially he didn't even want to make the trip. When God commanded Moses to bring the Israelites out of Egypt, Moses replied, "Who am I that I should go to Pharaoh?" He became committed after God assured him, "I will certainly be with you." Moses challenged Pharaoh to free the Israelites from slavery, and when Pharaoh refused, ten plagues fell upon the Egyptians, proof that God existed and could work miracles.

Moses encountered many obstacles as he led the Israelites out of bondage, not the least of which was the Red Sea. When the Israelites reached its shores, Moses probably didn't have a game plan. With Pharaoh's soldiers not far behind, promising certain death, and the prospect of drowning straight ahead, he may have felt some uncertainty about which way to proceed. But Moses trusted God to guide him, and the waters parted, allowing the Israelites to pass.

Moses was committed. He moved toward his dream, and in so doing, obstacles literally fell away before his eyes. You cultivate your dream every day by listening to a higher intelligence that directs you how to order your life in accordance with the dream. That intelligence will guide you step by step if you listen. We have to be pliable. Our new life doesn't drop down on us. We have to be steered into it.

Moses and the Israelites wandered around in that desert for forty years. They ultimately reached the Promised Land, but Moses himself never entered it. He only glimpsed it before he died. He was not bitter or negative, for he died knowing he had done what God intended for him, even though it took forty years. These stories from the Bible are not just dry theology; they are about you and me. That forty years is symbolic of whatever time may be required for our own dream to manifest itself. None of us knows if we will reach our own Promised Land in forty days or forty years. We must remain committed, fueled by passion, until we reach our destination. We each have that part of us who is Noah, willing to build an ark, and that part who is Moses, willing to remain committed to the dream no matter how long it takes to come true.

You are coded with the greatness of your Creator and endowed with capacities to be discovered, developed, and directed. Your dream may be a quality relationship, a garden of orchids, or a singing career. Any dream you deeply desire can come true. Put your dream to the highest test. Let God direct energy through you. Just as God creates the universe, so you too have the ability to mold and shape your life. You cannot see all the possibilities from where you stand. You may find yourself lost and wandering in the desert, but remain committed to the dream. Retain your energy and passion, and you will be guided. Then take the next step.

Growing Your Dream

Your mind may play host to a myriad of wishes, but you need to distinguish your deepest desire from whims and passing fancies. You are endowed with the power to choose that dream closest to your heart, and by co-creating with God, you can embark on a path that will bring that dream to fruition.

1. Set your intention. What is the life you want to be living? Your focused intention will move through the energy field of all possibilities and draw to it the substance that will produce the crop of your life. Thoughts held in mind reproduce after their kind. That's the nature of the universe. Practice telling yourself: "Where I place my attention, I place my intention." Buy a "dream journal" and commit to paper the deepest longings of your heart.

2. Test your dream with five essential questions: Do you feel passion for your dream? Does the dream align with your core values? Do you need God for your dream because the dream is bigger than something you can accomplish on your own? Will the dream bring good to you by moving you closer to your true self? And finally, Will your dream bring good to others?

3. Commit to your dream mentally, emotionally, and spiritually. We find ourselves breaking commitments all the time, disappointing others as well as ourselves. For your dream to come true, you've got to stick with it, pledging yourself to a particular course of action. As you commit, you willingly take steps toward your dream, proceeding even as doubts arise, even when you do not have all the answers.

Chapter Three

DESERVING:

Building a Deeper Belief in You

> Life has to be lived forward but can only be understood backward.
>
> —SÖREN KIERKEGAARD

- ♦ *Focus on the Good—Even When It Is Invisible to the Eye—and the Good in Yourself Will Be Revealed*
- ♦ *Stop Dragging Harry; Let Go of Limiting Thinking*
- ♦ *Practice Gratitude to Bolster Your Sense of Worthiness*

It was a rainy night in the fall of 1971. My husband and I had fed our two boys early and then sat down at the dinner table to try to hammer through the wall that stood between us. Words didn't work for us anymore. It didn't matter if we screamed, pleaded, or sweetly cajoled; we couldn't seem to get through to each other. It was as if a soundproof glass barrier separated us, and the harder we tried, the thicker the barrier grew. I couldn't eat. I couldn't speak. The frustration gripped my heart like a vise and squeezed me until I felt unable to breathe. The pain was so big that it encompassed every part of my life, every cell of my being. I could not stay in that house a moment longer.

I stuffed my bare feet into a pair of penny loafers and threw an old sweatshirt over my blouse. With barely a backward glance at Haven's startled face, I ran out into the dripping darkness and wandered aimlessly down darkened streets. Within minutes, the downpour turned my sweatshirt heavy and dank; I felt similarly weighted down. Rain filled my shoes, and cars whipped past, spraying arcs of water over me as if I were invisible. I thought about suicide. Maybe one of those faceless sedans would run me over and not even slow down, as if striking a twig in the road. It would be over in a moment, and all my unbearably heavy pain would vanish.

What had become of my dreams? I was now a twenty-one-year-old mother of two who so much feared living forever in the life I had created that death seemed preferable. It seemed amazing to me that just a few years earlier I had chosen life, triumphing over a serious kidney disease. I had felt the beginnings of a spiritual awakening, and I had enrolled in the university to pursue my dream of teaching. But now those stirrings lay dormant. I loved the classroom but was miserable in my marriage. On that walk, as water sloshed in my loafers and I shook in the chilled, weighty folds of my sweatshirt, every pore of my being screamed, "Help me! Help me!"

I felt as though I were right up against an insurmountable wall. I was deeply unhappy; I saw myself as a victim of unlucky circumstance. I wanted a better life but didn't believe I deserved one. I had no idea how to give my life value. Many of us have had such an experience in one form or another. Such a turning point may arrive, as it did in my case, as the result of great emotional anguish; it may dawn as the simple realization that our life is devoid of deeper meaning. Whatever the origins of such a moment, we're at an impasse. We've tried everything. Nothing has worked, so something inside our hearts rises up and screams, "Help me!"

That wall can be a very powerful and positive place; it is the boundary of who we thought we were up until the moment of crisis. Our willingness to pass through the wall and reach our higher power brings us to a greater life, one in which we can begin to believe in ourselves. During a birthing, the walls of the uterus tighten, and the little being inside feels the pressure to move outward. The butterfly in the cocoon also feels its encasement becoming intolerably confining and struggles toward freedom. So too we struggle on the verge of new life, of transformation.

Nice metaphors, but they didn't exactly pop to mind that agonizing night. Even if they had, I would have dismissed them as spiritual mumbo-jumbo. In that moment I knew only that I could tolerate my pain no longer. Was divorce the answer? Maybe. And yet as shameful as a teen pregnancy had been in that conventional community, the stigma of a failed marriage would be worse.

Those who preach from the lofty security of a pulpit may describe the emergence of self-worth as if it were as simple as doing the laundry. Rinse the dirt from your life with a little agitation and you're instantly clean, fresh, and wrinkle-free. It is so much more difficult than that. You may be moving toward your dream, as I had by taking classes toward a teaching certificate, but if you neglect to nourish your own sense of worthiness, you are not fully committing yourself to the dream. A part of you holds back, saying, "I'm not worth it."

When I heard myself scream, "Help me!" something important happened. The spark had not quite died out in me. My mind was flooded with a new thought: "There must be a better way." Things began to change inside me at that moment, though I didn't realize it at the time because the pain was so all-pervasive. Nothing dramatic happened that night; I simply walked home and emptied my shoes. But something held me back from the urge to end my life.

The next day I saw an advertisement in the Portland State University school paper. It read: "Wanted: Couples for Communications Encounter Group." No matter what became of our marriage, I figured Haven and I should at least be able to talk to each other more freely. I signed us up.

We had never been in counseling before, and neither had any of the other five couples present. Julia, a visiting professor, was the counselor in charge. A gray-haired grandmother in her mid-sixties who did volunteer counseling at my university, Julia had a deceptively mild manner that seemed at odds with her considerable position as head of the psychiatry department at the medical school nearby. She began by asking one of us to share our story, but we all tried to blend into the background instead.

Finally I stood up. I had been hurting for so long that I figured unburdening myself might release some of the pain. "I'll do it," I said.

Haven winced.

I began a lengthy diatribe against my husband. He was so inconsiderate, so selfish; if only he would change, if only he were different, then I would be happy. With all eyes upon me, I warmed to my subject. On and on I went, calling up every slight, every argument. When I finished, Julia looked at Haven and asked if he'd been listening.

"Of course," he said. "There are a few things I'd like to say—"

She cut him off. "If you've been listening, you'll be able to repeat what Mary just said."

"Well, she said . . . well . . ."

"There's a difference between authentic listening and merely waiting for your turn to talk. If you've spent this time preparing your own comeback, you can't have been listening to your wife's concerns."

I laughed to myself. I was thoroughly puffed up. The counselor was on *my* side. She understood what I had to put up with each day, this husband who never listened, who never—

"Mary." That sweet, grandmotherly gaze was aimed at me now. "Mary, because of your hurt, you're telling your husband you don't love him. You're punishing him by withholding your love. How long are you going to punish him? One day? One month?"

"Well . . ."

"The rest of your life? How long must he pay for your hurt?"

"Well . . ."

Julia convinced me to give the marriage another try. She wanted me to commit for one year; we compromised on one month. For the next thirty days, Haven and I would listen to and acknowledge each other. We would support each other by doing whatever the other person felt was important.

A few days later, on Sunday morning, Haven burst into our room when I was still half asleep. "I've just been to church," he said. "There's a new minister. You've got to come hear him; there's another service at ten-fifteen."

What I wanted to do was go back to sleep. But I had made a commitment, and Haven looked so alive and enthusiastic. Grudgingly I agreed to go, and I dragged myself out of bed.

I do not recall much of what the minister said that morning, except for one thing. He said, "Nothing is bad unless you perceive it as bad. Because God is everywhere and God is good, there is good even in the midst of tragedy or situations we do not understand. But we will not find the good if we keep our mind closed to it. Ask God to help you see the good; open your mind and you will find the good."

My mind argued vehemently, "He's wrong. Murder is bad. War is bad. Poverty is bad. My marriage is bad."

The minister concluded by offering this spiritual practice: "The next time you begin to perceive something as bad, delay for three days. See if you can find some possible good in a situation you regard as totally negative. Look for the good."

I remembered my experience with Dr. Warn. I had held tight to the image of a perfectly healthy kidney, even as doctors told me it was diseased. Perhaps this minister had a point.

The next day Haven lost his job at the dairy. He and another milkman had requested pay for the overtime hours they'd worked, and their supervisor responded by deciding that their services were no longer needed. I was devastated. How would we survive? Would I have to drop out of school? My life was miserable enough, and now this.

"Look for the good," the minister had said. "Delay for three days." Fine. I would wait. If God didn't come through for me in three days, then I would panic.

For two days I withheld judgment. Although I had learned to change my perspective with Dr. Warn, I hadn't been panicked at that time; I had already accepted death. This was the first time, however, I had taken control over my own panic, and it wasn't easy. Several times a day I would catch myself beginning to tense, curse, or pick up a dinner plate so that I might hurl it across the kitchen. Then I would stop, take a deep breath, and tell myself, "Mary, this is not the end of the world. At least, not yet. I will not panic. I will wait for God to show me the good."

On the third day Haven found a better job at a dairy closer to home. He could ride his bike to work (which made him happy, as he never had time to exercise anymore), and the new job paid considerably more than the last one had. And I hadn't tormented myself in those three days between his loss of one job and his finding a new one. Because I was not in my own suffering, I was able to support my husband more in his endeavor.

Remember the tiger that lived as a goat? This was my roar of awakening. Tremendous power in me had lain dormant until I took charge of my emotions. When I stopped perceiving myself as a timid goat—a victim—I let out a tiny roar. It wasn't a great roar full of confidence and triumph, just a sign that I was opening myself to receive the meat, the good. Choosing to focus on the good is a spiritual freedom that literally lifts you. Finding the greater good outside yourself leads you to recognize your innocence within. God is in the midst of every situation, and when you are ready, He will reveal the splendor of your own life.

The dream that you envision for your life is a gift. You cannot experience that gift unless you receive it. No matter how wondrous the bequest, to the person with hands clenched, the gift remains unopened, unappreciated. You may have honored your discontent and acknowledged that the impossible can happen. You may have chosen and tested and committed to create your dream. But if you do not deeply believe that you deserve your dream, your life will still fall short of its potential. Even as your dream begins to take shape, unconsciously you will find a way to sabotage that which you deeply desire.

♦ **Focus on the Good—Even When It Is Invisible to the Eye—and the Good in Yourself Will Be Revealed**

Now, when I look back on my cry of "Help me!" I see that I had been living asleep. It was as if my pain pushed me through a doorway. I felt so excited, I was ready to learn more. I had begun to realize that life is not happening to me; rather, life is proceeding from me!

That recognition began to transform my life. During those early years of my marriage, I went through a process of looking squarely at that part of myself steeped in self-hatred. My new freedom came through discovering my own innocence. I recognized that everything I had done up until that moment had

truly been the best I knew how to do. As I exercised my ability
to control my thoughts and seek the good in any kind of
situation, I stepped out of feeling like a victim long enough to
recognize myself as the architect of my own life. With God as
my partner, there were no limits. With God as my partner, I
must deserve abundance, because if I open up, God will work
through me to manifest good. This is the basis of co-creation.

Haven and I continued marriage counseling, learning to
communicate and cooperate with each other. Although we
never did find a deep compatibility, we shared important interests. We both loved our children and wanted the best for our
family, and we both recognized a newfound commitment to
God. That minister's words had so impacted our outlook, we
wanted to know more. We began attending church regularly.
Then we started going to workshops, classes, and retreats.
Haven and I became like thirsty sponges absorbing every drop
of theology in our midst.

He began studying for the ministry immediately, while I initially hung back from formal training, telling myself my role
would be as a mother and enlightened minister's wife. I had begun to appreciate my own innocence and felt more alive than I
had in a long time. Yet I too felt a calling to lead a larger family,
a church family. I had reached the point where I wanted to
share my knowledge with others. So, two years later, I joined
my husband in ministerial school. Along the way, we quite literally expanded our family by having two more children, our
daughter Jenny and son Mathew.

Go look in on a classroom of kindergartners. What do you
see? Children that age are bursting with spontaneous feeling;
they bubble over in wonder at a simple paper airplane. Their
innocence is so near the surface, we cannot help but celebrate
it. But when those same children have grown to adulthood, we
automatically become suspicious if they display even a shred of
the joy that brimmed over in them as youngsters. We doubt,

questioning, "Now, what do they want? What's their angle? Why do they behave that way?"

We lose sight of our own core of innocence as we age, buried as it is under layers of self-protection, self-doubt, or disappointment. We hide our true selves. It is rare to find that adult who has retained a purity of heart, for others have been trained as we've been trained. We are trained to believe we are unworthy. We cannot have been raised in this country and failed to be influenced by a theology that teaches that we are basically bad. Regardless of our religious upbringing, some version of "original sin" seeps into our being. We operate out of a paradigm that there's something fundamentally wrong with us and thus we do not deserve what we deeply desire. That belief is like a negative magnet pushing away any good we might attract. For instance, we might engage in a relationship, but not a deeply fulfilling one. If those we love grow too close, they would recognize our badness, so we push them away to prevent them from finding out. Similarly, we fail to fully express our talent. Taking risks in a career makes us vulnerable to error, and we fear that stumbling will expose us as phonies. Despite what anybody says, we know the truth: We're basically bad, and no one must discover our ugly secret. We become so careful, so fearful of making a mistake, that we remain on a short leash, never venturing into a realm wherein our greater life resides. This is a very draining, diminishing, and frightening version of reality.

We ache from feeling empty. There's a hole inside us that we need to fill in order to be whole. But our longing sets us off on a frantic search for specific objects outside ourselves—money, material goods, or meaningless relationships—to fill the void, when true fulfillment lies in reconciliation with our true self. So the hole broadens because we are trying to fill the void from outside ourselves. We tend to operate out of guilt and shame, conforming to somebody else's code of behavior, always trying to atone or to make up for our flaws. This is the way I operated until my own roar of awakening.

Contrast for a moment original sin with a theology I like to call "original innocence." The former decrees that we err because we are inherently bad, while the latter allows that we make mistakes out of ignorance. We are ignorant of the power of our choices and the power that results from what we choose to create. We are ignorant of our connection to one another. If you hold hatred for another, you learn self-hatred. If you use immoral means to acquire, you do your world and yourself an injustice. We abuse our planet because we are ignorant of the fact that it is alive and we are a part of it. We are ignorant of the truth of ourselves, of God, and of one another. All our unskillful behavior results from our ignorance; it is not indicative that some dark, unworthy being resides at our core. We are unskillful as a child is unskillful, and we can grow more adept over time. This does not mean we always do good things; we may flounder and offend and fall off track. It does mean, however, that you are *inherently* good. You are inherently good because God created you. You can keep that good hidden or you can learn to uncover it.

St. Francis of Assisi, who had grown up wealthy and indulged in all the vices young men of his time indulged in, was once asked by one of his companions, "Why you, Francis? Why you? Why did God choose you as a lighthouse to bless the world?"

St. Francis smiled and replied, "Why me? I'll tell you why me. Because there could hardly be anyone who has made as many mistakes as I have. I have done and been everything you can think of that is abhorrent and unholy. I had absolutely nothing to offer the world. That is precisely why God chose to glorify me—to give hope to people who feel they have nothing to give, for if the Holy Spirit can work through me, it can work through anyone."

⸺

Carla, a woman in our congregation, spent most of her life feeling unworthy. She got the message loud and clear in the third grade from a narrow-minded nun. Outgoing and a touch rebellious, Carla always seemed to be in trouble at school. One day Carla said or did something that annoyed the nun—she can't recall precisely what—and was called to the front of the room. The nun instructed Carla to stay there as, one by one, her classmates stood and announced something they did not like about her. Everyone obeyed, including Carla's best friend. She can still see the faces of her classmates; she can hear the disdain in their voices as they picked her apart. Yet she cannot recall a single word of their denouncements. She blotted the painful comments from her mind. The image that remains clearest is that of the nun urging those third-graders on, branding Carla with shame.

"To me, the nun was God. That was God telling me I was these bad things. So I grew up believing I was a bad person."

That afternoon Carla packed up her books, went home, and told her mother she had quit school. She didn't explain why, figuring her mother would think Carla had deserved the humiliation. Carla's mother made her return to school.

As a teenager, she numbed her pain with drugs and alcohol. She wouldn't allow herself to take advantage of opportunities, because she didn't believe she was deserving of good fortune. She vetoed college and shunned the man she loved. She punished her body by stuffing it with food and then vomiting it back up. For years Carla was bulimic.

At age thirty-five, after several failed attempts to quit drinking, Carla finally became sober. Treatment included extensive counseling, during which Carla began to look at herself more objectively. She realized she was not despicable or unlovable. It was a single confused nun, and not God, who had deemed her bad. It was a confused Carla who believed the pronouncement.

Forgiving the nun and recognizing herself as a worthy individual has profoundly affected every relationship in Carla's life. Although she still feels pain over all her missed opportunities, she's grown closer to her family and put herself through college. Most important, Carla says, she now trusts God to deliver her greatest good.

In the eternal dimension, each of us is whole and perfect and complete. Power springs from that place where we locate our divine dimension. We can find that place in ourselves or miss seeing it entirely. Amplify your feeling of deserving by reminding yourself of your true identity. If you recognized yourself as a living image of God, how much more would you believe you deserved? You cannot *be* any more deserving, but you can learn to *feel* more deserving.

Jesus tells us: "You are the light of the world." Let's take a look at that for a moment. You are the light of the world. Who is this you? Your personality? Your profession? When you're asked "Who are you?" do you answer "My name is . . . ," "I'm a . . . ," or "I'm so-and-so's wife (or husband)"? No matter your answer, that is not the "you" to whom Jesus is referring.

Now, for a moment, notice your shoes on your feet; just feel the pressure of leather on your soles. Notice the weight of your clothing on your body. Notice the air gently touching those places where your skin remains exposed. Notice, for a moment, your thinking. What thoughts are moving through your mind? Probably you're wondering, "Where is she going with this?" What were you thinking before you turned to this page? What thoughts interfere with your concentration? Whatever thought disrupts your concentration is one that your mind has labeled more urgent than the task at hand. Notice the thoughts you've been entertaining. Notice your emotions. Are you feeling joyous or sad, mellow or anxious, hopeful or full of despair?

Now that you are aware of everything going on inside at this moment, ask yourself one more question. Who notices your body, how it feels to have those shoes on your feet, notices your clothing, notices the air against your skin? Who notices the body but isn't the body? You can cut my hand off, but you haven't taken any of *me* away. Who notices the thinking but isn't the thought? Who notices the emotion but isn't the feeling? The one who can notice is the you Jesus is talking to when He says, "You are the light of the world."

There is a you that is pure life. There is a you that is spirit, indestructible, undying. Jesus says, "Let me tell you about you. You are . . ." That is a very powerful word: *are*. Present tense. He didn't say, "Under certain conditions *you can* or *you will be* in the future . . ." He didn't say, "*You might be* . . ." He said, "You *are* . . ." Regardless of how you define yourself at this moment—despairing, undeserving, self-despising—to the one who sees you as God does, you are the light of the world.

Whatever you focus on expands. Focus on God, the source of all good.

During workshops, I sometimes present this concept through an exercise I call the "Victim/Creator Game." Each person chooses a partner, someone they do not know well. Then all the participants close their eyes and think of a time when life treated them unfairly. Maybe you think of the time you parked your car carefully and returned from a meeting to find your vehicle sideswiped and no note left. Maybe you think of the time you gave your heart fully in a relationship, and then, without warning, your loved one announced, "Sorry, but I care about someone else. See you around."

The partners tell each other their stories and sometimes get a trifle competitive, each trying to outdo the other's ordeals. Then I invite them to consider that we contribute to every event in our lives. Every event is part of our co-creation with God and therefore contains an element of good. By denying our responsibility, we short-circuit our ability to claim the good and move into heightened power. When we remove ourselves from our own experiences, we cannot possibly profit from them. The participants need to decide, "Am I a victim or am I a creator?"

I tell about being nine years old and returning home from a basketball game with ink on the back of my calves. My dad asked, "How did you do this?"

"I don't know," I answered honestly. I hadn't even noticed the stains until my dad pointed them out.

"Come on, now. What happened?" he persisted. As hard as I tried to convince him of my innocence, he refused to believe me. Finally he said, "There's no way you could get all that ink on your legs without knowing it. Go to your room and think about this. When you're ready, tell me the truth or you'll be grounded."

I slammed the door after me. What a raw deal! Still, no way did I want to be grounded. I finally emerged from my room and falsely confessed that I'd covered my own legs with ink.

"There, don't you feel better now for telling the truth?" he asked.

Of course not. I felt victimized. I had told the truth the first time, and my father hadn't believed me. He had forced me to lie.

Many years later, using the co-creative model, I began to revisit those times in my life when I'd felt victimized. Only then did I realize I was responsible in part for the mystery ink.

You see, I used to lie to my father all the time. It was my job to walk a quarter-mile each day to our mailbox and retrieve the mail. But I was too lazy. I'd tell my dad the mailbox was empty. A few days later, he'd come home after driving by the box, his arms full of bills and letters that had collected over the past week, and I'd say, "My gosh, we sure got a lot of mail today."

I had contributed to my father's doubt in me that day I came home with inky legs, because I had a history of lying. Why should he have believed me that time? In my pain of being disbelieved, I made in that moment a powerful decision. I decided to start telling the truth.

Unpleasant experiences offer opportunities for growth, but we're blind to the good unless we recognize our own participation in those bad experiences. How much simpler to isolate the moment and feel victimized. The bashed-in car leaves you feeling distrustful, vindictive, or reluctant to park on the street. Acknowledging your contribution helps you recognize yourself as a co-creator. Some people in our workshops have discovered that the sight of their dented car sends them a message to curb their own reckless driving or makes them more tolerant of traffic delays caused by accidents.

What about when injustice takes on a more heinous form? People who were abused as children in no way consciously chose that experience. Yet if they heal, their compassion and their motivation to reach out to others help their souls to grow. They possess an empathy that those who have not suffered similarly find impossible to imagine. Their roar of awakening is indeed an awesome sound. This is not an easy concept to understand or adopt. Yet the co-creative model—"life is not happening to me, life is proceeding from me"—allows you to make sense of the senseless. You cannot undo what has already been done. But you can become bigger than the tragedy that befell you by accessing unlimited power from God. The victim who clings to the victim role expects lifelong mistreatment. Creators free themselves for a life of abundance, confident they will receive what they deserve, which is God's greatest good.

This section of your dream-building dynamic cannot be skipped. I have known many people who launched a dream without first developing a sense of worthiness. Even when they finally attracted into their experience a desired dream, they managed to sabotage it before long. Their dream was not built on a solid foundation of divine deserving. As we are told by Jesus, if you build your house on sand, the wind and rain erode it from under you. Wind and rain are challenges. Build your house of dreams on rock, and you have something more solid to sustain you when the elements threaten to undermine your efforts.

Grace is a gift of God. You cannot earn it. You are born deserving it. Want to know whether you're worthy? If you're still breathing, the answer is yes. Saying to yourself, "I'm too fat, too ugly, too dull, too uneducated to be granted my heart's desire" will result in a self-fulfilling prophecy. Act as if you're worthless, and the universe will verify your belief. The universe becomes an unfriendly place because you have chosen to perceive it as such. You blind yourself to the good.

You can learn to affirm your feeling of worthiness. I tell my congregation about a little boy who began affirming: "I want to be the greatest baseball player in the world. I am the greatest baseball player in the world." He threw the ball up in the air, swung, and missed. He picked up the ball. "I am the greatest baseball player in the world," he said, and he threw the ball up, swung, and missed. He picked up the ball again and said, "I am the greatest baseball player in the world," and he threw it, swung, and missed. At this point he exclaimed, "What a pitcher!"

This little boy believed in his own worth even when he literally missed what he set out to achieve. He perceived his inability to connect with a baseball not as evidence he was a lousy ball player but rather as an opportunity to discover a greater talent within himself. When we stop responding to situations as if they're horrible, we might just pause long enough to look for the good. And in so doing, we discover a greater good at work in our lives and in ourselves.

♦ Stop Dragging Harry; Let Go of Limiting Thinking

Eight golfers go out to the fairway and break up into foursomes to play. The first four men play eighteen holes, then sit in the clubhouse waiting for the other group to come in. It seems they wait forever.

Finally, here come three men from the second group. These men are just a total wreck. A member of the first foursome asks, "My gosh, what happened to you guys?"

One of them responds, "Oh, it was just awful. On the second hole, Harry had a heart attack. After that, it was hit the ball and drag Harry . . . hit the ball and drag Harry."

So who is Harry? Quite simply, Harry is our deadweight.

There are parts of ourselves that we've long since needed to discard; they have died, but we're still hanging on. We're still dragging our childhood story. We're still hauling about what our spouse did yesterday or ten years ago. We're still lugging around the notion that we are not lovable. We're still dragging limiting ideas.

I spent a couple of days in Bangkok once and brought back a tiny brass elephant to remind me of how the elephants are trained as beasts of burden. The trainers capture the elephant and tether one of its legs to a giant tree. The elephant struggles to get away from the tree, and it pulls and pulls and pulls, feeling the tug of that chain. Finally, after a month of struggling, that elephant gives up. Then the trainers tie the elephant with a rope and repeat the process. Later the trainers can tie the beast with something even lighter, until finally they can take the elephant into the jungle, where it labors uncomplainingly, tethered with the reed of the lotus flower. That elephant will not even think of making a break for freedom, because it feels a little tug on its leg. The elephant is trained to believe that with that tug, it is captured.

I bought that trinket to remind me that I am like that elephant. I am trained to accept limitation that has no more power than my own belief in it. A lotus reed cannot restrain the elephant, except in one way, and that is by the animal's own conviction. The elephant's belief binds him. If I'm feeling limited or tethered in one area of my life, I can break free at any moment. I am free to choose a new thought and thus a new life any time I shed my old training.

A man called Brad was visiting our church one day when I told the Harry story. He returned to see me about a month later. He told me the idea that we can choose how we respond to circumstances had been entirely new to him. He had expanded the concept to fit his own life, and he called his Harry "the werewolf." Brad described himself as easygoing until the moment stress struck. Then he would explode with such rage that he became a different person. It was Brad's kids who had nicknamed him "the werewolf." But the very notion that he could stop reacting automatically, that he could respond differently, had filled him with a tremendous sense of freedom. He'd told himself that the next time he felt himself turning into a werewolf, he would remember what was truly most important to him: his family. He decided to remember these words: *Celebrate your family*.

Brad was feeling pretty powerful until he actually had to wrestle the werewolf. One day Brad's old car died. He had very little money, and he was sitting on the hood of his car, trying to figure out how to afford repairs, when he felt the familiar rage rising in him. He cursed aloud. His kids would recognize the usual signs when he would get home. They'd say, "Don't get near Dad—the werewolf is back."

It was difficult, but he stopped himself from losing his temper entirely. Instead, he thought about how else he might choose to respond. Sitting there on the hood of his dead car, he remembered the words *Celebrate your family*. When the wrecker came, he had his car towed to a junkyard, and he hitched a ride to the bus stop. He rode the bus into town, where he bought a bottle of sparkling apple juice and a bouquet of wildflowers. He walked all the way home, carrying his gifts, and opened the front door yelling, "I'm here, honey. I want you to know something—the car's dead, and we have no money, but I love you." His wife stood there for a moment, stunned, asking herself, "Who is this man?" Then she gave him a big hug.

All week long he lived in an amplified space of deserving. Ideas and resources became available to him that he would not have noticed had he been depressed or angry. Minus the deadweight of the werewolf, Brad had more room for God to maneuver in him, and he was led to find, and ultimately purchase, a far more reliable used car at payments he could afford.

It is never easy to let go. Brad's werewolf resurfaces from time to time, just as your own old sense of worthlessness or self-disgust may be resurrected. If you were a homely adolescent, it doesn't matter how attractive you became as an adult; the moment your significant other rejects you, boom, you're that ugly kid again. When the church I serve was initially evicted from its building and we had nowhere to go, I took the rejection personally. Some of the shame and humiliation I had felt as an ostracized pregnant teenager came flooding back.

You drag Harry despite the discomfort because at least he's familiar. There's a place in ourselves where we all feel unworthy or impure, despite our divine purity. Whenever I begin to drag Harry, I catch myself and remind myself that I am a child of God. The truth is, I don't know that I'll ever totally bury Harry. But I do know I don't carry him nearly as long or as far. And over the years, I think he's lost some weight.

Another man in our congregation, Scott, got rid of his Harry by moving into service. Scott told me that during the Vietnam War he had tried to register as a conscientious objector. This had not been an easy decision. Scott wanted to serve his country, but he could not reconcile the concept of service with the violence of war. He went through the difficult application process and was turned down. He appealed and was rejected again. In the midst of his second appeal, the war ended. At first he was relieved. Then, as his friends began coming home, he felt horrendous shame over his choice. His friends had risked their lives in war; some had lost limbs, and many were sick physically or sick at heart. All of them had sacrificed. Scott, on the other hand, remained safely at home shuffling papers. Despite the sincerity of his intention, he now felt unclean and deeply ashamed.

His urge to serve, however, had not diminished over time. Service is a tremendous spiritual practice that amplifies your inner good so that it blots out those pieces of yourself you perceive as bad. A contractor by training, Scott joined a service group with other contractors who contributed time, talent, and materials to community projects. He eventually worked his way up to become president of the organization. He heard about a Vietnam veterans group that was struggling to raise funds for a memorial to fallen soldiers. Scott recognized a golden moment in time. God was giving him a chance to make peace with himself and his world. As his group's president, he was instrumental in enlisting its support for the memorial. Once the contractors stepped in, other community groups followed. Scott put his whole self into the project, contributing his own money and becoming a driving force in the creation of Oregon's Vietnam War Memorial.

During the last phase of the project, Scott attended a meeting with the veterans. He knew he needed to tell the truth about his attempts to become a conscientious objector. Crying, he poured out his shame, expecting disgust and disdain from those who had gone in his place. Instead, what he received was overwhelming love and understanding. These veterans, many of them still battle-scarred, reminded him he had done what he truly believed was right, and that his shame was self-inflicted. Scott said he felt as if a huge weight had been lifted from his shoulders.

During the dedication ceremony, as Scott stood before the

monument to men who had lost their lives, he saw also a living monument of his gratitude to God for providing him an opportunity to give back, in a way that made a difference.

God does not care about your past or your perceived blemishes. You are created in the likeness of God. You are already perfect. Often we cannot see this simple truth from where we stand, so it's necessary to move. Service is a spiritual exercise that literally works off your excess baggage. Whatever method you use to identify Harry, whether it's by creating a symbolic reminder or moving into service, begin by telling yourself that the Creator of this universe has found you worthy by bestowing upon you the greatest gift of all: life. Tell yourself, "I have already received my birthright of worthiness. I will honor this great gift by lightening my load and living fully and freely."

◆ Practice Gratitude to Bolster Your Sense of Worthiness

A third and essential way to help you feel more deserving of your dreams is by practicing gratitude. Your mother may have raised you to say please and thank you, but that teaches mere politeness. There's a world of difference between saying thank you and giving thanks. Gratitude is a way of living that releases a dynamic spiritual energy, allowing you to exert a mighty influence in your world. As Plato said: "A grateful mind is a great mind. It eventually attracts to itself every great thing." Gratitude forms a connecting link, a bridge between you and every possible channel of good in your life.

There's a Hindu story that reminds me of the impact gratitude—or lack of it—can have in my life. In this story, a man who roamed the world came, in the course of his wandering, to a forest and there sat under a tree, feeling himself becoming very calm. A gentle breeze was blowing. As he looked around, the man thought, "If I had a companion, I would be completely happy." Now it just so happened that this tree was a wish-fulfilling tree. A wish-fulfilling tree is divine; if a person sits beneath it, his every wish is instantly granted. At that very moment, a beautiful woman appeared, and the man was enraptured.

She joined him, and for a while he remained content. Then he thought, "What a pity that the two of us have to sit under a tree exposed to the elements. It would be much better if we had a house with a few bedrooms and a dining room, equipped with all the amenities. Then I would lack nothing." Immediately the house he had wished for appeared. Delighted, he went into the house with his sweetheart, sat down, and had a loving chat with her. Then he said to himself, "What's the point of living like paupers in this house? I'd like to live like a lord. If only we had a butler and a couple of servants." In the twinkling of an eye, a butler and two servants appeared. The man called the servants over and said, "Prepare us two delectable dishes." Before long, the butler brought trays of gourmet food. The man tasted the food, and it was delicious.

Yet he began to wonder, "What's going on? I wished for a wife, and she arrived. Then I wished for a house and got a beautiful house. Then I wished for a butler and two servants, and they appeared. Then I wished for delectable dishes, and they too materialized. What's going on here? No way can all this be happening to me. There must be evil here."

And so evil manifested. A demon appeared with its mouth wide open. "Oh, no! He'll eat me up!" the man cried. And that's exactly what happened.

This fellow got swallowed by his own thoughts. At first he thought of good things, but he could not trust them, and his self-doubt conjured a demon. If instead he had thought, "I must deserve this goodness and I will be grateful," his life wouldn't have ended as indigestion for a demon. The manifestation of his wishes led not to gratitude but suspicion, rendering his own dream a nightmare.

We too are seated in the shade of a wish-fulfilling tree. We create our own worlds of experience out of thought and imagination. When we shun our gifts, thinking, "So what's the catch? There's no way all these good things can be happening to me," we're being ungrateful. I have a friend who was very lonely and dreamed of a loving relationship. He met a wonderful woman and for a time seemed content. But then he began to think, "If only she lost about five pounds . . ." and "If only she didn't laugh so loudly . . ." Over time, bit by bit, his criticism pushed her away. She didn't feel cherished, and eventually she left him.

A thankful person is thankful under all circumstances. A complaining soul complains even if he lives in paradise.

In 1990 I had the honor of going to Russia (then still the Soviet Union) as part of a Soviet-American dialogue mission. Our group had difficulty just getting around, and even the most ordinary goods were hard to come by. People waited in line for the bread and milk we take for granted. A store such as Wal-Mart or Kmart, where we might go to pick up bedding or cat food or any of the kinds of things we assume are always available, was simply unimaginable.

One night, four of my colleagues and I were invited to dinner with a local family. The elevator in the building had long since been broken and couldn't be repaired because of a lack of parts, so we had to climb fifteen flights to get to the family's little apartment. The living room had so little furniture that we sat on pillows on the floor, and the tiny, antiquated heater sputtered in fits and then stopped. The main course at dinner was boiled potatoes. At the end of the meal, the woman of the house, with eyes that were absolutely sparkling with excitement, said, "And now we have dessert." She came out from the kitchen and set a platter in front of us as if it were gold. There, carefully arranged, were five fresh pears. What sacrifices in terms of time and money she had made to please a group of Americans far from home! I never enjoyed a pear quite so much in my life. What nourished me beyond anything else that night was a renewed realization that the truly wealthy at the dinner that night were our hosts. Such givers as these were abundantly rich in what matters most. They were abundantly grateful.

Notice your own feelings of aliveness as you focus your thoughts with gratitude. Notice what happens to that feeling when you focus your thoughts strongly with resentment. One way of thinking gives life, the other diminishes it.

Linda, who was our church's first volunteer and went on to perform every job here—from cleaning the toilets to heading the staff—was an angel to her mother. But sometimes Linda found it hard not to resent this extremely difficult woman. From the time Linda was thirteen, she had taken care of her mother as well as her younger siblings. Linda's mother was mentally ill. She would sit and rock, day after day, chanting, "I can't go on. I can't go on." She deteriorated to the point that one day Linda found her in the bedroom with scissors at Linda's younger brother's throat. Linda was terrified and ill-equipped to manage such a situation. Finally her mother went into a hospital.

She was in and out of hospitals over the years. It didn't matter if it was a holiday or Linda's birthday—Linda and her mother never connected. If Linda gave her mother a present, she would complain and whine that it wasn't big enough or it was the wrong color. The woman found fault with everything her daughter did. Yet Linda was the one who took care of her.

Eventually her mother became physically ill as well as mentally ill. Linda searched for a safe, secure place, eventually putting her in adult foster care and becoming her legal guardian. Still, this woman continued to sap Linda's energy. On most of Linda's days off she took her mother to the doctor or some other appointment, buying her shoes, taking her for a drive, whatever she needed. And all day long her mother criticized.

Linda began to pray for a transformation; she did not want to resent the woman who had given her life.

Then one day when she came in to work, I looked at her and said, "You're looking great."

She said, "I had a miracle in my life."

"Tell me. What's the miracle?"

"I was sitting at lunch with Mother yesterday, and all of a sudden I felt myself lift up, and I viewed the scene from above. And I saw this differently. I literally was transformed by the renewing of my mind. I know now what this means."

She wrote a poem about her miracle:

For a moment, in the midst of her chatter, the scene in front of
    me went mute.
I watched her chew her food, her cheeks a bit bulged, mouth
    opening, closing, opening, closing.
I saw my mother's lips move, but I could no longer hear her.
It was as if I had left my body and become a witness.
A witness who saw a frightened, elderly woman
Who knew only how to ask for love through criticism,
Who knew only how to ask for love through complaining,
Who knew only how to ask for love through illness.
A woman who never found her voice, never experienced her
    personal power, never learned the true language of love.
A woman who would never understand that she was one of my
    great teachers.
The only thing I truly saw at that moment was her innocence
    and her purity.
I felt a wind blow through me and on its breath it carried away
    all the years of resentment and unfulfilled expectations.
I knew then what an honor it was to take care of her, this child-
    like creature of God, my mother.

This renewal is available to everyone. Linda's gratitude wasn't sugar-coated. She still saw her mother clearly. And her gratitude didn't transform her mother's life. But it did transform her own. You could see the change the minute she walked into the room. Adopt an "attitude of gratitude." Attitude is the filter through which we experience life. Pause in the midst of your life and give thanks for your good fortune. This attitude of gratitude enables you to construct your dream on a rock-solid foundation of deserving.

Gratitude is not passive, and it's not nicey-nice. It's an active spiritual practice. When we practice gratitude, we move into a different state of mind. Remember the words the Apostle Paul wrote while imprisoned for teaching the tenets of Christianity. Abused and alone, he wrote, "I have learned in whatever state I am in, to be grateful." The most important word in that scripture is *in*. He did not say to give thanks *for* all things, because there are some experiences we don't appreciate. He did not say to give thanks for sexual abuse or a fatal disease. Rather, Paul said, whatever situation you are in, give thanks *in life*. Give thanks right now, and you will be elevated to a state of consciousness that attunes you to opportunities that were there all along, opportunities missed by an ungrateful mind.

The universe bestows the good things of life in proportion to a person's readiness to receive. A person who goes to the great ocean of life feeling undeserving will take only a teaspoon with which to receive. More believing persons, filled with gratitude, run to that same ocean with a bucket, knowing the ocean delights in filling any container it is offered.

We begin to see not only ourselves but others as vastly worthy when we practice gratitude. Anyone who has ever loved another unconditionally can recall how the loved one appears radiant and beautiful. If we love another person fully, we may not always like his or her behavior, but we are always grateful to have that person in our lives.

Christine is an inspirational speaker who gave a talk at our church. She told us about a man she knew with a bulbous nose that rivaled Jimmy Durante's famous proboscis. Every time she looked at him, all she saw was that nose. Its sheer size riveted her attention. It was as if the rest of him were invisible. She didn't even notice the color of his eyes. Then one day, while looking at him critically, the thought hit her, "It's as plain as the nose on *his* face. I tend to look at what's wrong instead of focusing on what's right. Not just with this man's nose, either, but with my whole life."

Christine began to practice gratitude for the kindness displayed by this man with the big nose. She appreciated his intelligence, his concern for the environment, and his work ethic. Over time, the two became very close friends. Then, sitting across from him one day while having coffee, she found her heart overflowing with love for this dear man. She could see only his innocence and beauty. She blurted out, "John, you have the most wonderful nose." His profile had not changed; the change came in Christine. To her, his nose had grown distinguished. It shrank as her heart expanded. Eventually the two married. And yes, each of their beautiful children has a very strong proboscis.

Such a seemingly small step as not criticizing someone, even if it's as simple as looking beyond a big nose, can portend great leaps in our own sense of worthiness. As we grow in gratitude we are renewed, and the energies of love literally transform our old life into the life of our dreams.

Should you reach age eighty, you will have lived 701,280 hours. Why not invest twenty-four of those hours to begin forming a stronger foundation for the whole rest of your life? Practice giving thanks for being alive. During this time, make a list of every person you have criticized or condemned in some way during the past week. This might include a coworker, a politician, your spouse, or your next-door neighbor. Next to that person's name, write down something for which you give thanks. Your coworker may talk incessantly at the office to the point where you say, "I wish someone would just shut her up!" Cease your criticism. Stop expecting the worst, and you'll stop receiving it. What about this coworker makes you smile, brightens your day? Ask yourself if perhaps she chatters at work because she has no one at home with whom to talk. If you are fortunate enough to have a confidante, be grateful for that. Then move on down your list. For twenty-four hours, practice exercising a grateful mind, a grateful heart. We cannot *not* criticize without turning our attention to something of a higher nature. God gives us an absolutely unconditional guarantee of grace. Recall the words of St. Francis: "If the Holy Spirit can work through me, it can work through anyone."

I once read a story in a newspaper about a little boy whose father, in a fit of psychotic rage, set his son on fire. Much of the boy's body had third-degree burns, and yet that little boy lived. He was six years old when that happened. It's estimated that by the time he's thirty, he will have had dozens and dozens of surgeries. Every year doctors must operate on him to allow him to grow, and yet, on his seventh birthday, he wrote this:

I am alive!
I am alive!
I am alive!
I didn't miss out on living! And that is wonderful enough for me.

Growing Your Dream

Deeply believe that you deserve your dream, or you will fall short. God already knows you are perfect; now is the time for you to believe in yourself. With God's help, you can find that exquisite core you've kept hidden away and bring it out into the light.

1. Focus on the good to enhance your sense of worthiness. Circumstances are bad only if you perceive them as such. Instead of panicking when life appears to throw you a curve, wait and invite God to reveal the good. Then give yourself the same benefit of the doubt. Believe in your "original innocence." You make mistakes out of ignorance, not from a core of evil. You are inherently good because God created you. Beginning now, stop being a victim. Decide to become a co-creator—an architect of your own life—who benefits from each step of the process.

2. Stop dragging Harry. It's hard to move confidently into the life you have imagined if you're lugging deadweight. When you persist in carrying the baggage of your childhood, your shame, or your belief that you are unlovable, you have no room for greater possibilities. Let go of encumbrances by identifying and releasing your own Harry.

3. Practice gratitude to increase your sense of deserving. An "attitude of gratitude" enables you to construct your dream on a solid foundation of deserving. Begin by spending a day giving thanks to those you've criticized. From there, build a pattern of daily gratitude. When we begin to appreciate those we once condemned or took for granted, the field around the object of our appreciation broadens, attracting to itself even greater good.

Part Two

PLANTING THE SEED

Chapter Four

INTRUSION:

A Companion Called Fear

Our doubts are traitors,
And make us lose the good we oft might win,
By fearing to attempt.
—SHAKESPEARE

♦ *Learn to Recognize Your Delilahs*
♦ *Feed Your Faith and Starve Your Fear*
♦ *Be Willing to Be Wrong on Your Way to Being Right*

One of my favorite stories from the Old Testament is about a man named Samson, who was blessed with the gift of strength. Samson's might was so immense that the Israelites depended on it to defend them against the oppressive Philistines. But Samson did as many of us do: He toyed with the enemy of his gift. He flirted with a woman in the enemy camp named Delilah.

She asked him, "Samson, how do you get all that strength?" He pretended to give away his secret, confessing that if he was bound with new ropes, he would be rendered as weak as the next guy. So Delilah arranged to have Samson tied up, and of course he broke through those ropes as if they were thread. Delilah kept trying to entice the truth from him, and he kept showing off, breaking free of his restraints whenever she thought she had him trapped.

You'd think at some point Samson would have figured out this woman was bad news, but he chose to ignore the obvious. One reason I like this story is that I too sometimes tend to miss cues. I get distracted by an idea that sounds attractive, even when all messages point to trouble.

Finally, one night after she had besieged him relentlessly to reveal his secret, Samson blurted out, "If I am shaven, then my strength will leave me, and I shall become weak, and be like any other man." Delilah wasted no time in getting news of her discovery to the Philistines. Then she lulled Samson to sleep on her lap and called for a man to shave his head. When the Philistines arrived, the weakened Samson could not fight them. They plucked his eyes out (this is one of those grisly Bible stories) and took him to prison, where he was harnessed to the millstone to grind grain.

Samson's story is a metaphor for each of us. For one reason or another, most of us fall off course from our dreams. And if you allow yourself to play with the Delilahs in your life, you will live at the millstone, grinding away, going round and round in circles, getting nowhere.

Now, our Delilahs don't come waving banners saying I Am Your Destruction. They come looking good. Samson's Delilah was gorgeous, a true temptress. For many of us, comfort looks pretty alluring. We'd rather stay in a place we perceive as secure than stretch toward our dream, even when our safety is only an illusion.

Remember the old story about how to cook a frog? If you put a frog in hot water, it'll jump out, immediately recognizing a nasty situation. Should you, however, place the frog in lukewarm water, it settles in and gets comfortable. Then you turn up the heat a little at a time until the frog boils to death.

We too get comfortable, cocky even, refusing to acknowledge we're up to our necks in boiling water. We refuse to acknowledge Delilah as the enemy of our dream, even after she binds us with rope. Delilahs block the path to our dreams. As long as we're distracted, we cannot move into the next phase of our awakening. And that seems just fine at the time, because as we step closer to our dream we will be guided to take some risks. We fear risk; it can lead to rejection, ridicule, and failure, and it can feel uncomfortable to stretch and grow. We fear risk, yes, but if we really want our dream, we will find a way to grapple with our Delilahs so that they cannot stand in our way.

♦ Learn to Recognize Your Delilahs

A friend of mine who is part of a circle of women writers was talking with her colleagues about how they all feared facing a blank screen each morning, and how some days it was easier to clean the refrigerator than to turn on the computer. If they didn't attempt to write, then they wouldn't have to acknowledge the possibility that they might have nothing to say.

"I sometimes feel that way," said one of the women in the group, "but I've learned a great lesson from my aunt." The aunt had died recently, willing her niece the contents of her house, including a book collection amassed over her last twenty years. In this collection the niece found dozens of well-worn instructional manuals and books on writing—how to write a screenplay, how to write children's books, how to get published. It was amazing, because the niece had had no idea that she and her aunt shared the same love of writing. So the niece began sorting through boxes and scanning files, eager to see her aunt's work. Although she looked for days on end, all that emerged was a single paragraph that began "Once upon a time . . ."

Finally it hit her: There was nothing more to find. Her aunt had started and stopped. She must have possessed tremendous desire—after all, she'd had forty books on writing! Yet something stood in her way. What blocked her? What distracted her? No one will ever know for sure. The aunt's dream died with her.

Samson, with eyes plucked out, had lost his vision, just as we lose sight of the great plan that God has for our lives. We disconnect from our vision and veer off course. Something happened for Samson, however. Grinding at the millstone, he began to realize that his hair was growing back. God was giving him a second chance to do what he was meant to do.

During this time, the Philistines and their leaders, feeling pretty triumphant over having quashed Samson, ordered him brought to their temple so they could mock him. They ordered him to stand between two pillars.

There, standing between the pillars that supported the temple, Samson called to God, "Remember me . . . and strengthen me." He reached out his arms and, with every ounce of his renewed power, brought the temple down, killing all those within, and himself with them. Samson, dying a triumphant death, did not abandon his people. In his final moments he defended them as never before. Samson fulfilled his destiny.

What are your Delilahs? What stands between you and the fulfillment of your dream? Delilahs are disguises for fear. They manifest themselves in an array of costumes: distraction, doubt, confusion, and procrastination. Because our Delilahs come dressed so cunningly, we often fail to recognize them. They seduce us, lulling us into a false sense of security to the point where we grow fond of our fears. We cling to them.

A friend of mine has an eighty-year-old uncle who was born with an olfactory dysfunction, which meant he couldn't smell properly; in fact, he couldn't smell at all. If you can't smell, you can't really taste, and so he lived with only three of his five senses intact. A doctor told him, "You know, to repair your senses requires only two simple operations. The first will provide you a sense of smell temporarily, and then in about six weeks we could do another surgery and you would have your sense of smell permanently." The uncle, then a farmer in his twenties, agreed. He had the first surgery, stayed overnight at the hospital, and went home the next day. First thing the next morning, he went out in the barnyard and got sprayed by a skunk. Never having had the sense of smell before, the farmer made a decision in that moment: "The world stinks."

He refused to return for his second surgery, and so he spent his entire life not being able to smell a rose or savor chocolate or breathe in the scent of brewing coffee, all the incredible fragrances and delicacies life has to offer, because he experienced a whiff of something awful. He chose to remain secure inside his odorless little world, protected from skunks and all that exists beyond them.

Many of us have unconsciously plugged our nose to life's aromas, foul and fabulous alike. Rather than face the full dimension of our possibilities, we shut down. We narrow ourselves, carefully avoiding anything that stinks or stings, never getting close enough to our dreams to really inhale them or experience them.

One way to confront your Delilahs is by sharpening your senses. Your senses indicate the degree to which you are alive. Heighten your awareness of all you see, smell, taste, hear, or touch. Feel the rope tighten around your wrists as Delilah binds you. Tune in to the message. Does this feel like freedom to you? It doesn't do any good to deny doubt when doubt persists. It doesn't do any good to deny fear when fear strikes. We cannot move toward our dreams if we ignore the turmoil within.

Our ability to feel, touch, and taste is a gift from God. God has given us an eighty-eight-key piano with which to experience the full dimension of feeling, and we often play only chop-sticks. What sounds resonate in your mind when you shrink from a challenge? Consider how your face burns when you've told a lie. What's that sour taste in your mouth when you lose your temper? Consider the ache in your belly when you mis-manage your money. How does your body feel when you fail to care for it, stuffing yourself with cookies, neglecting exercise or sleep? You feel less alive, less connected, less at peace.

A woman from our congregation shared a story with me about how she recognized her Delilah. Lisa dreamed of having a loving relationship. She had been through a divorce and for a long time afterward had feared opening her heart to another man, keeping herself so busy at work that she didn't even have to think about dating. All those overtime hours were her Delilah until she met someone wonderful, her dream man. Lisa found herself falling in love and had the courage to tell him so. She could trust again. Good-bye, Delilah.

About a month after they started dating, the man called her and said, "Lisa, I need to tell you I'm not going to be calling you anymore. I've really enjoyed our time together, but there was a previous relationship that I don't feel finished with yet, and I need to finish that up and find out what's going on there."

Lisa was devastated. She thought, "I put my heart out there, and what happens? Bam! Someone comes along and crushes it again." She shut down and spent three days thinking, "I'm not going to do this ever again. This hurts too much. No more trust. No more hope. I'm not going to lay myself out like that."

On the third day, which was a Friday, she came home from work to a bitterly cold house. She went to turn up the thermo-stat, but nothing happened. It was less than fifty degrees inside. She called the gas company and was told, "We can't send any-body tonight. We'll be there tomorrow morning between nine

A.M. and noon." She went upstairs to her bedroom, crawled under her down comforter, and spent the evening thinking about living in not only a cold house but a cold heart as well. The gas company repairman arrived about ten-thirty the next morning and said, "There's nothing we can fix. The ignition switch on your furnace is broken. You're going to need to get that replaced, and for that, ma'am, you need the furnace folks, not us."

So Lisa had to call a company that repairs furnaces and was told, "We'll be out sometime in the afternoon; it could be as late as five o'clock."

"Great," she thought. "Now I can freeze all day." But the icy feeling started her thinking: Maybe the furnace malfunction was a metaphor for her life. Perhaps she had turned off her own ignition switch when she had said, "I'm not going to let myself get hurt again." She realized that by turning off the switch, she would live in a frozen condition; in not allowing her heart to be broken again, neither would she let it be touched. She said to herself, "I don't care if I get hurt again. I'm not going to shut down, because if I do, I'll always remain hurt. And you know what? Maybe this month-long romance didn't turn out the way I wanted, but in those thirty days I got in touch with feelings that I hadn't felt for a long time. I got in touch with parts of myself that I had forgotten existed, and even the way this relationship ended was honest. He didn't just stop calling with no explanation. We communicated, and that too is something to celebrate here." She said that once she came to her senses, the furnace man arrived two hours later. She didn't have to be cold all day after all. The heat was turned back on, both inside and out.

All aspects of our lives are a metaphor for what's going on inside us. We all experience fear as we grow into our greater selves. To avoid the fear, we may numb ourselves, we may shut down our hearts and minds and senses so that we cannot envision the divine life that awaits us. Lisa, for instance, came close to shutting down her heart for fear that it might break again.

Yet had she shut down that way, her dream of a loving relationship could never have become a reality, because her dream, like anyone's dream, must be pursued with an open heart. Tune into your senses so that you can sniff out the fear lurking behind your distraction. Ignoring the warning signs can stunt your dream; even as you go through the daily rituals of life, the dream begins to slip away from you, unnoticed.

Someone once asked me what was the worst thing I'd ever done, and I answered without hesitation, "I was so self-absorbed that I didn't nurture Rich enough when he was a baby." Rich is the second of my four children, born when I was nineteen years old. I certainly cared for him in all the physical ways that a mother cares for her child. I fed him properly, changed his diapers, cleaned his clothes, and ensured he got the proper amount of sleep.

Still, if you're a parent, you know that's not enough. Recall your own experience, or stop and watch a new mother and her infant gazing at each other. The intimacy is almost palpable. I loved my son, but our relationship lacked that bursting abundance of feeling. That sense of rapture, the connection, was missing. Frightened that I would never be able to live my own dream and become a teacher, I had turned myself off. I felt dead inside. I attended to Rich's needs meticulously, but in many ways I was simply going through the motions of motherhood.

Rich developed infantile diarrhea at the age of six months. His body could not retain any nourishment. He ran very high fevers doctors could not control. No matter what we did, Rich continued to lose weight.

The time arrived when the doctor told me my baby would not likely survive the night. In the early hours of that morning, I was sitting in a hospital room adjacent to where Rich struggled to survive, tubes protruding from his tiny arms. An attending physician told me how Rich would go, trying to prepare me for the worst, when suddenly I realized I was watching our conversation from the other side of the room. What I had come to identify as "me," my everyday consciousness, was hovering in an upper corner, observing this sterile white room and the people in it in a way that was curiously unattached yet compassionate. I had read about out-of-body experiences but shrugged off those stories. Now I could clearly see the doctor speaking with a young, frightened mother: me.

At the same instant I could sense my consciousness hovering in Rich's room. Gazing down at my baby, I was overcome with the realization that he was not starving for physical nourishment; rather, he needed the sustenance of the unconditional love I had denied him. His body hungered in that absence, unable to thrive.

In a flash I found my consciousness back in my body, and I thanked the doctor for his words of condolence. Immediately I started down the hall to Rich's room. Every sense in my body felt keenly aware and awake. As I approached the crib where he lay, I felt as if my energy grew and expanded to surround my ailing baby son. Suddenly I felt as if I were once again pregnant with my child. I completely enfolded Rich with my love, my being. Careful not to disturb the tubes, I reached into the crib and began stroking his face, reassuring my son that I would never again deprive him of the love he needed. My heart opened completely. I connected with how much I loved him and wanted him in my life. I matured a great deal in those few minutes. For the remainder of the night I sat next to Rich's crib, praying and feeling his soft skin against my hand.

Rich survived the night, and slowly the symptoms of his illness subsided. But doctors warned us about permanent neurological damage. When he was one year old, Rich still could not pull himself up. His arms and legs had little strength. In the weeks and months that followed, Haven, our parents, and I concentrated on nothing but pouring love into him. He grew stronger but didn't recover fully until he was almost three.

As I watched him play football in high school years later, I could hardly believe that as an infant this vital young athlete had been barely able to move his limbs. We both had experienced our own miracles. His was the miracle of physical healing. Mine was the miracle of moving past fear and doubt into a realm where I was free to love my son.

You cannot master a foe you don't recognize. Becoming more attuned to your senses will help you ferret out fear, even in its many disguises. Then, as you recognize your fear, you can speak to it directly: "I know you, fear. I know this doubt. I know this feeling. I will not let you guide my life."

The point is not to get rid of fear. Anything you oppose only grows larger. Acknowledge your fear. Accept it as your companion, not your master. Then shift your attention by reminding yourself: "There is something in me greater than this fear. That something is the power guiding this universe. And when I allow it in, that power guides my life. With this power, I can move past my Delilahs and onward, building my dream."

♦ Feed Your Faith and Starve Your Fear

There's an old Native American story I like to tell myself whenever I feel myself falling prey to fear. Like the biblical tale of Samson, it emphasizes the power of belief to overcome.

An Indian brave approaches his chief and says, "I feel like there are two dogs at war inside me, a white dog that is good and a black dog that is evil. What is going to happen?"

"Do not worry," the chief says, "the white dog will win."

"How do you know?"

"Because," the chief assures the young brave, "you will feed him."

Negative, fearful thoughts control our lives only to the degree that we empower them. If you have an unwelcome guest in your home, what do you do? Quit feeding him and he goes away. And so it is with the unwanted guests that try to live in our minds—fear, dread, and anxiety. Quit feeding them and they vanish. At this moment, what are you nourishing with your attention: your dreams or your doubts?

Feed those thoughts that nourish your dream. Serve them several heaping servings of loving kindness every day. Feed them with energy. If you had an unpleasant or fearful experience, starve it out by redirecting your thinking and nourishing the good. Steer all your energy in that direction. This is an important practice, because if you could somehow tally all your thoughts in a given day, one column for your dream and another for your doubts, which list would be longer?

Notice the unkempt house, with food and garbage left everywhere; see how the lowest life forms come in to feed off the waste. Your own life form feeds off the nourishment you provide with your thoughts. Thoughts of fear draw to us experiences that feed off that negative energy. Thoughts of love, acceptance, and faith respond in kind.

Take, for example, a fear that haunts many of us: getting old. Can you stave off old age and death by feeding your faith? Of course not. But you can, if you desire, do something equally miraculous.

I performed a funeral for Emma, a woman who had truly mastered her fear of death. Over her lifetime, she started nursery schools in the United States, Canada, and Japan. Emma taught English at an esteemed college until her late sixties. She was still jumping horses in her eighties.

When Emma was eighty-seven, her money manager found that she had $90,000 he hadn't known existed and asked why she'd tucked away so much money. She responded, "I was saving that for my old age."

"You're eighty-seven. When does old age start?"

"Not yet."

In her final days I visited her at a nursing home, where she remained concerned about others whom she deemed much worse off than herself. She told me, "Why, some of them don't even know God! They can't appreciate the smell of fresh coffee or the sun shining through the window." I asked her how she had developed such a positive attitude. She told me that when she turned sixty-five, her friends had strongly urged her to retire from her college teaching job. This prospect threw her into a deep depression, and for a time she became obsessed with death and old age. She prayed for help with the last chapter of her life. Three days after she began her prayers, she came across a passage called "Youth" by the turn-of-the-century poet Samuel Ullman in a collection called *A Treasury of the Familiar*. From then on, she read that passage every day to empower her to build new dreams as she grew older.

This is "Youth":

Youth is not a time of life; it is a state of mind. It is not a matter of rosy cheeks, red lips and supple knees; it is a matter of the will, a quality of the imagination, a vigor of the emotions; it is the freshness of the deep springs of life.

Youth means the temperamental predominance of courage over timidity, of the appetite for adventure over the love of ease. This often exists in a man of sixty more than a boy of twenty. Nobody grows old merely by a number of years. We grow old by deserting our ideals.

Years may wrinkle the skin, but to give up enthusiasm wrinkles the soul. Worry, fear, self-distrust bows the heart and turns the spirit back to dust.

Whether sixty or sixteen, there is in every human being's heart the lure of wonder, the unfailing child-like appetite of what's next, and the joy of the game of living. In the center of your heart and my heart there is a wireless station; so long as it receives messages of beauty, hope, cheer, courage and power from men and from the Infinite, so long are you young.

Emma fed her faith and died young at ninety-two.

Fear of old age, fear of failure, fear of loneliness, and fear of disease: You face all of these in the course of a lifetime. You cannot avoid them. Yet your response—do you feed your fear or your faith?—determines the outcome of your dreams.

The Book of Matthew contains a powerful story about faith and failure. Peter and the eleven other disciples of Jesus, all experienced sailors, set out one afternoon to cross the Sea of Galilee. Now, the Sea of Galilee is only seven miles wide, a pretty small body of water. But during the crossing a howling storm arose, sending great waves crashing against their boat. Soaking wet, the disciples were stuck in the middle of the sea, fearing for their lives, when they spotted Jesus walking toward them on the water. At first they thought He was a ghost.

> But immediately Jesus spoke to them, saying, "Be of good cheer. It is I. Do not be afraid."
>
> And Peter answered Him and said, "Lord, if it is You, command me to come to You on the water."
>
> So He said, "Come." And when Peter had come down out of the boat, he walked on the water to go to Jesus.
>
> But when he saw that the wind was boisterous, he was afraid; and beginning to sink, he cried out, saying, "Lord, save me."
>
> And immediately, Jesus stretched out his hand and caught him, and said to him, "O you of little faith, why did you doubt?"
>
> And when they got into the boat, the wind ceased.

I've heard several interpretations of this story. Some people believe that the message is that if you lose your faith, not only does Jesus scold you, but splash! you sink underwater. I believe the true meaning is more challenging.

When we are trying to stay afloat in a rocking boat—which

is what we cling to, thinking we'll be safe—something greater calls us to step out. This isn't like stepping out onto the sidewalk. You're being called to step out where you cannot see, where no solid ground exists beneath your feet. Only a fool would not be afraid.

Peter, however, feeds his faith. He says, "Lord, if it's You, command me to come to You." He asks his Creator for direction, just as you ask direction for your dream. Jesus replies, "Come to me." Focusing on Jesus, Peter lifts one leg out, then the other, and he walks on the water.

Then the Bible says, "He saw that the wind was boisterous."

At that moment Peter feeds his fear of drowning more than his faith in Jesus, and he starts to go down, just as any of us sink when we're overcome by fear.

So did Peter fail? Not at all. There are two more key points to this story. One, Peter asks for help. He calls out, "Lord, save me." Immediately Jesus reaches out to him. When you begin feeding your fear, ask for help. The Spirit of God will not hold back when you ask authentically. And two (we tend to forget this point), just for a moment, Peter walks on water!

Many have criticized Peter for losing his faith, for sinking, but remember, he was the only one of the twelve willing to get out of the boat. His willingness to move beyond where he sat demonstrated a faith beyond that of his companions. Peter walked on water and so was forever changed. He stepped out of fear and onto a plane where he was kept afloat by the power of his faith. Peter did not fail. He moved one step closer to his greater self.

Now, to come back to dry land, imagine your own dream is being challenged by fear. Let's say you envision your greater self as part of a twosome. Your dream is for a loving, nurturing relationship. Yet as hard as you try, that kind of bond eludes you.

"Have faith," your friends say. "Someone will come along." A platitude? On the surface, yes, but what if you were to take their advice quite literally? What would you need to do?

You could start by expressing love right where you are. Shower friends and family with love at this moment. Send your parents or best friends cards telling them what they mean to you. Practice random acts of kindness to strangers. Bake cookies for the new neighbors. When you're at the supermarket, ask the grocery checkers about their day. Feed your faith in love by becoming a living example that love exists. This is not always easy. If you haven't been on a decent date in a year, you may feel more inclined to radiate bitterness than love.

The problem is that so many of us withhold our love, thinking we'll wait until a prospective partner materializes. When nobody appears, our loneliness makes us stingy toward the people who do care for us—especially if we resent their being in a happy relationship. We hoard our love, in essence starving our faith.

Now suppose Mr. or Ms. Right does finally appear. You nab this prospective mate before he or she can get away. You pour out your pent-up love so eagerly that what you convey is not celebration but desperation. And Mr. or Ms. Right goes, "Whoa!" and gets scared off. Either that or, despairing of meeting anyone decent, you grab the next available person who comes along, blind yourself to any danger signals, and wind up settling for a poor facsimile of your dream.

Turn the tables for a moment: When someone *else* is looking for love, do you feel more attracted if your presence causes that person to celebrate or to hang on for dear life?

There's a law of attraction in this universe that holds that in response to the energy I generate, the universe responds in kind. Those who love life are loved. People in satisfying relationships feed their faith almost unconsciously; they radiate a loving confidence that draws to them even more warmth.

Those who nourish love see the world—and fill the world—with joy. Feed your faith by being loving and nurturing right where you stand.

Don't get me wrong. Loneliness so profound it physically hurts to see a pair of strangers holding hands cannot be trivialized. You long for what others seem to take for granted. Generating love toward others may not whisk the perfect man or woman into your life right away; but if you live lovingly, you cannot help but attract other loving people to your field.

Fear of loneliness, fear of old age, fear of failure—all these we will encounter, but we need not let them devour our lives. We may even take comfort from the fact that so many others share them. The prospect of death from a fatal disease, however, is different. Illness strikes at random and always, it seems, unjustly. We feel singled out, cut off from everything that has anchored our lives. How can we feed our faith and build our dream when we may have little time to live?

Mary Ellen and Rick, two of my closest friends, were married in March 1982. I met them six months later when Mary Ellen, then thirty-six, was diagnosed with lymphoma. The doctor showed her a study indicating that people with her condition lived an average of three years from the onset of the illness. He recommended radiation and chemotherapy.

Mary Ellen was warned that the particular chemotherapy drug she would take would cause all her hair to fall out within a few weeks. But Rick and Mary Ellen are a couple of tremendous faith, and Mary Ellen felt very strongly about her dark, wavy hair. In the midst of her daily prayers, she visualized little helpers tying knots in every cell of her hair to keep it on her head.

The doctors were surprised by Mary Ellen's hair, which did not fall out as expected. They were even more startled by her life. Mary Ellen did not die after three years. Instead, her cancer went into remission for over eight years.

In the spring of 1991 it came back.

Once again Mary Ellen recovered. At this point the couple felt they had beaten the odds. Their faith in God had been tested, and through it all, their faith had emerged stronger.

In 1993 Mary Ellen felt a pain in her groin. Thinking she had pulled a muscle, she went in to see a doctor. Within a few hours she was lying in a hospital bed: The lymphoma had struck again. Mary Ellen was only forty-eight years old, and she was battling cancer for a third time.

I was at the hospital with Rick when the doctor made his diagnosis. We sat there in a tiny waiting room, holding hands, as he told Rick truthfully that his wife might not survive.

Rick, in a flash of fear, wondered if his faith had all been a sham: "I thought to myself, 'My God, what's happening? This doesn't make any sense. We had all those years free of cancer. We had all these miracles, and now this.' It was a moment of sheer, overwhelming terror."

My heart broke for both of them, but I knew that once again they could call on their faith to see them through. I pointed down the hall to Mary Ellen's room. "There's a woman in there who hasn't given up," I said to him.

Rick said that even in his tremendous despair, he recognized he would not abandon his faith. "I was either going to self-destruct or make space enough to see all the possibilities. Nothing is a disaster until you call it a disaster," he said.

Rick and Mary Ellen both harnessed their faith. It was never easy. Mary Ellen underwent a painful bone marrow transplant and more radiation. Once she remained in a coma for twelve days. During her treatment, not knowing whether she would live or die, she told me: "I'm a spiritual being having a cancer experience. You know, I think I rejected cancer as my teacher, and I just didn't want to ever really look at cancer as my teacher again. Yet there's something in me that knows what I need most, and it's bringing me this experience. It is for some reason—I just don't understand it. Cancer is not what I as a human being would choose, but for some reason cancer is again offered to me as a teacher. And what I know is, I would not be where I am today if I had not had cancer as my teacher along the way. My being knows more than I know."

Mary Ellen did not see herself as a victim of cancer. She saw herself as a student of cancer. Of course she wanted to live. She believed her faith in her relationship with God was bigger than any disease. Mary Ellen prayed daily for a recovery, but she also accepted that she might not recover this time. In so doing, she reflected on her life and could honestly say she had no regrets. She had tremendous love for her husband, her friends, and God. If she missed time by dying before she reached her fiftieth year, at least she had wasted not one moment of it while living.

"I'm not saying I wasn't afraid," Mary Ellen now explains, "but I know that when I'm in that space feeling fearful, I don't make very good decisions. There are moments in the hard times when you fall on your knees and your faith is diminished. That's when I feel the weakest—when I think things aren't going to work out. I don't want to stay fearful. I remind myself of all the little miracles in my life and how God has always been there to support me.

"I keep my eye on the gifts I already have. If we remember the good things, our faith is fully restored, and we're motivated to go on again."

Mary Ellen did go on again. Her cancer went into remission. But her story does not end there.

In August 1995 she was diagnosed with cancer a fourth time. Unable to face any more invasive treatment, Mary Ellen is looking at her options and reflecting on her life. "You know, when I look back at when I was diagnosed the first time, it was an absolute disaster for me. Yet when I look back over these last fourteen years, I have grown so much and enjoy my life so much more, I realize I wouldn't be the person I am today without the cancer."

"When something like this happens, you have two choices," says Rick, "love or fear. If you choose fear, it's, 'Oh, my God, the bone marrow transplant didn't work,' and your life ends. You're in misery, waiting for death to come.

"We chose love. I notice how she does her makeup, how she looks when she's sleeping in the morning. I went from feeling totally in despair to noticing how magical our loving relationship is.

"The chances of us being the people we are now with the faith we have now—it's absolutely impossible. Cancer was our teacher. We had to make a conscious effort not to hate cancer but to embrace it, to let it teach us what it has to teach us and then to leave us. We're ready for it to go."

This dear couple have been my teachers. Rick and Mary Ellen have taught me that it is possible to live a full life in the midst of cancer. Their faith was tested as Job's was. And they too emerged more faithful. Through cancer, Mary Ellen stepped into a greater dream. The immensity of love the two of them experience for each other daily is evidence of God's presence.

♦ Be Willing to Be Wrong on Your Way to Being Right

Rick and Mary Ellen freed themselves by recognizing that their inner peace did not hinge on her recovery. They do not know if she will recover a fourth time. They have come to recognize that viewing only a particular outcome as success would render everything else failure. Their lives have not been about failure. They believe that remaining flexible gives God more room to work in their lives.

It is very easy to get locked into a particular map of your dream. What happens when you pursue a dream only to find you've taken off in the wrong direction? If you're rigid, you panic and thus miss out on the greater dream awaiting you. I heard somewhere that the Apollo 11 spacecraft was off course 90 percent of the time during its long voyage. But the destination was preprogrammed, and the spacecraft kept correcting and adjusting its bearings until finally it reached the moon.

Don't be afraid to change course midway through your journey. Your inner guidance mechanism is set toward your dream. You'll find your way to a greater good if you are willing to take the occasional side road, knowing there's a lesson in the detour and that you will find your way back.

Once when I was complaining to a friend that I wished my life had a few less detours, that I occasionally grew weary of struggle, she told me a story about a man who tried to help a butterfly. One day the man was in his backyard and noticed, on a tree limb, a butterfly emerging from its cocoon. He watched that little being struggle and strain and press up against the walls of its prison. The butterfly was having such a difficult time, and the man wanted to help, so he sawed off the tree branch and brought it into his house. He used a pair of very fine scissors to delicately clip the cocoon and create an opening for the butterfly. Sure enough, the butterfly emerged easily. Then, as the man looked on in horror, it flopped around on the table, unable to lift its wings. Within a short time the butterfly died.

The man knew he must somehow have interfered with nature, and so he went to the library to do some research on butterflies. He learned that as it emerges from its cocoon, the butterfly presses and strains, which pumps fluid from its large body into the wings. This process strengthens the wings and shrinks the body. Without that struggle, the butterfly emerges with weak wings and an unwieldy body, and cannot survive.

This is our own life process as well. We emerge from a chrysalis state to become our real, divine selves. We may fear the struggle and wish to remain safe little caterpillars, yet the more we open, the greater our rewards. For us it's not a single experience; we emerge over and over again, growing into a new way of being, exploring one way and then trying another until we find the right fit. No one can cut open your cocoon for you because it is through the struggle that you develop the strength to fly free.

Be willing to be wrong on your way to being right. You may head so far in one direction that you feel there's no way back, but there is always a way.

Jim, a member of our congregation, told me about what he called "a near death business experience"; that is, the near death of his construction company resulted in an experience that changed his life. It started when Jim bid on a $5 million project, his firm's biggest ever. Jim got the job; in fact, his was the only company to offer a bid.

"Then we got a little deeper into the process, and I realized I had underbid the cost by seven hundred and fifty thousand dollars. If we did the work at the price we had bid, that would kill our business," Jim said.

Naturally Jim was terrified. He had been so meticulous about building his company—his dream—slowly, taking on small-scale projects. It had been in just the past year or so that he'd begun to show a profit. Then this $5 million job materialized, and he said to himself, "This is it; this is my sign that it is time for me to move into something bigger." Now he was cursing himself for reaching too far; if only he'd steered clear of the multimillion-dollar job, his company wouldn't be facing bankruptcy. He was also cursing himself for entrusting the details to a new assistant. The numbers on which he based his bid had been wrong.

Jim's dream had been to own and run a successful business. He began on course with a clear plan, then veered off in the wrong direction when he underbid the project. Now he had to make some choices about which route to follow.

Fear led him down some pretty tricky paths. Perhaps if he didn't pay himself, put off paying the crew, he could . . . Forget it. He needed to pay the crew. Maybe if he used cheaper materials and . . . No, Jim was an honest man. He would never cheat a customer. Jim needed to take action of some sort, so he thought about what was true in his situation. First, the responsibility for the erroneous bid lay with him; he was the boss. Second, he was terrified of losing his business. Third, he had made a wrong turn and wanted to get back on track. Fourth, he needed help.

Jim asked God for guidance, and a thought came to him: What would he do if the tables were turned?

"I'd want to know the truth," Jim told himself. Now he knew what his next step must be.

He made an appointment with the client and confessed his error. He sat before a room full of frowning men and women who didn't hesitate to point out what Jim already knew: Legally he could be held to complete the project for the amount bid.

He remembered the words of Jesus: "And you shall know the truth, and the truth shall make you free." Jim had come to a place of surrender. "If it is God's will that I lose this business, then I will accept that. But in the meantime I'm going to do everything I can to save it and maintain my integrity. I will keep moving vigorously in the direction of my dream until I am unmistakably redirected." Despite his terror, Jim kept reminding himself of the truth.

Suddenly, Jim said, the director of the project took a deep breath and said, "Let's do the right thing here. You've been fair with us. We'll pay you what's fair and what really belongs on this bid. I appreciate your truthfulness." He then signed off on the additional funds.

Jim didn't make a penny on the deal, but neither did he lose his business. He realized that if called upon, God was always available to him and would work in his best interest, no matter what form that took. Don't marry yourself to a particular outcome or you may doom yourself to disappointment. Remember that sometimes you plant in one field and harvest in another. As Jesus said, "Behold, I say to you, lift up your eyes and look at the fields, for they are already white for harvest." Your harvest may arrive early or late or may not look precisely the way you anticipated, but if you remain constant in your faith, eventually you will gather your crop. Regardless of what you're going through right now, a harvest awaits you. Fear may always accompany you, but so long as you remain pliable, willing to move, you can proceed toward your greater good.

When my daughter Jenny was four years old, she had a fear common to many of us as children. She was terrified of water. Our family would go to the local swimming pool, and Jenny would not just hang on to the edge of the swimming pool—she would cling white-knuckled to it. No matter how much her father and I encouraged her to trust the water, telling her that it would support her if she would only let go, she wouldn't. She clung to the side of the pool, watching the rest of the family splash around and enjoy the water.

Not believing that throwing Jenny in would be a good idea, we had long conversations with her trying to convince her she could let go and remain safe. We kept telling her, "Jenny, it's okay. You can let go of the edge of the pool."

"But I'm afraid."

"I know, sweetie, but you don't have to let your fear run your life. It's okay. Look at the other kids. They're bouncing in the middle of the pool, and they're the same height as you. You can, too."

One day we said, "Jenny, don't you want to let go?" And she said, "I don't want to, but I'm going to."

This is the moment of transformation for all of us. None of us relishes facing our fear, but our dream exists beyond the borders of that fear. We tell ourselves, "No, I don't want to deal with the fear, but no longer will I let it stand in my way."

Finger by finger by finger Jenny unfastened herself from the edge, and we carried her to the middle of the pool. Her toes touched the bottom. She moved her arms and took a little bounce. Her eyes lit up.

Then she looked me right in the eye and said: "I've got the power!"

That's what the four-year-old did. She let go of the edge. That's the experience that awaits each one of us, discovering the power within as we release ourselves from fear.

Growing Your Dream

Anyone who dares to dream knows fear. If you're endeavoring to make your dream reality, you are required to step beyond the borders of your fear. That cannot help but be scary. Accept fear as a companion on your journey. You block your dream when you allow your fear to grow bigger than your faith.

1. Recognize and master your own Delilahs. Fear can doll itself up in some pretty alluring disguises, and if you're not careful, you can waste all your precious dream-building energy on a losing proposition. What is distracting you from your dream? So long as we allow our fear to busy our fingers or numb our minds, we don't have the energy available for building the reality of our deeper desires. When you shut down your senses, you're less alive. By the same token, when you sharpen those sensations that let you know you're alive, you begin to master your own Delilahs.

2. Feed your faith and starve your fear. Help your dreams grow by serving them several helpings of loving attention each day. Should your fears shove their way to the table, refuse to serve them. At the very least, say no to a second helping. If

nourished, fears tend to develop gluttonous appetites that can swallow your dreams whole.

3. Be willing to be wrong on your way to being right. The trail leading to the mountaintop is full of switchbacks. It may seem that you're covering three times the ground as you slowly ascend the mountain, but imagine how difficult your climb would be if you had to hike straight up. We are guided first in one direction and then the other for good reason. As you move vigorously in the direction of your dream, remain pliable so that God may guide you to your true destination.

Chapter Five

ABUNDANCE:

The Gift of Constant Circulation

If you build it, he will come.
—THE VOICE IN *FIELD OF DREAMS*

♦ *Take the Good You Have and Bless It*
♦ *Recognize that There Is One Source but Many Channels*
♦ *Circulate to Accelerate: Begin with Tithing as Training Wheels*

After graduating from ministerial school in Arizona, we moved our family to a farm Haven's mother owned in Oregon. Haven's two brothers joined us, drawn by the lush greenery and acres of gently rolling hills. Only God could have rendered property so magnificently pristine; clearly this was the ideal setting from which to launch our ministry. We planned to live off the land, raising marionberries, a special blackberry used primarily in pies and jam. We had great romantic notions of the earth sustaining us, of simple toil bringing us closer to God.

We forgot one thing: We were children of suburbia, and none of us had ever farmed before. The first year, we worked endless, back-breaking hours only to end the harvest $10,000 in the red.

Perhaps, we reasoned, a second year of farming would provide us the income to clear up the debts accumulated from the first, "failed" year. Then we could earn enough from farming to further our ministry, which was about as stunted as the crops. Frequently, no one even came to pay a visit Sunday mornings, so my husband and I would take turns holding services for each other. Even close friends kindly told us we were only "playing" at being ministers.

We did this year after year for five years, thinking, "One more year. This time we'll make it. We'll do it one more year." One winter, a severe freeze cut the marionberry crop to half its normal size. One spring, it rained relentlessly during blossom time. Each berry flower has to be pollinated five times in order to achieve a full-size crop, but the downpour scared away the bees before they completed their task. A third year, excess rain while the berries were on the vine turned the fruit moldy during harvest. This was not a field of dreams we were growing but rather a thicket of nightmares. If the earth is available to anyone willing to plant, why did the soil so shun our repeated efforts? We put every penny that came our way into farming. We nurtured our crop, we lavished it with care, we sought to harvest so that we might better serve God—how much more honorable can you get?—and instead of reaping the earth's bounty, we were stone-cold broke.

Finally I heard myself accusing God, "We're trying to do this so we can give this land as a ministry home for You, and You're not supporting us." How dare God welsh on the bargain I had designed! We were up against the wall. We hocked the tractor. By 1980 our debts had mounted to the point where we had to refinance the farm and lease it to others just to pay our bills. Our career as fledgling farmers had ended. I had knocked and knocked and knocked on a door that refused to budge.

Not so many years earlier, desperate over the difficulties in my marriage, I had cried out, "Help me." At that time I didn't know whom or even what I was calling on, but a response had come anyway: "There must be a better way."

Perhaps there was a better way now.

So I looked closely and saw another door slowly opening. From the other side of the threshold, my inner voice told me to take our ministry on the road. This is what some people refer to as intuition and what I call a still, small voice of inspired insight. My first reply was, "We don't have any money."

Undaunted, my voice replied, "Take your message on the road. Leave with your four kids and two cats and travel for a year."

"How can we do that?" I argued in my mind. "We have barely enough to live on."

The voice answered, "Take what you have and go."

My third reply was, "Yes! I'll do that!" And the door swung open.

With the door to farming bolted shut, I craved new direction. Besides, over the last year and a half my enthusiasm had diminished, and I had fallen into that familiar pattern of dullness, planting and picking and tilling by rote, lacking the thrill, the sense of aliveness that had seen us through the initial years of disappointing harvests. And yet I plodded through my farming chores, convinced that since we had committed to farming as the vehicle for our ministry, we ought to just keep at it. I wasn't allowing myself to co-create with God and imagine another alternative.

There's a story about an old man who was fishing off a dock.

Next to him stood a bucket and a ruler snapped off at the ten-inch mark. He would throw out his line, and every so often he'd reel in a little fish. Then he'd carefully unhook the fish and lay it down next to his ruler; any measuring eight or nine inches he'd toss in the bucket. Pretty soon there was this big tug on the line, and the old guy fought with the fish for quite a while. Finally he reeled in a real beauty; it must have been over a foot long. He laid it on the dock next to his ten-inch ruler. Then he threw the fish back in the water. A guy who was fishing next to him broke the silence: "Gosh, I've been watching you fish all afternoon, and that was the biggest fish you caught. I don't get it. Why did you throw it back?"

The old man responded, "Well, you see, my frying pan is only ten inches wide. Anything that doesn't fit my pan goes back."

Our frying pan is the size of the life we know. Our Creator sends us fish, ideas, to nourish us, to build the life we want to live. When an idea comes that's bigger than the frying pan we know, we toss it. We throw it back into the ocean of ideas, saying, "No, that won't fit, so that idea isn't for me." God's currency is ideas. The people who realize their dreams are the ones who are careful not to discard ideas that can nourish them and lead them to a more abundant life. They realize the frying pan does not span a mere ten inches; its breadth is infinite. My yearning for a new direction was so great that this idea of going on the road felt right, even though I had no idea how we could pull off such a feat. When an inspired idea hits fertile soil in you, it won't leave you alone; it grows and pulls at you until you either follow it or know no peace.

At first Haven and our two oldest children didn't want to go, but they couldn't ignore the spark in my eye, and eventually they were persuaded by my enthusiasm. It wasn't as if we had much to leave behind.

Haven bought window-washing equipment and took a quick study in the art. We agreed we would wash windows in neighborhoods along the road to pay our way while we conducted workshops at churches around the country. We bought a trailer and a Checker cab painted blue, which we decorated with rainbows. Our quasi-psychedelic dwelling for the next year would hardly qualify for *Better Homes and Gardens*, but what it lacked in taste was compensated for in heart. Besides, everybody could see us coming.

A few months earlier we'd started a self-esteem workshop for children in our local school district. Incorporating music from such diverse talents as Kermit the Frog and Pink Floyd, it introduced the concept that we all contain a rainbow of feelings and that what we do with those feelings builds a wall ("Just another brick in the wall," sang Pink Floyd) or builds a bridge. The kids had nicknamed the workshop "Rainbow Bridge." Parents were thrilled when their children came home and, for the first time, spoke openly about their feelings. They asked if we could put on a similar workshop for grown-ups. Why not both? I thought. The Rainbow Bridge workshops had been the one part of our ministry that had caught fire, and we decided to make them the basis of our traveling ministry. Hence our colorful motif for the road.

In August I went to the school district office and took our kids out of school for the year, planning to teach them during our trip. We had a seventh-grader, an eighth-grader, and a kindergartner and a preschooler. So with four kids, two cats, $300 cash, and a dream, we hitched our trailer to a rainbow and headed south.

We were just shy of the California border when the brake system on the trailer locked up, causing our home-on-wheels to fishtail at fifty miles an hour down the freeway. Fortunately no one was injured. But when I opened the door to the trailer, it was like a scene from the movie *The Long, Long Trailer*, with Lucille Ball and Desi Arnaz: dishes broken all over the floor, clothes scattered every which way. Only we weren't laughing. It took $172 to fix the brakes, more than half our stake. I started to get really scared.

The lack of money confused me. After all, weren't we devoting our lives to delivering God's message? I was essentially saying to God, "I've put my whole life on the line for the Spirit. Why does my dream feel as though it's on the verge of extinction?"

As we went on, we always seemed to have just enough money, just enough to put gas in the car and just enough to buy food. There was never anything left over. Then, on the road in south Florida, even this equation stopped working.

We had worked our way through California, across Arizona and Texas, and on through the South. We presented about ten workshops during the first four months, spending more time with squeegees than in sanctuaries. Congregations enjoyed our workshops, and word spread to other ministries. Still, we left Texas with a forty-day stretch until the next scheduled workshop. We drove to south Florida, believing that God would send us the work we needed to survive.

We had failed, however, to take into account the economic and sociological differences between south Florida and the other areas we had visited. Many people retire to Florida, and crimes against the elderly flourish, leaving senior citizens wary of strangers. Thieves and con artists abound. Folks are not eager to open their doors to people with rainbows painted on their car roving through their neighborhood looking for work. At house after house, we heard "No!" from behind closed doors.

Our money ebbed away, until one morning we had only three dollars left. I knew I could call my parents in Oregon and say, "Please send us some money until we can get to the end of the next workshop," but I couldn't bring myself to do that. There's absolutely nothing wrong with asking others for help, monetary or otherwise; in fact, you frequently need assistance to manifest your dreams. But it's got to feel right. I had a sense that if I asked for a loan at this point, I would miss out on an important learning experience hovering on the edge of my consciousness. Besides, I was too proud to admit to my parents that this latest escapade—like the farming—was ending in disappointment.

That afternoon I walked along the beach, feeling desperate about money and furious at God. My anger and feelings of separation intensified. This state of mind usually leads us to look down, the direction in which we are emotionally headed; it was no different for me as I kicked angrily at the sand that day.

At exactly the moment I began thinking, "I need a sign that we should continue with the workshop," I saw a small, shiny object staring back up at me from the beach. A bright, sparkling penny glistened in the sun. A single penny; it wasn't much. At one time I would have left it lying in the sand. But now the appearance of this humble coin at the exact moment I requested a sign gave me faith that I was on the verge of my lesson. God sends out signals all the time, but we tend to overlook them. As we grow increasingly aware of these signals and heed their significance, we are engaging in the process of co-creating with God.

We still had a little food, but not enough, so I took our three remaining dollars into a nearby grocery store and bought two packages of split peas, one green and one yellow, for thirty-seven cents apiece. The two different-colored peas would allow the kids to think we were having something different for supper each of the next two days.

As I headed for the checkout counter, the thought "I'm doing all I believe is right, so where is the support?" continued to rattle around in my head. Just as I dug in my pocket for a single bill, one of those moments of clarity we learn to recognize flashed through my mind. The still, small voice within, that very quiet, calm resonance that we know is deeper than our conscious mind, said to me, "You are tithing your time and you are tithing your talent, but you are not tithing your dollars."

It was instantly clear to me that my experience of abundance had diminished in the one area of my life where I held back. It wasn't the universe that was withholding its abundance from me. I had made little room to receive by my unwillingness to give financially. I wasn't sharing what had been given to me, however paltry the sum. That was the significance of the penny. It had value. If I wanted an abundant life, I needed to recognize my own wealth.

♦ Take the Good You Have and Bless It

We bless our material good by recognizing we have something to give. I knew the Bible teaches us to tithe 10 percent of our income. Somehow I had excluded myself from this principle, reasoning, "Yes, but I am giving my whole life to God, and we really do have very little money. When we have more, we'll give more."

Now as I stood in this critical crossroads, I heard the voice within encourage me to open up and give in the very area I most needed to receive. So I counted out thirty cents of the three dollars we had that day and put it in the donations box at the chapel of the Christian campground where we had parked our trailer. Then I prayed.

"My entire life is now on the line, God," I whispered. "We need a bit of money to survive. This, or something better. Thy will be done." This simple affirmation of our surrender to God, deeply felt and believed in, allows a power greater than our own to move in our lives.

By donating thirty cents, I was infusing the universe with my treasure. Many of us think, "I can't afford to be generous right now. I'll start giving once I get that promotion, that inheritance, that lottery jackpot." That attitude goes contrary to the principle of abundance, a necessary step to dream-building.

Abundance evolves through giving. A person with an abundant life is one who first shares his or her own wealth. You replenish the world around you with a portion of your worth and thus move forward yourself. If you're going to accelerate in a car, you first have to fill it with fuel; if you want heat from a wood stove, you must first put in the wood. It does no good to stand outside the stove screaming, "Give me some heat and I'll give you some wood." And yet we treat the universe that way. To accelerate your life, give.

Try this experiment. Take a deep breath and hold it. Just hold it. No, don't breathe. Hold it. Pull in a little more, even. Hold on to it. This is your life. This is all the good that you have now. Hang on to it. Don't release one drop. Keep holding it. You know what happens if you never let go? You turn blue and pass out. That's what has happened to many of us. We have become unconscious because we haven't learned how to let go. We cling to what we have, and we think that we can run our lives ourselves. When we move into the illusion of self-will, we become oblivious to the activity of God and to spiritual law in our lives. So many of us want only to inhale, to take, we forget that the life-giving act of breathing itself requires us to exhale, to give, in equal measure. Bless the good you have and share a portion of it.

A few hours after I donated the thirty cents, Haven returned home, and I braced myself for more stories of rejection. Instead, he walked into the trailer with a broad smile on his face.

"This afternoon," he told me, "everything turned around. I knocked on a door, and the woman in the house said, 'I'd love to have my windows done!' "

The job paid $80. This seemed like an enormous amount of money to us. We had gone from our last $30 to our last $3, and now we had $80 and felt quite rich! I explained the happenings of my afternoon and, without hesitation, we took eight dollars and sent it to the church where our next workshop was scheduled. The next day, a $160 window-washing job materialized.

Again, we tithed $16. After six years, harvest time had arrived and, like a farmer who returns the best seed to the ground to ensure another good crop, we were seeding our abundance with faith.

What made the difference? As farmers, we gave our time and our labor but held on to every penny. We had so little money, I thought we needed to keep it all for ourselves. I thought I could withhold myself financially and still fulfill a dream. But God doesn't work that way. If you hoard your best seeds instead of planting them in the earth, your crop always remains stunted. Now we were offering a portion of our treasure to a greater good.

In that moment of clarity in the grocery store, I had discovered the need for constant circulation on every level. It is the circulation itself that makes us prosperous. Prosperity is a way of living and thinking, not just the possession of money. Poverty is a way of living and thinking, not just the lack of money. Fear of economic insecurity evaporates as we move into an awareness of abundance.

The Old Testament tells the story of a widow deeply in debt. According to Talmudic law of the time, if you had no money, you paid your debt by sending your children into bondage. The widow was desperate. Imagine how you would feel. Your husband is dead, you owe a fortune, and you're about to lose your kids to boot. She went to a prophet called Elisha and begged for help. Elisha said to her, "What shall I do for you? Tell me, what do you have in the house?" And she said, "Your maidservant has nothing in the house but a jar of oil."

The widow was caught in "nothingness consciousness." Instead of looking at what she had and blessing it and multiplying it, she looked at it and said she had "nothing in the house but . . ." In that kind of consciousness, she could only see lack.

When Jesus had the five thousand to feed and there was only

a little bit of food, He didn't say, "Oh, my gosh, I've got only a little bit of food, I can't feed anybody." He blessed what He had, and the food multiplied.

Elisha taught the widow the same lesson. He told her to go and borrow every container she could find and take them to her home. She was then to take the oil she had and pour it into the new containers. The widow knew that the little oil she had would never fill even one container but she faithfully followed the instructions.

The story tells us that as long as she had empty containers the oil continued to pour. When there was no more room to receive, the oil stopped. She then sold the oil, paid her debt, and she and her sons lived on the rest.

This is how the spiritual principle works. If you have a capacity, open yourself through giving. The Spirit fills you. If you don't open, there's no room for the Spirit to pour anything into your life. The Spirit moves and fills your life according to the dimensions of your belief.

Do you want to change your life? Start inside. Refuse to be victimized by old thinking that moans, "Life is happening to me." You can't blame poverty on lack of education, or loneliness on a weight problem. You are absolutely, abundantly free to create what you choose. A prosperous person is one who gives. If your pocketbook indicates you are impoverished, defy that thinking with your generosity. What happens? As you circulate your good, the circle broadens to include you. What you think today is a prosperous life, what you think from your present viewpoint is the abundant life, will change as your dream-building matures. Your dream of prosperity will grow and mature as you grow in spiritual maturity. What I thought of as the abundant life twenty years ago is very different from the abundant life that I feel and embrace today.

I felt prosperous when I gave my thirty cents because I grew closer to God in the process. This heightened state of awareness opened me to gratitude and grace, a place where I awakened to the abundance already in my life as well as the potential for all that God had in store for me.

During our stay in Florida, we met a minister named Roy Fox. We were going to leave the area temporarily but were planning to conduct a workshop at his church when we returned in a few weeks. I called him to clarify details before we left town, and he said, "I'm just on my way out to get coffee and pie. Why don't you meet me?"

Despite our recent rash of window-washing jobs, we were still just making ends meet. We had so little money that my scarcity thinking dictated, "Oh, no, we're going to have to go to a restaurant and have coffee and pie. We don't have the money to go to a restaurant." But I knew we needed to confirm our workshop, so I told myself, "Well, we'll just have water or tea or something, and we can get by."

But Roy insisted on buying our dessert, and as we were scraping the last bits of blueberry from our plates—marionberries, fortunately, had not yet found their way to Florida—Roy told us, "Here's how to amplify your good. Give ten percent of everything that comes your way. Give it back. Circulate it. And then bless everybody you ever encounter. Bless them. You will emanate a radiant field of energy. That energy will attract to you ideas, inspirations, substance that you can't possibly imagine."

Roy told us that he asked waiters and waitresses in every restaurant he went, "Do you want to increase your tips by fifty percent or more?" Of course they would say yes. He'd say, "Okay, here's what you do. When you come up to the table, bless that family in your heart, bless that person, silently extend the energy of a blessing, and then keep track of your tips over a month's time." Some of these people thought Roy was a crackpot. But others did not. He showed us a file of letters from servers reporting their results: "You know, all I've done differently is bless that table, and you wouldn't believe . . ."

Roy told us that when you start putting out a blessing, when you bless the good you have, you're more fluid; you're more porous to the inspiration of God moving you.

Then when you least expect it, the good you project will return to you tenfold.

After Roy paid our bill, he stood up and said, "You know, right now I'm feeling a prompting from the Holy Spirit that I'm supposed to give you kids some money. So I think I'll give you twenty-five dollars. Why don't we go across the street to the bank and I'll give you twenty-five dollars, buy your next tank of gas and send you on your way." I thought, "We can accept that." Then as we headed across the street, he said, "Gosh, I think I'm going to have to give you more than that. The Holy Spirit's not leaving me alone. It's telling me to give you more money."

Now I felt really awkward and tried to protest. But he waved our protestations away and went into his bank. When he came out, he said, "I've argued with the Holy Spirit all the way up until It finally shut up. I thought I'd give you twenty-five dollars, and the voice said, 'More,' and then I thought, 'Okay, fifty dollars,' and the voice said, 'More,' and I said, 'Okay, seventy-five dollars,' and I was writing the check and the voice said, 'More,' and I wrote a hundred dollars, and the voice got quiet, so there, that's all you get."

Generosity is a powerful, magnetic energy field in which you attract ideas, substance, and circumstances and align them with your deepest dreams. It has nothing to do with how much you have; it has everything to do with who you are being. Are you being generous? To build a greater dream, we must first step into a greater energy from which to draw prosperity into every area of our lives. We live in a generous universe. We can align with God by becoming God-like in our expression. Infusing our lives with the energy of generosity opens the doors to God's unlimited supply of ideas, opportunities, and substance.

After circling Florida and returning to Tallahassee to conduct the workshop at the Rev. Fox's church, we headed north along the coast. When we reached upstate New York, our long-awaited tax refund of $400 finally caught up with us, and just in time. The old rainbow Checker lugging our trailer had burned up a lot of rubber, and we desperately needed new tires. As we prepared to dash off to the tire store, I called my mother in Oregon. I was curious about the response we had received to a letter sent out across the country informing people about our workshop. Ministers would respond by calling our Oregon phone number (my mother took the messages) and I returned the calls, charging them to her phone. After a few minutes of conversation, I asked about the current phone bill.

"How much do we owe this month?" I asked.

"Well, it's three hundred dollars," my mom answered.

"Oh, my!" I said, anxiously thinking, "There go the new tires." Our phone bill had been running about $100 a month. Now what? Tires or the telephone? I knew my mother would let us make small payments until we paid off the bill. But my experience in Florida had taught me a lesson. If I remained open and trusted God's timing, we would be presented with a solution. Unquestionably our debt came first.

After my phone call to Oregon, I mailed a check to my mother for $300. I felt better for having paid the bill, but I was also wondering how our trailer would make it the rest of the trip on bald tires. Our trailer was parked just outside the church where we had been giving our workshop that week. I wandered into the sanctuary, praying for guidance. A woman who worked at the church approached me.

"I didn't mean to eavesdrop, but yesterday at the workshop I overheard you talking to somebody about needing tires. Do you still need them?" she asked.

"Oh, yes, we sure do!" I answered immediately.

"Well, I might be able to help" was her mysterious reply. I had no idea what potential solution she had in mind.

The workshop that night was well received by the congregation. Early the next morning, we walked outside and found five new steel-belted radial tires, exactly the size we needed, leaning up against the trailer with a note attached to them. A man who had attended the workshop wrote: "I was very inspired by your work, and I heard you needed tires. I wanted to contribute."

If I had put off paying the phone bill, using the money for new tires instead, we would have missed God's solution on two fronts; the phone bill would still have been unpaid, and the gift of the tires would not have been made available to us. The willingness to trust, to stay open, and to let go of our preconceived notions of how things should work creates a peace of mind and a spaciousness in which God can provide abundance in our lives beyond anything we have imagined for ourselves.

Jesus said, "Do not fear . . . for it is the Father's good pleasure to give you the kingdom." He also taught that God is love. An abundant life means the full experience of love, the experience of peace, in all areas of our lives—health, relationships, and finances. The experience of love, our awareness of the abundance in our lives, can surface even when we are ill or in the middle of a divorce, or when we worry about getting a flat on the expressway. For no matter what the circumstances of our lives, God is still our source. Settling peacefully into this realization gives the universe room to co-create miracles with us. Conversely, without this acceptance and peace of mind, no accumulation of treasure will satisfy the hunger deep inside us. No matter what we have, it will never feel like enough.

In all, our year on the road took us 37,000 miles and into a hundred churches and religious centers, the last of which was in

Calgary, Alberta, Canada. We had tired of living in a trailer and were anxious to go home. What we would do when we got there, we had no idea. Our dream was still to head our own ministry, but we lacked the seed money to get one started. While we were conducting our final workshop in Calgary, a massive storm pelted the cab with hailstones, pockmarking the once polished surface. We headed home in now what was truly a sorry sight, a steel shell of dented rainbows, which we affectionately renamed the "Dimpled Darling."

The Almighty sometimes signals through the least likely messenger, and this time it was through our automobile insurance carrier. When we arrived in Oregon, we immediately put in a claim for the battered cab. A few weeks later the insurance company sent us a check for $2,500. Written at the bottom of that check was the notation "Hailstorm. An act of God."

The message couldn't get any clearer than that. Our dimpled darling never regained her smooth complexion, but our dream had been infused with radiant life. We took that $2,500 and opened a bank account. We leased a two-hundred-square-foot office and found ourselves a dingy little Odd Fellows Hall that somehow felt to us like a sanctuary. We dusted off the antique pulpit that I had purchased at a garage sale five years earlier, moved our stereo system from home to the hall, and spent $100 to have a banner made that read Living Enrichment Center. We took that banner and hung it outside the building. Six years after we had been ordained ministers, we were finally on our way. The church had been born.

♦ Recognize that There Is One Source but Many Channels

Ask yourself how well off you are at this moment, and you may automatically reach for your last bank statement for an answer. The reality of our culture is that we tend to equate abundance with how much money and material comfort we possess. Collectively, we've been trained to believe that our checkbook represents our source. Our bank account, our CDs, our IRAs, our job—we have translated where we draw our financial good into the source of our security.

We tend to define who we are either by what we earn or what we do, particularly if what we do is considered prestigious and pays well. The problem arises when our perceived source disappears—the company closes down, we get laid off, or the Dow-Jones average suddenly drops a hundred points. If you believe your entire worth is contained in your job title or your stock portfolio, you cannot help but feel worthless—without value—in such a crisis.

A friend told me about her friend Tim, who had been an art director for a leading advertising agency. Word came of major layoffs, but Tim wasn't worried. He knew the layoffs were his company's way of eliminating dead wood. Tim felt fortunate to be among those whose talent was readily recognized; he believed he was immune to the ax.

Imagine how Tim felt when he received his pink slip. His coworkers thought he must be joking. Tim experienced the gamut of emotions: fury, humiliation, hurt, and denial. He believed his talent had been a sham. He took a nearly identical job hundreds of miles away, one that he didn't really want, in part to reassure himself he still had what it took. A prestigious job can be highly rewarding, but it is a channel, not the source. It wasn't until Tim realized that the talent within him came from God—no business needed to validate his talent, nor did any business possess the power to take his gift away—that he found the courage to do what he truly wanted to do all along. Tim went into business for himself. And yes, he prospered.

Some people mistake their source for a job or a savings account; others of us measure our worth through relationships with others. Our source does bring us good through many channels, such as love from friends, marriage, and the birth of children. Do not confuse, however, these channels of love with their source, which is God. If we do, we feel cut off from love itself when someone leaves us. We distort our sense of security. Circumstances change, and if we don't know our true source, we are left feeling abandoned, insecure, fearful, and alone. When a loved one leaves, for whatever reason, we may feel as if our feet have been knocked out from under us. But when crisis strikes, we can remain in a field of prosperity by reminding ourselves that we have but one source.

I read an article about a little boy who wrote a letter to God. A postal worker found an envelope addressed to God written in a young person's handwriting. He opened it and found a letter from a young boy saying his father had been ill and the family had no money. They needed $500 to pay the rent and buy food. The letter said, "God, please send us $500." The postman was so touched that he took the letter to the post office and circulated it, creating an opportunity for people to give to this cause. Within a week, $300 had been contributed. He put the $300 in an envelope and delivered it to the boy's house. Two days later, another note addressed to God arrived at the post office. This letter read, "Dear God, Thank you very much for the $300. Next time bring it to me directly; the post office took $200 of it." Unlike many of us, that kid had no doubts about his source; it was the channel that confounded him.

Are you focused on the source or on the channel? In any given circumstance, ask yourself this question: Are you thinking in terms of "us" versus "them"? Tim mentally pitted himself against the former employer he felt had robbed him of his dignity and opportunity, until he recognized that what was most valuable could not be taken from him. When you align yourself with God, your source, there is no divisiveness.

I once took my old car to a dealership for new brakes. While talking to the service writer about how much the repairs would cost, I noticed a funny odor. "Smells like something is burning," I said.

We looked around, and the fellow said, "It's you!"

My coat was pressed up against a little space heater, which had burned a hole the size of a mason jar lid clear through the fabric. The man felt bad and arranged for his dealership to pay for a new coat. "Go pick one out and send us the bill," he said.

I thought, "Great!" and headed straight for the mall. In the midst of trying on various styles, I noticed an interesting process taking shape in my thinking. A $300 coat had more appeal than a $50 coat, and not just because I could get wool instead of polyester. I could allow myself the luxury of a more expensive garment when I spent someone else's money. "This is not my money," I thought. "I can get the coat I've always wanted."

Suddenly I realized I was making the people from the car dealership "them." There is only one source, and by setting myself against "them" in buying that new coat, I would have to lower my consciousness from the unity of all life. Unless I was willing to spend "their" money as if it were "my" money, I would have to live in separation. As soon as I recognized my temptation to draw lines, I began to feel more peaceful. The dealership was a channel; it did not possess infinite pockets. As I made the decision to act in integrity with my values, I came around a corner and saw a sale rack. I found a beautiful blue wool coat that had originally been marked $300. It had gone on sale for half price. The day I went shopping, it had been marked down another 50 percent. I tried on that coat, and it fit perfectly.

When I returned to the car dealership and presented the bill for $75, the service writer looked at my receipt and said, "Is that all?"

"I shop," I told him, "with a careful eye."

He paused, looked at me, and said, "Thank you, ma'am."

I kept that coat three years. Every time I wore it, I felt wonderful. The coat was a gift of abundance that kept giving itself to me every time I buttoned it up.

You and I are creating our experience of abundance at every moment of our lives—either an abundance of scarcity or an abundance of prosperity, whichever we choose. We tend to create, over and over again, the same unwanted experiences because we fail to heed the levels of thinking in operation. We forget that we can change our thoughts and thus alter our results.

There's a story about a man who was an old-time logger. He heard of something called a chain saw and wanted to try it out. He went to the hardware store in town and told the sales clerk, "I want to try this newfangled chain saw."

"This will probably cut twenty trees a day for you," the clerk said, handing him one.

Two weeks later the logger returned. Angrily he threw the chain saw down on the counter, saying, "This thing won't cut more than four, maybe five trees a day. I've had it!"

The perplexed clerk said, "Let me try it." The clerk then pulled the starter, and the chain saw fired right up with a roar.

The old-timer's eyes grew wide, and he asked excitedly, "What's that noise?"

Why do we so often attempt to hack our way through life without connecting to the source of the strength that will allow us to cut through to its essence? We get stuck in one pattern of thinking and doing, a way that is no longer efficient, then curse the universe when what we want fails to materialize. Matter must obey the intent of consciousness—automobiles, money, food, jobs, and relationships have no particular bias about where they go. To receive abundance, you must participate in its flow. Align yourself with your Source, from which all abundance flows.

When you align yourself with your paycheck or bank account, you get stuck. The paycheck is a channel, not a source. If you treat it like your source, placing your security there, you're going to be disappointed. If the paycheck dries up, what then?

When we honor the true source, we locate channels in the most unexpected places. My oldest son, John, discovered an unlikely channel to abundance during our family's year on the road with Rainbow Bridge. John, then an eighth-grader, hadn't been keen on this journey in the first place; like any kid his age, he wanted to hang out with his buddies and play football. To make the trip even more loathsome for him, we couldn't afford entertainment—no movies, no amusement parks, nothing to perk up a grumpy adolescent. Nothing, that is, except a pair of boogie boards we'd brought with us from home. All along the California coast, after a day of window-washing and church meetings, we'd spend our October evenings gliding through the surf, laughing and screaming as the slippery rounds of fiberglass shot out from under us and we landed on our backsides, covered with wet sand.

After one such afternoon we were eating dinner at our campground, when John sprang up from the table with a look of panic on his face. He had left one of the boogie boards in the rest room when we went to wash up. John raced over to the rest room, but the board had disappeared.

So too had half the family fun.

John grieved for the lost boogie board. He saw only two answers to his problem: He could earn enough money for a new board (not likely), or we could find one used. We hunted through garage sales and secondhand stores looking for a replacement, but even the most battered boogie boards went for $120, way beyond our budget. Finally we gave up looking but not dreaming. Halloween came and went, and we at last had enough money to buy John a new pair of shoes. Inside a mall, John was trying on sneakers, and I commented to the salesman that he looked like a surfer. He was, and we shared with him the saga of our stolen boogie board, asking if boogie boards were ever available for under $50.

When we finished, a man who had been standing nearby approached us. He said he had a brand-new boogie board hanging in his garage.

"I don't know why, but I want to give it to you. This is something I know I'm supposed to do."

John and I followed this stranger to his home. Sure enough, there in his garage was a shiny red board far superior to the one that had been stolen. The price tag was still hanging on the leash strap.

John had tears in his eyes as he carried his new board to the cab. On the drive back to the trailer, he told me that on Halloween, after he and his brother had finished their trick-or-treating, he had noticed a Snickers bar in Rich's bag. John had really wanted that candy bar. Snickers bars were his favorite. John had reached into the bag when his brother wasn't looking. After all, there was so much candy, who would know? But just as his hand touched the wrapper, something had made him stop.

"I just couldn't do it, Mom," he said. "I knew that even if no one ever found out that I stole Rich's candy, I would know, and I decided that feeling right with myself was more important. And now look—God found a way to help me!"

John didn't tell himself, "Gee, if I don't take the candy, maybe a boogie board will magically pop up!" Abundance isn't about quid pro quo. You don't behave with integrity merely to coax your desired trinket from the universe. You choose to live honorably because you recognize honor as your true nature. When John refused the temptation to steal his brother's Snickers bar, he aligned himself with his source. And John became available to one of the infinite number of channels that flow from the source.

In *The Empire Strikes Back,* Luke Skywalker asks the Jedi master, Yoda, "How will I know the good from the bad?"

Yoda replies, "You will know through calm and peace. This is the way of the Force; a Jedi does not need to attack; the Force will work for him."

The Force is available to work for all of us, and we will know what is right through peace and calm. As you build your dream, notice those moments of serenity. They come not when you're frantically searching and asking, "Can I get . . . ?" or "What's in it for me?" Those moments arrive when we align ourselves with our source.

As we begin to open the door for a greater experience of life's flow, we begin to sense a security that is unshakable, a kind of love that never leaves us and a sense of being alive that grows and expands with the passage of time, because there is one relationship that is eternal, and that's our relationship with our source, our Creator.

♦ Circulate to Accelerate: Begin with Tithing as Training Wheels

When you are truly in the giving spirit, you willingly give your time, your talent, and your treasure. Leaving any one of these elements out throws you off balance. The parents who buy their children every material good but neglect to spend time with them are in fact depriving them. By opening our minds to abundance, gifts flow back to us in often startling ways. Do you want to accelerate? Circulate. Many people are unsure exactly how to go about this. There's more involved than merely saying, "Hmmm, I earned fifty thousand dollars this year, and taxes are going to eat me alive. Hey, maybe if I write a check to charity for five or ten percent, I'll get a tax break and feel better about myself to boot!"

Circulation is a way of life, a constant process born of practice, not an isolated gush into the universe.

As a child, you probably didn't learn to ride a bike by perching a two-wheeler at the top of a hill and hoping you'd figure out how to control the pedals on the way down. First, you opened your mind. Many kids are terrified of learning to ride, but they get this mental image of themselves pedaling down the block, fast and furious, whizzing past the neighbor kids, and so they say, "Okay, I'm going to give this thing a try." Then they venture out tentatively with training wheels. Eventually, when they find their balance, they remove those wheels. Pedaling has become automatic, and the kid who once shrank at the sight of handlebars is racing full tilt down the road, yelling, "Look, Mom, no hands!"

So we begin with the willingness for abundance. Do you consider yourself prosperous? Jesus said, "For to everyone who has, more will be given, and he will have abundance; but from him who does not have, even what he has will be taken away." This means that people who celebrate whatever good they possess by sharing it with others enjoy a more abundant life. If all you can see is what you do not possess—your former college roommate has a better-paying job and a bigger house, everyone but you drives a decent car—you fail to honor what you do possess. That which is not appreciated decreases in value. The ill-tended car breaks down. The ill-kept house goes unsold.

Learn to celebrate the abundance of others. When you see someone else having what you want, what happens inside you? If at that moment you contract into envy, resentment, or self-pity rather than celebrate that person's good fortune, you narrow your own receptors. If you are alone and see someone else in a beautiful relationship, celebrate for that couple. Hold that relationship as a model for yourself. If someone else at work gets the promotion you sought, rejoice for that person and resolve to work even harder. I'm not saying this is easy or that the next opening is guaranteed to go to you. Yet by contrast, bitterness and envy will surely shut you out of opportunity.

You increase your cardiovascular capacity by working out. It's the same thing with the spiritual aspects of your life. If you want to increase your capacity to receive abundance, you have to increase your capacity for giving. You cannot receive more unless you give more. People delude themselves into thinking that the amount they give is tied to what they have. In fact, the opposite is true: What you have is tied to what you give. We can put ourselves in the mind of the abundant giver.

Give more than you think life gives you. If you're giving out only what you think you are getting, you will continue to receive just that. Make space in your life for good to move into you and through you. Underpaid at work? You won't get ahead by watching the clock and scrambling out the door every day at 5 P.M. Undervalued at home? Give your relationship more love and watch it blossom. A friend once shared with me the difficulties she was experiencing in her relationship with her husband. "We seem to be at odds with each other over everything," she lamented. We mused together about how when you start a new relationship, you feed it, pouring time and energy into it. You send flowers and cards; you say nice things, you caress. When you gradually stop doing all those endearing things, soon you may find yourself saying, "This relationship is no fun. I don't think I like what's going on. In fact, I don't think I like *you*," and then you search for someone new, not recognizing that most often the relationship merely reflects what both of you contribute to it.

The next powerful step for abundant living is tithing, a conscious form of consistently circulating material good. When I first began giving, I gave by how I felt; I would look at my checkbook to decide how much to circulate. Over time I began to understand that by circulating money in this way I always stayed at the mercy of my checkbook—I was looking at my checkbook as if it were the source of my abundance. I finally learned that my checkbook was nothing but a leather repository for the money God helped me to create. By tithing we join consciously with God at the material level, which can take a great deal of courage. We too are channels of God's abundance. God can only do for us what God can do through us. I realize now that God contributes through me, and I am fulfilling my purpose of allowing the flow of energy in the universe to move through me. One example of this flow is the flow of funds. As I allow the current to move through me, I recognize more each day that I am worthy of having the flow move to me as well.

Many of us, at one time or another, have not had enough money in the bank to cover the checks that we had to write on Friday in order to get to Monday. When we started the Living Enrichment Center, we sometimes had to decide whose light bill we were going to pay—mine, my assistant's, or the church's—just to get through the week.

Jesus taught us to think beyond our present beliefs and to feel beyond our present feelings. In order to break out of scarcity thinking—to experience more peace of mind, greater and more vibrant health, enriched relationships—we can begin with self-examination. We ask ourselves, "Am I willing to open to abundance?" Then we can begin to see that the universe can supply us in ways that we had previously discounted.

Put on your training wheels and start practicing percentage giving. Take the very thing that can cause distortion and a frightened sense of separation from God—your very sense of worldly security—and give a portion of it away. That very act requires one of the greatest steps in faith that you will take. Most of us who choose a spiritual path of living find we're willing to give our love, and we're willing to give our friendship, and we're willing even to give our time, but we're much less willing to give of our financial good. We are trapped by the belief that our security is in the world. So the prophets of old gave us training wheels, if you will, in a pattern for growth called tithing. A tithe literally means 10 percent. In the old days the smartest farmers took 10 percent of the best seed of their crop and reserved it for the following year. They then sold the balance for their livelihoods. This idea of seeding the future with your present good began to be understood as a universal principle of growth and prosperity.

Now, there's no magic in these training wheels except that they teach you when you begin to slip away from a balanced flow of giving. There is an energetic principle here. The energy dynamic you experience while in the flow of giving lifts you to an amplified abundance. First you use training wheels to help you get comfortable. If you're learning to ride a bike, those training wheels are very helpful. They teach you what it feels like to be in flow, to balance.

We get confused if we start measuring results immediately in our financial world. We think, "Well, I gave fifty dollars, so I should get five hundred dollars." Instead, start to notice your sense of well-being. Wealth is so much more than financial good. There is a sense of security that begins to be seeded and nurtured when one enters into a life of trust. Trust is not passive but active.

To experience the full benefit of the flow, try circulating 10 percent of your current income. If that amount interferes with your paying basic living expenses, then begin with a percentage that's more realistic. The key is to move into percentage giving. In this way you learn to give as you breathe, regularly and easily. The universe continually gives of itself. As you practice a higher level of giving, you align with the very nature of the universe and open wider to its flow. Channels of greater good open to you: ideas, opportunities, and the peace of being right with life grow in the most amazing ways. After a time you will find a new balance, so you don't always have to think about giving 5 percent or 10 percent or 15 percent. You can remove those training wheels. Once we find true balance, we find a whole new freedom from financial insecurity, living in the flow of giving ourselves into life and holding nothing back.

Remember, we are created in the image and likeness of our Creator. Our Creator gives unceasingly. It is almost as if our very DNA is coded so that we feel really, deeply good and right with ourselves when we are giving.

One man I know travels all over the country conducting organizational development seminars for various businesses. People in his field tend to hang on to their teaching materials, protecting them, because that's how they make their income. He has a different approach. "Whenever I'm with other consultants who want ideas, I give them copies of everything I have," he says. "Once I was doing that with another person, just giving away all these copies of things, and the person said, 'I'm just amazed that you could give this away.' I replied, 'Oh, it comes back to me.' Two hours later I got a phone call in my hotel room from someone else who said, 'I got to thinking about you this afternoon after being in your seminar. I've got three referrals for you.' They were major corporations, clients worth a great deal of business. The income from those referrals more than tripled my income."

We learn to let the energy flow because God is the inexhaustible source of it all. You cannot give more than God; God has a bigger shovel.

A man named Mark who attends our church received a $600 sports watch from his sister. Her wealthy former boyfriend had left the watch at her house one night and never retrieved it, even though she called frequently to remind him. Apparently with no regret, he discarded a watch that cost more than the average American earns in a week. Mark, however, was thrilled. He already owned a dress watch, but he didn't have anything for casual wear. He felt quite chic jogging along the riverfront each evening after work with a $600 timepiece strapped around his wrist.

He was wearing his new watch at the home of a close friend one day when the friend confided that he was broke. He and his wife had just had a baby and bought a new house. The move and family addition had wiped out their savings, and the husband's employer was sending him to Washington, D.C., for an important conference the following day.

"Here I am, going to this conference with all these hotshots, and we're so broke right now, I can't even afford to buy a twenty-dollar watch," the husband said. His old watch had broken recently.

Without a second's hesitation, Mark said, "Well, here, take this," and he unstrapped the wristband.

Wearing that watch while running had made him feel rich. Jogging bare-armed after he gave it up, Mark became truly wealthy. "You don't need a six-hundred-dollar watch to go jogging," he said. "I got that watch and passed it on into the universe."

A close friend, Steve, travels a great deal. When he comes to a tollbooth, he automatically pays for the person behind him. When he pays his bill at a coffee shop, he hands the waitress or cashier an extra $10. "The next people who come in through the door," he says, "give them a pie. Whatever kind they want." Frequently the cashier gives Steve a funny look, as though he's up to something. Some people don't trust anonymous generosity. No one's going to thank Steve. He'll be gone by the time the new diners get their pie. The car behind him on the expressway probably won't catch up to beep a thank-you.

"What is it you're after?" more than one waitress or tollbooth collector has asked Steve. They assume he wants something in return. And he does, but not a quid pro quo. He's not expecting free lemon meringue at the next Denny's. Steve has learned that his greatest joy in living comes from joining himself more fully with his source, which blesses him with so much. No matter what he gives, the universe always gives more.

I'd like to close this chapter with one more story. It's about Nancy, a woman from my congregation who taught me a lesson in giving that I will never forget. I helped Nancy plan her sixtieth birthday party. She sent invitations to all her friends. "This is my last birthday," she wrote, "so please bring me something very, very special." Her friends knew this to be the truth; Nancy was dying of cancer.

The day of her party, Nancy sat with friends gathered round her and slowly, gratefully, opened every present. There was a beautiful scarf, and she tried it on, relishing the luxury of the silk. She opened a candle and inhaled the delicate floral scent. Then she laid all her presents out on the table and looked around at her friends. "Right now I'm not in a gathering period in my life; I'm in a relinquishing period, and I'm learning how beautiful this can be. What I want for you each to do now is select a gift that you didn't bring and take that gift home with you. All the years you live, remember my love for you whenever you see this gift."

Nancy died six weeks later. Maybe her days were fewer than she and her friends and family would have liked, yet her life was abundantly full.

Growing Your Dream

It matters not if you have only pennies to give. When you infuse your life and the lives around you with giving, you cannot help but have a greater good circle back into your life.

1. Take the good you have and bless it. To build a greater consciousness of abundance, through which you can build your greater life dream, turn your attention from "only" thinking—"I only have this or that"—and replace those thoughts with blessing. If you hold your breath too long, you become unconscious.

The life-giving act of breathing requires you to exhale as much as you inhale. So fill the world around you with a portion of your worth and you yourself become replenished.

2. Recognize that there is one source but many channels. Your source has infinite ways to bless you. If your bank account is high, you might feel prosperous. If an emergency wipes you out the next day, you may label yourself poor. Yet you have not changed. By aligning ourselves with our source, from which all channels flow, we remain prosperous, regardless of our circumstances.

3. Circulate to accelerate. Put yourself in the practice of giving without worrying what you'll receive in return. Give your time, talent, and treasure. Think of tithing as training wheels. Begin with 5 or 10 percent of your income, and once you establish a balanced flow, you'll be able to take off those wheels and live freely in a spirit of giving that feels as natural as riding a bike.

Chapter Six

ILLUMINATION:

Lighting the Path to Forgiveness

Forgiveness is a gift we give ourselves.
—ANONYMOUS

♦ *Learn to Separate the Being from the Behavior*
♦ *Recognize that You Don't Know the Whole Story*
♦ *Ask for Help in Removing the Poison of Resentment*

In the early years of my ministry, I had the honor of working with an amazing woman—I'll call her Julie—who had been abused as a child. Julie had been repeatedly raped—physically and emotionally—by her father. She spent her entire childhood without one single moment of feeling safe. At any time this girl's father might burst into the room and attack. He was always threatening to set the house on fire with his family inside. Her mother was terrified of him and did little to protect her children.

Julie's most vivid memory of growing up in that home was of when she was ten years old and sitting motionless for hours on the living room sofa with her mother, brothers, and sister. The father, drunk, held his family captive with a gun in his hand. He would walk up to one son, hold the barrel to the boy's temple, and say, "This one's for you." Then he would point the gun at the girl. "This one's for you," he said over and over, until he finally passed out.

At age sixteen Julie had a nervous breakdown. While she was hospitalized, she began telling herself, "I am going to get better." Still a teenager, she moved away from home to build a life for herself. Seventeen years later she began coming to our church. She had indeed built a life independent of the horror she had suffered, but not one that even came close to fulfilling her dream. This woman dreamed of one day having a loving, caring marriage. But at age thirty-three, intimacy so terrified her that she had never felt close to any man.

During the seventeen years since she'd left home, she'd had no contact with her father whatsoever. After attending church and becoming intrigued by the concept of forgiveness, she wrote her father a postcard. In it she simply told him that she was doing well and asked that he contact her.

He never responded.

The silence hurt her anew; the daughter who had been so violated by her father had actually reached out to him, and he had rebuffed her. Her initial reaction was rage: "How dare he ignore me, after all he's done!" She nursed her new hurt for a time, as any of us might, and then she returned to work. I say "work" because forgiveness can be an arduous, challenging process, and sometimes we're tempted to skip work and stay home. Or we perform our jobs absentmindedly, our hearts not really in the task before us. Forgiveness may be the most difficult work you ever do. It also promises the greatest rewards.

Most of us have no difficulty wanting a different life. Our difficulty lies in our willingness to be different ourselves. Only as we change ourselves can our lives have more meaning and fulfillment. You can't grow a healthy dream in toxic soil on a hill where the sun never shines. Any farmer knows that the soil must be as healthy as the seed for the crop to prosper.

Over time, as you practice forgiveness more regularly, you begin to notice how much easier it becomes to keep building greater dreams for yourself. Your inner soil, the deep recesses of your heart and mind, enriches the seed of a well-loved idea.

So whether or not her father responded to the postcard, Julie needed to forgive him—not for his sake but for her own. Forgiveness was the only way she could release herself from her past. As long as she refused to forgive her father, she would feel like damaged goods.

Forgiveness is a process. We forgive a piece at a time as we go on with our lives. Often, after we think we have finished, more pain arises from the same circumstance, and we must work through that next layer. Each time we become that much more liberated.

If anybody had an excuse for staying stuck, paralyzed by circumstances, Julie did. Do you have a story, an authentic grievance? Of course you do. We have all been treated unfairly; we've all been diminished in some way or another. You may have every justification for hanging on to your anger and grief. Who can blame you? Still, hanging on takes so much effort—it saps our aliveness, shuts us down, and keeps the abundant life out of our experience. Forgiveness frees. Eventually our lives arrive at the juncture where we are no longer willing to hold on to our pain, fear, resentment, and hatred. Those emotions create a tremendous void in us and around us. If you refuse to forgive, all those toxic feelings of hatred and resentment stay bottled up inside, eventually seeping into other areas of your life. The offender doesn't suffer. It is your own life, your own dreams that are stunted. Julie wasn't created to live a sad, empty life, and neither are you. In order to free the dream inside you, practice forgiveness every day.

♦ Learn to Separate the Being from the Behavior

In order to forgive her father, Julie needed to separate who he was from what he had done. She needed to separate him as a being from his terrible acts. To forgive means to give up one way of thinking for a higher way of thinking. We may not forgive the act perpetrated against us, but we can forgive the perpetrator, recognizing that behind every hurtful action lies a hurting person. The meanest, angriest person in the world still wants to live in love. This goes back to the principle of original innocence. We are created by God and are therefore inherently good; our true nature is good. Remember, even Anne Frank, who had every reason to believe that some people were despicable, said that she believed all people were basically good. Because they have suffered through injurious experiences, some people cover their true nature with layers and layers of hurt and wounding until the good is no longer visible or reachable, until they can do nothing but act out the hurt and wound others. But in the very act of hurting others, the ones who wind up most wounded are themselves.

One forgiveness technique Julie practiced was to pray specifically that she stop seeing her father as a monster. She began asking God daily to allow her to envision her father as a hurting individual who knew only one kind of behavior: hurting those closest to him. He didn't reach out; he lashed out. Her father had no idea how to show love or affection. Perhaps, his daughter reasoned, his own pain ran so deep, he knew of no other way to communicate than to hurt others.

For a long time she hoped he would ask her forgiveness so

that she might feel magnanimous in granting it. Gradually she learned to release herself from any expectation that he would contact her, or that if he did, it would be because he had changed. Maybe he simply would not change. But she and her life could. She recognized that her hatred would only bind her to him in an extremely unhealthy way. The Buddha likened resentment to a burning coal a person retrieves from a fire with the intention of throwing it at the object of his anger. Pick up that coal and it is your own flesh that is seared.

This does not mean that we do not need to protect ourselves or seek justice when someone behaves dangerously. It is natural to feel outrage in response to seeing someone hit a child, blaming the violence on his own bad childhood or even a bad day at work. Those who commit harmful actions—particularly criminal ones—need to be held accountable for them. And frequently they're not. How many newspaper stories have we read about child molesters and rapists who manage to escape prosecution and go on to abuse others? When Julie first told me her story, I felt so enraged on her behalf that I wanted to track down her father myself and haul him off to prison. But ultimately, holding blame and holding resentment hurt only the one burdened with the negative emotion. If we meet hatred with hatred, we perpetuate the life-damaging consequences of the original act.

I watched Julie release herself from her past and build dreams deep in her heart. It was not necessary for her to forgive the heinous things done to her. Yet she forgave the person who had committed them, something that may be difficult for many of us to imagine. The result, however, was that by her mid-forties she was happily married with children. She has a family and work that she loves.

Does that mean she has never again resented her father? Of course not. She is human. Does her enormous forgiveness mean that she automatically pardons lesser or less personal transgressions with grace? Hardly. Like any one of us, she frets and fumes if her spouse forgets an anniversary. And she particularly boils with rage every time she picks up a newspaper and reads about another abused child. Forgiveness is not like the chicken pox, which has to be dealt with only once. The act of forgiveness does not bestow sainthood upon you. It bestows freedom. Julie forgave her father and, in so doing, freed herself to step into her dream.

Don't feel bad if you cannot forgive others easily or readily. After all, it took Julie more than two decades to forgive her father his atrocities. The bigger and more outrageous the wrong, the more challenging it is to envision the person who committed it as a being apart from his or her deeds. This does not mean you cannot heal in the interim. Help yourself heal by focusing on your own needs, asking yourself how forgiveness might benefit you personally. Think about it: If you carry around a grudge, it gets mighty heavy at times. Do you really want all that extra weight? If you nurse a hurt indefinitely, you come to perceive yourself as wounded; it's tough to touch others with warmth and affection if your hands are busy bandaging and rebandaging old wounds.

One of my mentors, the late minister Jack Boland, told me how he had worked to separate what his former brother-in-law had done to him from the man himself. For years Jack felt tormented by their relationship. Not only had this man cheated Jack in a business venture, he then turned around and tried to sully Jack's impeccable reputation for integrity. Every chance he had to put him down, he did.

"I had a list of grievances a mile long," Jack declared. "Anyone who heard that list of what he had done to me could easily jump to my defense, and I was very good at using that story to get people on my side."

Jack said he nursed that hurt, cursed it, and rehearsed it for many years. Then one day he thought, "Who is this really hurting? I haven't seen the guy for years, but he lives inside me every day of my life. Who is this hurting? It's hurting me!" Jack had been withholding his forgiveness because he felt the man didn't deserve a pardon. He deserved punishment, he deserved retribution, he deserved . . .

And Jack—well, he himself deserved a major apology.

Jack suddenly realized forgiveness really had nothing to do with his former brother-in-law. Forgiveness was needed in order to free Jack's life. Every prisoner needs a jailer. You think of yourself as the jailer of the person you have condemned, but the truth is that you are the guard who is also stuck in that prison every single day.

So Jack asked for help in learning how to forgive. After a period of sincere asking for guidance from God, an idea came to him. Jack's experience shows that all you have to do is have one tiny spark of willingness, and the universe will rush to support you. In the words of Jesus, "It is your Father's good pleasure to give you the Kingdom." You must work hard to manifest a new life, but the support is always available once you begin the effort.

So Jack asked for support, and he got an idea. The idea was to hold the image of his former brother-in-law in his mind and just pour love on him, to learn to see him in the image of love. There is a Hindu word, *namasté*, which is often translated as "the Light in me recognizes and honors the Light in you." That was the spirit of Jack's practice.

So Jack thought, "I'll hold my former brother-in-law up in my mind and I'll see him in this forgiveness light, in the divine light." He envisioned the man's face in his mind, and all his anger surfaced. He told himself, "I'm going to think love; I'm going to think love." He thought of that man again, and once more negative energy poured forth.

"Now what?" he asked, perplexed. Again an idea came to

him. Jack brought to mind the face of his son when he was a little boy. He immediately felt a surge of love for that child, that sweet grinning face with the front tooth missing. Then, right in its place, he slipped in the face of his former brother-in-law. His energy of love decreased, but not as quickly as before. He practiced diligently for weeks until he could see the man's face in his mind and began to feel real love, not for what he had done but for the being that was this man, for the child that he once had been. I know others who have been successful using a variation of this technique: They look at a childhood photograph of the person who has wronged them and practice imagining their nemesis as an innocent child.

Jack said he knew the process had worked when, several months later, he was driving down the street and a brand-new Cadillac pulled up next to him. He thought, "Wow, that's a nice car." He glanced over and saw the driver was his former brother-in-law. Jack hadn't seen him for years. His immediate, spontaneous reaction was, "He must be doing pretty well, at least financially. That's nice." In that moment Jack knew the healing had taken place in his own heart. He was now free.

You have to put your old hurts behind or remain trapped forever. Throughout this book I've offered numerous metaphors for getting stuck. Dragging Harry, carrying the deadweight of your past, slows you down as you move toward your dream. Flirting with your Delilahs, fear's distracting masquerades, makes you veer off course. Failing to forgive others causes yet another delay because you are relegated to living in a small portion of yourself. When you fail to forgive, you cannot grow. Sometimes you shrink from forgiveness—but when you do, your soul shrinks.

Yet your dream calls upon you to evolve; it cannot come true unless you grow into it. I'm not suggesting it's easy to change a lifelong pattern. Forgiveness is not easy. The human part of us has a great deal of difficulty in letting go. The human part wants to hang on; that's why we need divine help in letting go. With higher help, you can begin to expand instead of contract in the way you regard others. Remember what Thoreau wrote about making your dreams come true: "If one advances confidently in the direction of his dreams, he will meet with a success unexpected in common hours. . . . He will live with license of a higher order of beings." Forgiveness is not a pardon produced by a judging or vindictive mind. Forgiveness is not logical. It emerges from a sincere willingness to choose love over condemnation. The grace of forgiveness heals our hearts when we are truly willing.

♦ **Recognize that You Don't Know the Whole Story**

One thing that can help your forgiveness work is acknowledging your ignorance. You don't know everything about the person who has wronged you. Even if you consider yourself an authority on your spouse or mother-in-law or best friend, there's bound to be something hidden from you that affects that person's behavior at times. You cannot know what happened the day before or even the minute before that might have provoked someone to lash out or behave in a hurtful way. They might not even know themselves.

How often do we condemn strangers based on even a single glimpse of their lives? I was in line at the grocery store one day and watched an incredibly rude checker treat the customer ahead of me horribly. I was quick to think, "Wow, I can't believe this woman represents the store." When my turn came, I noticed she overcharged me for some grapes, and I pointed out her error. She got very upset, acted as if the over-ring were my fault, pulled the tape out of the register, and finally handed me back my change with a snarl.

When the box boy helped me out to the car with my groceries, I engaged in a little gossip. "That was really the rudest checker I've ever had," I told him.

"Yeah, I know," the young man responded. "Yesterday her

son was hit on his bike. He's in intensive care in the hospital, and she's a single mom and she didn't think she could take the day off to be with him. She's really worried."

All of a sudden I didn't feel anger; I felt compassion. Her rudeness over a pound of fruit was very understandable. Now that I knew her story, my feelings changed. If we truly knew one another's stories, how much more compassion would we feel? Since we don't always have a box boy to set us straight, perhaps we can simply forgive. We can learn to accept that if we knew the true story behind each hurtful action, compassion would be our natural response.

Start simple. Whenever I'm tempted to condemn, I try to remember how it feels to be judged myself. Consider how you felt the last time someone pointed a finger at you after you made an innocent error. Consider how you felt when someone condemned you for another person's mistake. You probably felt lousy. Remind yourself that you don't know the whole story, so you're in no position to judge.

My son Rich told me a story about a woman friend of his who recognized that she did not know as much as she thought about another person. While waiting for her plane at the airport, she bought a little bag of chocolate chip cookies and sat down to eat her treat. Then she decided to get a cup of coffee, so she left her carry-on bag and the cookies in the waiting area. When she returned with the coffee, she saw a disheveled, homeless-looking man sitting next to her carry-on. And what was he doing? Eating her bag of cookies!

She sat down, took a cookie, and gave him a dirty look, hoping he'd take the hint. No such luck. He took a cookie and she took a cookie, and he took a cookie and she took a cookie. Finally he took the last cookie, broke it in two, and gave her half. A little huffy, she snatched her last piece and thought, "This guy! What nerve!" She boarded the plane, sat down, and buckled herself in. As the plane took off she opened her purse, and there, tucked behind her wallet, was her bag of cookies. This shabby fellow, who had appeared so down on his luck, had most generously been sharing his cookies with her the entire time.

She thought about how she had acted while she shared his snack. She thought about how many times in her life she had stood in judgment simply because she didn't understand. She realized that once we understand one another's stories, judgment evaporates. We judge what we don't comprehend. And by condemning others, we are really judging ourselves; it's as if when you point one finger, three point back.

Eventually we realize we don't have to know the whole story to move into understanding. We all do the very best that we know how given the current circumstances of our lives. Forgiveness finds the place in our hearts where compassion and love abound without reservation.

It is not a place, however, that is necessarily easy to locate. For fifteen years Beth, a member of our congregation, could find no place in her heart to feel compassion for Marion, her mother-in-law. Granted, Marion was such a pain that even her own son didn't like her. She had a harsh voice, poor manners, and a perpetually negative attitude. Marion found something to complain about every day, and inevitably she called Beth with her lament right at dinnertime. You may know somebody like this; you may be somebody like this. Most of us know someone who is difficult to love.

"When she called me, chills ran down my spine," Beth said. That's the kind of relationship they had. Then Beth came home from a trip on a Sunday night to a message from Marion on her answering machine: "Please call me." That was it.

Beth thought, "I'm not calling." She was in a funk that night anyway, and her own mother called, so she never bothered to return Marion's call. She stayed in her pity party for a while and then went to bed.

The next day about noon, she and her husband found out that Marion had died of a heart attack that very morning. Beth felt as if a dark cloud had closed around her. She felt remorseful that Marion had asked to hear from her the night before but that Beth, feeling sorry for herself, hadn't returned the call. Now she would never have a chance to make up for her omission.

This dark cloud grew. It encompassed her, and she began to be filled with guilt for all of the "could haves" and "would haves" and "should haves" of those fifteen years. How many times could she have shown kindness? How many times had Marion wanted to be hugged but Beth didn't hug her? How many times had Beth focused on the harsh voice and missed the call for love? Beth saw that Marion's unskillful behavior wasn't directed at Beth to wound her; it was the only way Marion knew how to reach out to others. All those years, Beth realized, she could have forgiven her mother-in-law.

Beth's daily practice is to pray privately every morning. She has a special place in her home—a chair by a window—where she goes to pray. It is her sacred space, a place to build a connection between herself and God. When she goes to that spot, she immediately relaxes and opens her mind to feel God's presence.

On the third day after Marion's passing, all of a sudden a thought came to Beth: "I haven't had my quiet time today." So she went to her special spot and she began to cry. She cried for her lack of loving. She had thought of herself as a compassionate person. When others talked about punishing criminals, hers was the voice that urged rehabilitation. Yet with her own mother-in-law, all she had done was judge. As she poured out her heart and tears, she thought, "I should ask God for forgiveness." So she prayed, "God, I need forgiveness. Take this hurt from me."

Immediately she heard, "You're asking in the wrong place. God never condemns." She thought, "I need to ask my mother-in-law for forgiveness. I have been in this woman's presence for fifteen years. I know her. She is a very big woman. She has a very big energy."

Beth wrote me a letter describing her experience: "As I made this prayer, 'Marion, I need your forgiveness,' suddenly I felt that she was there with me. I felt her presence as much as I have ever felt her, only this time she was absolutely warm, comforting, supportive, caring. I asked for her forgiveness. I said, 'Forgive me for not calling, forgive me for not loving you, forgive me for my attitude. I could have just loved you, and I didn't.'

"I have never in my life felt such love and support, and I was absolutely washed clean, totally cleansed, in the presence of this love. That gray cloud was lifted—not a tiny ounce of it was left on me anywhere. The pain was totally cleansed from me.

"In that moment I saw I had not recognized her as a woman who needed to be loved because I was so busy judging her. Immediately I saw a couple of other faces, knowing that they were other people in my life that I was busy judging rather than loving. I recognized that the person who stood outside of love's presence when I was judging was me. I immediately moved into seeing love and a call for love in these other beings in my life. Marion had given me a great gift—a gift of perception.

"She also has given me another gift. I recognized that I had been so self-centered, so in my ego that night she called, that I was throwing a pity party and thinking about myself. I stayed stuck for hours when what I could have done was reach out to help somebody else and the funk would have lifted. I knew in that moment that every time I've been hurting and have turned that hurt around, it's been because I reached out to help somebody else. And I recognized that now when I'm feeling self-centered and sorry for myself and stuck, what I will do is say, 'How do I take this energy and transform it by loving someone else who needs love right now? For whom can I pray? To whom can I write a letter? Whom can I call and support? How can I be an instrument of God's loving right now?' "

Beth will never know Marion's whole story, why she so often behaved in ways that seemed designed to torment her daughter-in-law. But the moment she awakened to the knowledge that she had not been a target, that Marion had been calling out for love, Beth's perceptions altered; her mind stopped narrowing, and she stopped shrinking. When Beth realized forgiveness, she grew. She grew in compassion for her mother-in-law, and she grew in compassion for herself. Beth no longer felt the need to beat herself up for all those years she had condemned Marion. She had done what seemed natural and right at the time. From her now greater perspective, she knew she could do so much more.

There is an affirmation in *A Course in Miracles* that reads: "I can choose peace instead of this." Instead of judging people or nursing our grudges, we can choose to feel in harmony with God, even in harmony with someone who has hurt us. I think this is particularly true when it comes to our parents. We cannot hope to have a deep, lasting, fulfilling relationship with another human being when we resent or hate one of our parents. That hatred is like venom that leaks out into every other relationship.We don't know everything our parents endured; we can't possibly.

A woman from our congregation, Amanda, had been at odds with her mother for as long as she could remember. Yet she knew she needed to find peace with that relationship in order to be a better mother to her own children. As a child, Amanda had been sexually abused by her maternal grandfather. It wasn't until Amanda herself became a mother that she mustered the courage to tell her own mother what had happened—only her mother refused to believe her. The two didn't speak for a year.

Even in the midst of her anger and disappointment, Amanda knew she needed to forgive her mother. She wanted her own two children to know their grandparents. And she wanted to end the family tradition of hurt and hostility. Amanda wrote me a letter about their troubled relationship and her decision to forgive: "You see, we were both expecting someone else, and we each held fast to our own vision of what the other should be. My mother and I are separated geographically by 1,500 miles of ocean, different climates, different cultures, a five-hour plane ride. I have spent my life striving not to be my mother, and indeed I am not her, most of the time.

"A phone call was as close as we got to a real visit. We talked about her animals or my kids or my younger brothers or our health. Anything but ourselves. What we really wanted to do was tell each other our stories. Make each other understand why she was the way she was. But each other is what we didn't mention.

"Two years ago we weren't speaking. I spent hours rocking myself and crying, wrapped in my soft, nubby meditation blanket in my guest room. After days of rocking, I beat pillows with a cardboard tube from an empty roll of Christmas wrap. I closed myself in the only room in the house with no outside window, curled up on the floor among my daughter's shoes, dirty clothes, and naked Barbies, and screamed and yelled until I was hoarse. I rolled up all the windows in my car and talked to myself driving along the back roads.

"On the good days, I meditated every morning. I visualized my mother in a healing white light. Sometimes there was no light at all. Not even my mother's face. Just a darkness into which I'd tumble.

"In spring I go to a retreat in Mexico and wonder what in the world I am doing there. On the third day I begin to cry during a morning meditation, and I can't stop because I am thinking of all the people who have been kind and generous with me throughout my life. But I've been so busy resenting my mother, I haven't appreciated others. If she'd just drop by and tell me how much she loves me, then I could move on. I wouldn't have to wait here anymore. 'What's the matter?' asks Alan, one of the retreat leaders.

" 'Nothing,' I choke out.

" 'Why don't you come up here?'—'up here' being the front of the room.

"Fifty people wait. I rise, knowing this is a mistake.

" 'Pick someone to be your mother,' says Alan. I pick Mary because she is the woman in the room who intimidates me the most, like my own mother intimidates me with her I've-always-got-it-together look, which I have often admired and have never been able to emulate. Mary and I sit face-to-face on the slate floor, legs crossed. I am not used to looking people in the eye and have to glance away often.

"We role-play. Mary is the mother and I am the daughter. 'What is it you want to say to me?' she asks. I do not answer—my nose is running, and I am trying not to touch my nose. After all these years, here is my opportunity to say anything I want to my mother, and all I can feel is my runny nose. 'What is it you want to say to your mother?' Mary asks again. I wipe my nose with the back of my hand, and someone shoves a jumbo box of Kleenex into my lap.

"I tell her: 'I want to say that all that's happened doesn't matter anymore. I had to tell you the truth about your father, but I'm sorry that it hurt you so much.'

"Mary takes my hands and locks her eyes with mine, telling me about my mother, a woman she has never met. I begin to hear about a woman whose pain is so intense she cannot share it. She thinks that by keeping secrets she is sparing her daughter pain.

"I begin to see her side and am no longer so angry. I return home from Mexico, and during a meditation I see my mother receiving thirty-five yellow roses—as many as I am old—and reading the enclosed card: 'Here's to the first thirty-five years. Let's start the second thirty-five from here.' It takes me three days to remember to stop at the florist and order the flowers.

"I thank God for all my relationships and ask for healing, especially with my mother. I remember for the first time in many years the stops at Dairy Queen she made just for me. The Christmas magic she made for Dad and me and then my brothers, the way she talked Dad into letting me go to boarding school for the chance of a better education, even though Dad was dead set against it. The day after I send the flowers, a light on my answering machine blinks. It takes me a minute to recognize my mother's voice. Her words and tone are softer than I remember, and her message ends with 'Call me.'

"I fly out two months later to wish her a happy birthday in person. We hold each other and cry during the quiet of post-breakfast coffee during my three-day visit, each of us with only a vague notion of the other's struggle.

"The ocean still separates us; we still talk about her animals or my kids, everything but ourselves. We still don't agree on many things, but that doesn't matter anymore. We are two women who have met face-to-face, and nothing can alter or diminish that."

Amanda must live with the fact that some topics remain off-limits between mother and daughter. The whole story will never be told. Yet Amanda now says she admires her mother's courage for protecting her daughter the best she knew how. Her way is not Amanda's way, but in accepting her mother as she is, Amanda has freed herself to move on in her own life.

Remember, you cannot know the whole story. When you can accept that fact with a full heart, you experience true forgiveness. You cease to be a victim and become a participant in life with a mind and heart open to new possibilities. You move forward in your life and in your dream through expanded compassion and awareness.

♦ Ask for Help in Removing the Poison of Resentment

I once attended what was called a "Human Unity Conference" in India with two hundred religious leaders. As part of that conference, we meditated and prayed with the Dalai Lama at the Baha'i Lotus Temple in New Delhi. The Dalai Lama introduced us to a practice called the Loving Kindness Meditation. The words in this meditation are simple, yet in their simplicity lies great power. The words speak directly to my heart. Every time I repeat them, I feel as if I am praying not only for myself and those close to me, but for every person on the planet.

Some Buddhists repeat the meditation three times a day for twelve weeks to extend loving kindness to themselves, then out to the world. Here is a portion of the meditation:

> May I be happy. May I be free from suffering. May I be free from tension, fear, worry. May I be healed. May I be at peace.
>
> Just as I wish to be happy, so might you be happy. May you be happy and free from suffering. May your tension, may your painfulness of heart, fall away. May your joy increase. May you be free from suffering.
>
> May we all be happy. May we each come into the light. May we let go of the blocks. May we let go of our suffering and experience our perfect being. May we all be free from suffering. May we all be happy.
>
> May all beings be happy. May all beings be clear-minded. May their hearts open. May they be free from suffering.
>
> May all beings be free from suffering. May they love themselves. May they come to their happiness. May they uncover the joy of the true self. All beings everywhere.

Repeating this meditation has helped me in my forgiveness work. It has helped me direct the energy of loving kindness toward those I may resent. For instance, consider the line "May all beings be happy." As I say this with feeling, I sometimes immediately find myself editing: "Well, maybe not so-and-so, because, after all . . . May all beings be happy, but not you!" The practice has caused me to come to recognize anyone I have failed to forgive, or forgiven only partway.

Once you experience that powerful healing inside yourself, you begin directing similar energy outward. With practice, compassion becomes the lens through which we view the entire world. As we grow into our capacity to direct loving kindness, we begin to direct compassion toward the entire planet.

This meditation has helped me, but meditation is not for everyone. For my late friend Jack Boland, the practice of visualizing his antagonist proved most helpful. We all need to find whatever tool or process works best for us.

One woman in our church found love's presence with the help of a dictionary. Ruth and her ex-husband had been apart for years, but she still felt controlled by him. She had felt emotionally battered during their eighteen-year marriage, bullied, diminished, publicly humiliated. He treated her, she felt, as if she were stupid.

Ruth and her former husband shared custody of their two teenage boys. Every time the boys' father called her or wrote her a letter, Ruth felt intruded upon. She felt victimized. Even though their lives were separate, he still had a tremendous emotional hold on her. She felt he continually used their sons as a vehicle to manipulate and control her. Every contact with him felt like a blow. It wasn't fair. She had worked so hard to distance herself from him, but he was still managing to keep her under his thumb. Maybe if he could change, become a better person, then the phone calls wouldn't upset her so. She deserved a little peace. It wasn't fair.

One day, while she was taking a walk, she reached out and asked God, "Why is this still happening in my life?" And she heard, "It's to humanize you."

"Humanize me? What does that mean?" she wondered.

The Holy Spirit always knows how to speak in a way that you can hear if you're willing to do the work of interpretation. Honor the symbols given to you. They're specifically designed so that you may decode the next step of your life. Ruth is a very believing person with a highly inquisitive mind. So she did what came naturally: She went home and looked up the word *humanize* in the dictionary. To humanize, she read, is to become humane, and a humane person, according to her dictionary, is "one who embodies mercy." That really jolted her. So next she looked up the word *mercy*. Mercy, she read, is "kindness in excess of what may be expected."

Ruth realized that she had not practiced "kindness in excess of what may be expected." Her cold response was understandable, yes, perhaps even justifiable, but she was now being called to a higher level of existence. Over the next few months she began to practice kindness in her thinking. Rather than feel victimized when her ex-husband contacted her, she practiced feeling compassion. Her ex-husband was not an easy person to love, and never again would she be with a man whose behavior was so destructive. Yet so long as she continued to disdain him, he continued to remain powerful. "I do not have to let him have the power to take my peace," she told herself. "Kindness is more powerful than violence. I can be stronger by showing him mercy, and even if he does not change, I will." Forgiveness does not happen all at once; rather, it is part of a learning continuum. It's a skill and, like any other, requires diligent practice.

Ruth's former husband didn't change simply because his ex-wife saw him more lovingly. But Ruth changed. Although he continued to contact her and attempt to bully her, she no longer felt controlled by him. As she continued treating him with extraordinary kindness, she began treating herself more kindly as well. Up until that point, Ruth had been beating herself up for allowing her former husband to maintain an emotional hold on her. She saw that her reaction was understandable. Her feeling victimized was a starting point. From there, she was able to grow.

For some people, a beginning stage of forgiveness is anger, feeling outrage at the harm done them. We can stay stuck in this place for a long time, or we can choose to move beyond rage, learn to express anger in a healthy way, and talk about our pain. Healing begins in the simple act of finding appropriate verbal expression for our hurt. When we hold the pain in, when we get that lump in our throats and shove it back down, we dis-ease our own lives. Part of forgiveness means feeling the pain, being angry about the pain. Yet remember that the psalmist David wrote, "Yea, though I walk through the valley of the shadow of death, I will fear no evil." The key word here is *walk*. Do not pitch a tent and camp out in your pain.

Sharing our pain with God and with an appropriate person helps us release our suffering so that we can begin healing. One of my closest friends told me about a forgiveness technique that actually incorporates the expression of anger. It certainly worked for his buddy, Al.

Al was separated from his second wife and very much wanted to reunite. He confided his feelings and reconciliation plans in a trusted friend. Later, to his dismay, he found that this "friend," Bruce, had all the while been seeing Al's estranged wife. Furious at the betrayal, Al wanted to revert to old behavior patterns, which would have included doing Bruce physical harm. In-stead, Al asked for higher help. He was guided to talk to another friend about his resentment.

The friend listened patiently and then made a suggestion: "Don't prey on him. Pray *for* him."

Al was dumbfounded. "What?" he asked.

"Pray for the SOB."

"I can't pray for him. I hate him," Al said.

"You can start the prayer any way you want," said his friend. "So . . ."

"You must pray for Bruce's health, his well-being, and his happiness," Al's friend went on. "But remember, you can start the prayer any way you want."

So for two weeks, Al prayed this prayer: "If a truck doesn't run over him first, please, God, let Bruce be happy and do well."

After two weeks Al was able to drop the line "If a truck doesn't run over him first" and simply say the rest of the prayer. In time his resentment disappeared, and Al was able to find peace. He and his estranged wife never did reconcile. But two years later Al met the true woman of his dreams, and they have been happily married for many years. And as for Bruce, well, he was not hit by a truck. But he didn't get to keep Al's former wife, either.

When you practice forgiveness, you clear the field for a healthy harvest. You take the negativity, the condemnation, and let it go. You know how at times we'll rehearse a hurt, crank it up again, and bring it alive with a bunch of energy? We can feel that hurt all over again, or we can learn to let it go and see things differently. If you don't vigorously clear the field, if you leave weeds here and there, they will spread and choke out your harvest. Live in a state of inner condemnation, and soon you will have four, five, or six other reasons to condemn.

I remember a former employee who failed to show up for work one day. She didn't call in sick, and nobody could reach her. She had left work early the day before for a doctor's appointment, taking with her my notes for a eulogy I was to give.

She had promised to type up my eulogy, print it out, and bring it to me first thing in the morning. Not only was I personally embarrassed at the funeral as I delivered my impromptu eulogy, I felt horrible for the family. These people deserved better. And it wasn't as if I would get a chance to do it over the right way.

The next day the employee apologized, saying she had turned the phone off the night before and then overslept. When she realized what she'd done, she was too embarrassed even to call. I said, "That's okay, I forgive you," but I really didn't. What I really wanted her to know was how humiliated I had felt conducting the funeral. In other words, I wanted her to suffer. I did so by greeting her each morning with a forced smile and by withholding responsibilities from her. Without saying so directly, I wanted to let her know she wasn't trusted. The result was that I became less trusting in general, even of someone else on the staff who was consistently responsible. And so when this other woman failed to deliver an important report for a meeting, I really lost my temper. She looked extremely ashamed and then said in a weak voice, "Mary, the meeting isn't today. It's tomorrow."

We start holding grievances a little at a time. We start withholding love a little at a time. We get so full of resentment that we become toxic—a little at a time. Tender dreams cannot thrive in toxic soil. So what do you do? Look very carefully for the poisonous thoughts and begin, bit by bit, to replace them with more-nourishing ideas. Begin by practicing forgiveness with the easy hurts. Today someone will offend you in a minor way, perhaps cutting you off on the freeway as you're driving home from work. Try an experiment. The moment you feel that familiar resentment, tell yourself, "I'm not going to let this get to me. It's just not important enough." And move on. Start letting go when everyday occurrences do not go the way you want or when someone does not treat you the way you want.

As you seek out the toxins, you open to the dream of who

you want to be and how you want to feel when you've completed forgiveness work. Then you act as if you already are that person. That person is the real you, anyway. This transformative experience leads us to a commitment to put love first in our lives, recognizing that God, as love, is the source of our abundance, of life itself. Dreams can come true only when forgiveness shifts our perception to reveal love's presence.

A young man who has written meditation music for our church told me a story of how the forgiveness process unfolded for him. Joe had broken up with a woman he had lived with for two years, no longer able to tolerate her jealousy of his relationship with his son from a previous marriage. She would accuse Joe, "You love him more than you love me."

Instead of ending the relationship with compassion, one day he yelled at her, "Get out! I don't want to talk to you anymore. Get out of my life."

The next week Joe found himself in a situation he'd often been in before: ready to launch another romance before the dust had settled from the previous one. He asked God for a new girlfriend, saying, "You provide a relationship for me. It's in Your hands."

Joe waited for a week, but no woman materialized. Apparently, Joe thought, God wasn't listening. At first he was annoyed, then impatient, then resentful, and then suddenly he began to feel more at peace. Maybe there was a reason. Maybe he had some other work to do before he was ready for a new woman.

Joe began focusing on what he did best and what gave him the greatest peace: composing music. But he felt blocked in his creativity. A longtime professional musician, he had built an entire sound studio in one room of his house, equipped with various computers and synthesizers. He describes the room as a little orchestra that sits whispering, "Okay, maestro, tell us what to do." Always before, music had come easily to him. Now, nothing. One evening his intuition told him, "Play it in the key of F." Sitting before his equipment, he was puzzled about what this meant. Still the voice said, "Play it in the key of F."

He says he could feel his little orchestra calling to him, "Tell us what to do, tell us what to do," but still there was no music, nothing but the message "Play it in the key of F." Each evening for the next three days, Joe sat patiently waiting for inspiration. He sat quietly in his living room and asked, "Okay, what is it?" At last Joe realized he had forgiveness work left uncompleted, work that he had stuffed aside, denying his pain, cutting himself off. Suddenly the insight came to him: The key of F is forgiveness.

Joe considered the fact that every relationship up to that point in his life had ended with anger, resentment, and bitterness. Yes, this latest relationship was over, but he didn't have to be such a jerk to the woman he had lived with for two years. He wrote her a letter, explaining his hurt over her jealousy and asking for her understanding. He told her he should not have ended the relationship so harshly and hoped she would forgive him.

So Joe became a true maestro. He began playing his whole life as if it were a symphony. He learned that the master always plays in the key of F. And during this period of gradual awakening, each time he went into his studio an abundance of music flowed naturally through him.

We may not be musicians, but our job too is to play the melody of life in the key of F. That's how you make forgiveness happen: Look for ways to get the pain out, by writing about it, talking about it, moving it out into the open. You can ask God to assist in your composition. Ask your Creator to lead you in replacing your hurt with forgiveness. Remember, forgiveness means a shift in perception in which we actually come to see a situation or person through loving eyes. Where once there was discord, we now find harmony.

A man at our church offered to re-create our Living Enrichment Center logo in stained glass. Dan said he would seek out his father's assistance. Dan was an artist, but he did not have much experience with glass, whereas his father made stained-glass windows for a living. There was only one problem. Dan hadn't been home in over two years, ever since he told his parents he was gay. He planned to visit his family over the Christmas holiday, however, and asked his father for help with the logo. He hoped such a father-and-son project would provide the impetus for healing. Although the two men had spoken on the phone, the subject of the son's homosexuality was never discussed.

"My dream was that we would be able to talk, that it would be more than two bodies producing a piece of art," he said.

Only that didn't happen. Instead, they worked on the project mostly in strained silence. The artwork, however, was impeccable: a brilliant sun rising over a mountain, with a valley in the foreground. Just as they were cleaning off the finished product, the sun cracked. At first his father was unable to find another piece of yellow glass, but when he finally located one, he seemed irritated rather than relieved. It is far more difficult to mend something that has already been pieced together.

Dan was put off by his father's anger. He remembered how, as a little boy, his father had used anger to push him away. As they were struggling to fit the new sun into the sign, Dan said, "I just can't work like this," and went up to his old bedroom. He was very upset. He had been willing to forgive his father's past coldness, hoping their shared love of art would bring them closer, but they remained distant. Dan asked God for help. He wanted to love his dad and feel loved in return, not further distanced.

Dan's father came up to the room, and for the first time in both men's lives, they spoke honestly with each other. The father felt his son had always run away from him. Dan responded, "I'm afraid of your anger, and I have retreated from you all of my life. I thought you didn't love me, and Dad, I want you to know, I really love you."

His dad reached out and said, "I want you to know, I really love you."

As these two men, father and son, held each other, they forgave years of hurt. Then they went downstairs to complete the job they had started.

The sun was fractured in the artwork, the same way the son was fractured in his family. Both came to be mended. That stained-glass logo hangs in a front window of our church as evidence that there is no break so great that it cannot be healed, and that nothing is impossible with the power of forgiveness.

In the Bible, Peter asked Jesus, "Lord, how often shall my brother sin against me, and I forgive him? Up to seven times?"

"Jesus said to him, 'I do not say to you, up to seven times, but up to seventy times seven.' " In Genesis, we read that the heavens and the earth were created in seven days. Seven symbolizes a number of completion: seven days in a week. Forgive seventy times seven. Take the time you need. And in fact, it takes a lifetime to really learn to live in freedom. None of us have totally cleared all our grievances. We have someplace in us where we still harbor some resentment or hurt.

An affirmation that has helped me is "I will make no decisions alone today." When you are on the verge of judgment, open up your mind and heart and ask for help. Without forgiveness, without the ability to let go, we cannot possibly build dreams that endure. Our resentments taint our intentions and drain our energy. Imagine life as a slide show, with the slides in the carousel representing the events of our life. With each slide comes the question "Can I forgive this?" If we say yes, we have learned to accept that specific life experience. We may not forgive some horrible behavior or act perpetrated against us, but we forgive the person who committed it, and we accept the experience as part of our past. The experience does not have to intrude on our present life. When we reach that feeling of release, the slide comes out of the carousel and another slide enters the frame. As the slide comes into focus, again the question surfaces: "Can I forgive this?" If we say, "No, I cannot," then the slide goes back in the carousel and will come up again later. The experience may reappear from a different angle, but it is the same event all over again. We can't move on until we come to peace with that event.

Sometimes there's a spot of dust on the slide, and instead of wiping it clean, we curse the projector. You want someone else to change. You want a better life but refuse to make any adjustments to the show running through your head. The very life we're experiencing is a projection of the thoughts we hold.

When we hold the energy of love and compassion, we see beauty we might otherwise miss. Wiping the slide clean rewards us with a life of amazing clarity. We see ourselves more clearly and begin to extend compassion not just to others but to ourselves as well. We forgive ourselves. Sometimes we are the most difficult people of all to forgive. When we hold ourselves to impossibly high standards of behavior and then fall short, when we beat ourselves up for the slightest transgression, the slides in our carousel once again become scratched and distorted. How often have friends told us, "Hey, don't be so hard on yourself," and we say, "Yeah, yeah," and then dismiss their opinions as uninformed?

Forgiving yourself shifts your energy from pain to power. You step into a greater fullness of your own being with that shift and turn that enhanced energy toward building your dream.

I've found that spending a few minutes at the beginning of each day practicing forgiveness does strengthen me. First I quiet my mind, then ask the Holy Spirit, "What would you have me forgive today?" Listen and accept whatever your still, small voice tells you. Often I have found that the person I need to forgive is myself.

I remember one morning many years ago when I asked the Holy Spirit what I should forgive that day. Sitting quietly, I suddenly had an image of myself as ten years old, playing in a park with several girlfriends. My first reaction was, "This old memory couldn't have anything to do with my life now," but I have come to know that every experience has meaning. What you are asked to forgive on a particular day may seem at first to be a trivial event, but if you are patient, the significance will be revealed.

So I focused on myself as a ten-year-old in the park. I grew up in a traditional home: two parents, two kids. But my sister, Jackie, was eight years older than me, so by the time I was ten, she had gone off to nursing school. I missed her terribly. Both my parents worked, and during the summer I spent a lot of time either in an empty house or with friends in the neighborhood. I began to remember how I envied my girlfriends who had brothers and sisters at home. If only I had brothers and sisters around to keep me company, I thought, my loneliness would disappear.

The family across the street from where we lived had five children. One day two of the sisters collected quarters from all the neighborhood children to purchase candy for a rendezvous in the park later in the day. I surrendered my quarter, feeling good about being included with the other kids. During my meditation, my mind replayed the scene when the candy was handed out. Everyone in the park that day had at least one brother or sister present, except me. My heart ached for the little ten-year-old that was me as she excitedly unwrapped her candy only to find it broken. "If only I had a brother or sister to stick up for me," I remember thinking, "I wouldn't get the bad candy." Twenty-five years later, my mind brought the memory up for me—a broken piece of candy when I was ten. I thought, "This can't be very important."

I stuck with the process anyway. As I explored my feelings, I gradually understood that this ten-year-old girl had made a fateful decision that day. She thought the broken candy meant she was not as good as everyone else because she had no brother or sister to be with her, to defend her. The decision made that day over a seemingly small incident had helped foster in me, for two and a half decades, a sense of inadequacy. So I asked God to help me heal where I needed healing most: my perception of myself. I saw the light of forgiveness beaming into the past, and I gave that ten-year-old girl a loving hug from her future self. And then it was over. I got up and went back to work.

On the surface, my self-forgiveness had no great significance. Yet, over time, I began to see the fruit of the new seed I had planted that day. I noticed I began accepting myself more readily. I was less likely to snap at myself, "Mary, look, you've messed up again!" I also noticed that I was feeling more kindly toward others. As I became more comfortable with myself, I stopped holding myself and others to impossibly high standards.

Plain and simple: Forgiveness produces miracles. Forgiveness frees you to build your dreams.

Growing Your Dream

Through forgiveness you find the power to build lasting dreams. Without forgiveness, the negative emotions you carry leak toxic energy into every area of your life, stunting or entirely choking out your dreams. Forgiveness is a process requiring great willingness and commitment if you are to be released from the bondage of your past.

1. Learn to separate the being from the behavior. You may

never forgive some terrible act perpetrated upon you, but you can learn to forgive the perpetrator. When you move beyond your outrage, you can begin to heal. Practice seeing the other person as a child of God who has forgotten his true self. You can forgive someone who has amnesia and acts out of gross confusion. As you practice forgiving the being, not necessarily the behavior, you find yourself able to direct your creative energies toward building your dreams.

2. Recognize that you don't know the whole story. The next time someone cuts you off on the freeway or cancels a dinner date, create a plausible life story for the individual. This is not to say that you excuse rude, offensive behavior. What you're doing is empowering yourself. You can see, from your greater perspective, that the petty acts of an unhappy individual do not have to damage you.

3. Ask for help in removing the poison of resentment. Experiment with different techniques: meditation, visualization, or even an unorthodox prayer. Resentment taints our dreams; you cannot hope to grow a healthy dream in toxic soil. Even when we tell ourselves we've forgiven, we frequently have done so halfheartedly. Forgiving is done with your entire heart. Begin each day by asking the Holy Spirit, "What should I forgive?"

Part Three

GROWING THE
DREAM

Chapter Seven

GUIDANCE:

Recognizing the Voice of Inspired Insight

The Voice for God is as loud as your willingness to listen.
—A COURSE IN MIRACLES

♦ *Acknowledge the Inner Nudge Toward Outer Motion*
♦ *Build a Relationship with the Still, Small Voice of Inspired Insight*
♦ *Go to the Edge of the Light You See*

I was dreaming of a new life, but fear kept me boxed into the old one. I wasn't even stepping, creeping, or inching my way toward my dream. My soul must have grown so exasperated with my inertia, so weary of my excuses for standing still, that my higher power decided, "That slug Mary is never going to move unless she gets a big ol' kick."

Which explains how I one day found myself with nothing but 140 feet of air between my feet and the ground.

It had been eleven years since our family had spent a year on the road, eleven years since we used insurance money from a battered cab to found our church, and twenty-six years since two frightened teenagers had said their "I do's." The church, following many years of struggle, had truly begun to flourish. I could not say the same for our marriage.

I dreamed of a spiritual partnership, a marriage in which two souls melded into one. How to arrive at such a partnership was a mystery. Haven and I had spent nine years together in couples therapy and, as a result, had learned a solid level of cooperation. We loved our children. We loved God and devoted our lives to serving. Yet at the deepest level of our beings, something was missing, and we both knew it. Try as we might, true compatibility eluded us. Our relationship had stagnated long ago, but neither of us wanted to acknowledge it. Besides, I equated divorce with failure. So I determinedly hunkered down to live my life within the cramped soul space my marriage allowed.

As William Shakespeare wrote, "This above all: to thine own self be true." I didn't see that a person untrue to herself dies a little with each pretension, each tiny lie. I smiled, convincing myself everything was fine, and delivered rousing sermons on the power of love. To our congregation, we must have seemed a perfect couple, man and wife sharing the same vocation, devoting their lives to God and counseling parishioners whose own marriages were more visibly rocky.

Bit by bit, I noticed my sense of aliveness diminishing. The signals came subtly at first. They came from deep within, from what I call the still, small voice of inspired insight. We all possess such a voice; we all, at times, tend to tune it out. Often we don't even acknowledge its existence. My voice would whisper, "Mary, you are not happy." Almost immediately I would quash the voice and try to replace it with thoughts of gratitude and affirmation. "After all," I told myself, "you have so much to be thankful for: a healthy family, work that you love, wonderful parents. Why shouldn't you be happy? What's wrong with you?"

I did have much to be grateful for, and yet somewhere along the way I had lost myself. Rather than honor my discontent, I chose to bury it, and thus when my voice whispered, I shamed myself for having such longings. When my voice spoke up, telling me I had the right to happiness, that unless I embraced joy for myself I would have none to give others, I argued it back into a quiet corner. This tactic worked for years, until the strategy slowly unraveled and I with it. With no room to maneuver, I began to entertain thoughts of dying. There I stood in the midst of tremendous evolution in our church, and I was fantasizing about getting a terminal illness as the only graceful way out of my marriage!

Your knowing voice picks up this self-destructive chatter but does not condemn. The voice within us does not rant, rave, chide, or dictate. We sense instead a gentle nudging, moving us in the direction of our highest good, never denouncing us or keeping a running tally of our errors. God illuminates the path to greater fulfillment, and no matter what mistakes we make, God continues to guide us. Carl Jung had a sign above the door to his home that read Called or not, God is present. God is always present and available through the still, small voice.

You may choose to ignore your voice, as I did. Most of us stay so busy that we avoid hearing this voice until we reach a crisis. We don't want to face the pain. If you've got a cavity, it needs to be filled. When the drill hits the nerve, you wince, but that's also a sign the dead matter has been excised. It is the living tissue that hurts. Skipping your dental appointment, discarding your reminder cards, will not make the cavity disappear. In fact, the longer you put off treating it, the more severe the pain will be. You reschedule when the ache becomes unbearable, confident your dentist will always welcome you back.

My voice told me for years that my husband and I each deserved a happiness that our marriage could never provide. I tuned out my voice until the pain became unbearable. I heard the voice, and I recognized the source, but I didn't want to listen. One thing sustained me, however: I knew that my voice would not desert me. I had a standing appointment any time I was finally ready to listen.

♦ Acknowledge the Inner Nudge Toward Outer Motion

Some people call the still, small voice insight or intuition. They describe encounters with their voice with a kind of awe: "I just had this feeling I was supposed to come here tonight, and look who I met!" "I just had this feeling our numbers weren't quite right; thank goodness I double-checked the report." While we honor these confirmations momentarily, we also tend to forget about them pretty quickly. Some people attend to the voice only when they've deliberately ignored it and paid the price as a result: "I had a feeling this guy was all wrong for the job, don't ask me why, but I hired him anyway, and now, after I just got him trained, he's leaving!"

Our insight is a gift from God, not one to be taken lightly or for granted. It is a gift that offers access to tremendous power. If we acknowledge that the voice doesn't just pop up in our mind like some haphazard jack-in-the-box, that it is available to us always, we have the most important source of assistance in building our dreams. We can turn random intuition into regular inspired insight.

Puccini said, after writing *Madama Butterfly*, "The music of this opera was dictated to me by God. I was merely instrumental in putting it on paper and communicating it to the public." Brahms said, "Straightaway the ideas flow in upon me directly from God." The more we listen, the louder, more resonant our voice for God grows.

We learn the origins of the still, small voice from the Old

Testament. The First Book of Kings tells how the prophet Elijah is infuriated by those who worship Baal, a false god fashioned in the image of a calf. To make matters worse, Queen Jezebel wants Elijah killed, and the prophet flees for his life into the wilderness. Exhausted and alone, Elijah begins to feel sorry for himself. The people of his time refuse to recognize the true God, revering an idol instead, and Elijah is just about ready to give up trying to convince them otherwise. He spends the night in a cave, and then God speaks to him: "What are you doing here, Elijah?"

The prophet comes close to conceding defeat. "I alone am left; and they seek to take my life."

God assures Elijah he is not alone. He instructs the prophet to stand on the mountain. When Elijah climbs to the top, he encounters a wind so strong it tears into the mountain, breaking rocks into pieces. When the wind ceases, the earth begins to shake. Then flames erupt everywhere.

When the flames die down, Elijah hears a still, small voice. Overcome by his sudden awareness, he wraps his face in his cloak and goes to stand at the entrance of the cave. God has not been in the howling of the wind, the trembling of the earth, or the crackling of the fire. Elijah finds God only in the silence that ensues once the spectacles cease. He comes to know God in the still, small voice. We too can be guided by the still, small voice.

Many of us expect God to appear like Zeus, hurling thunderbolts, but the truth is that God is always present. You may be very impressed—but also distracted—by extraordinary phenomena. Yet it is in ordinary moments that we can really quiet ourselves and experience God's presence. In awaiting the spectacular, we overlook the obvious.

When I speak of this voice, I call it the voice *for* God, rather than the voice *of* God. God is love, a circle whose center is everywhere and whose circumference is nowhere. We are all inside God's love. God is infinite, so God's voice is speaking an infinite number of different messages. Every person has access to a message uniquely designed for his or her specific need at any given time. As Gandhi said, "The voice for truth is available to speak to every single person on the planet every single day."

The voice for God, then, is co-creative; the more we listen, the more there is to be heard. The voice lifts our individual awareness and knowledge through our faith. The voice for God is within us all.

Each step that has furthered my awakening has been prompted by the voice within. In moments of quiet, a warm feeling of insight reassures me, "Mary, this is right for you." My trust has been fortified as I find that following my voice for God brings me closer to my dreams. Each time I have adhered to my guidance—"Become a teacher," "There must be a better way," "Take your ministry on the road"—I have been rewarded. I have grown. Every time I have discredited the voice, I missed opportunities that offered themselves to me only through my trust.

The voice is available anytime we are willing to listen. It has a certain resonance we can feel and identify immediately as valid. Reverence for our guidance is critical. The voice for God in us knows best, even though we cannot always fathom its message.

I have learned to respect my inner voice tremendously, but I truly believed it had gone haywire the first time I heard the words "Take a bungee jump."

A what?

Now, this inner voice has guided me to some very strange things over the years. Taking a family of six on the road for a year when I had only $300 in my pocket defied logic, but at least it did not defy the law of gravity. A bungee jump? Bungee jumping was for thrill-seeking teenagers, not respectable ministers. My feet were planted firmly on the ground, and I fully expected to keep them there. That small voice persisted, however. You might even say it nagged, louder and louder, until finally, when I was showering one morning, I snapped back, "If you want me to jump, at least make it easy for me."

While toweling off, I flipped on the radio to catch the tail end of the news, just in time to hear the reporter announce that this would be the last weekend of a bungee-jumping program in Portland.

The message couldn't get much simpler than that.

So, that very afternoon, I journeyed to the bungee-jumping site and watched a video explaining the procedure and outlining safety measures. I paid close attention. Intellect is God's gift to each of us; do not bypass your intellect. The reasoning mind discriminates and distinguishes; that's its job. You can't jump off a building and hope to sprout wings on the way down. Your intellect is an important instrument of the soul, but not, however, the master of the soul. My intellect—and brief research—told me the company offering the bungee jumps was careful and reliable, even as I signed papers releasing the business from any liability should I die or become disabled as a result of the jump.

But something greater than intellect guides us when we allow it. When we live directed by our reasoning mind alone, we miss the grace available from a higher perspective.

Hafiz, the fourteenth-century Persian poet, cautioned: "Woe to he who would try to learn the marvel of love from the copybook of reason. He will surely miss the point."

Bungee jumping is not reasonable. No one decides to swing out over open space because it's the fastest way to travel between two points: "Hmmm, think I'll bungee to my meeting today; it's so much quicker than taking the Volvo."

At the base of the bungee tower, a man wrapped a towel

around each of my ankles and secured the towels with a large clip. The clip was connected to a cable that would attach to the bungee cord once I reached the jumping platform. I hopped like a bunny as the instructor pointed the way to the bungee basket and the expert to whom I would entrust my life.

I easily identified my guide. He was a nineteen-year-old kid wearing a sweatshirt that read Bungee Master.

As we rose 140 feet from the parking lot to the platform, the master spoke: "When you get to the top, hop to the edge of the platform. I'll say, 'Three, two, one, bungee!' As I say 'Bungee!' you jump—and do not hesitate! People who wait don't do well." He added confidentially, "Sometimes we even have to take them down."

I stepped out onto the platform, which looked like nothing so much as a flimsy diving board. The wind picked up, and the platform began to wobble. Every cell in my body screamed, "This is nuts. Don't do it. It's certain death!" Cells of the body have an impulse to stay alive. They send that message really well. I looked down, hoping that the sight of a pristine lake below would soothe my ragged nerves. Of course, there was no lake, only the paved parking lot I'd left moments earlier.

"Three . . . two . . . one . . . bungee!"

I hesitated a second, but this time, instead of looking down, I gazed straight ahead. There, a few miles in front of me, a huge cross loomed above the New Hope Church.

Fixing my eyes on the cross, I said aloud, "Into Your arms." I held my breath and jumped.

As I plunged into the air I exhaled, embracing the sky. I was at the end of a giant rubber band, being stretched all the way down and snapped back. Exhilaration rushed through me, and with the wind sucking tears from my face, I swung freely past all my barriers, cast off the heavy cloak of denial, and landed joyfully—although I did not know it at the time—into a whole new life.

༄

I was still riding on the exhilaration from my bungee jump, when I received some unexpected news: Our church, the Living Enrichment Center, was being evicted from its rented facility. We had thirty days to move.

Evicted? We'd planned to move eventually. We had for years dreamed of a permanent church home. But we weren't ready, not by a long shot. Even though our eviction was purely a business decision by the owners, I took the rejection personally. No one likes to be ousted from the familiar, even if the present circumstances are far short of ideal. Our house of worship, unlike more traditional churches, boasted no stained-glass windows, not even a pulpit. But it did have popcorn. Plenty of buttery popcorn. We conducted services in a rented movie theater in a suburban shopping mall. Each Sunday, with the smell of that stale popcorn wafting through the air, I stood on the stage and preached into the inky darkness. The theater was so dark, I could see only the front half of the congregation. For a long time I worried that my sermons were boring, as the few church-goers visible seemed to shift restlessly in their seats. But I later learned they were simply attempting to remove wads of gum from the bottom of their pumps and loafers or to find a comfortable spot where the busted seat springs did not stab into their backsides.

But I wasn't complaining. The theater had been quite a step up for us. Our first church home, in 1981, had been a dingy Odd Fellows Hall, where the weekly rent was offset by the $25 we received to mop the floors and empty the garbage. We had only a handful of congregants at that time but remained confident that we would expand. And we were right; in just under five years, we had grown by 500 percent. In other words, we had fifty members. Still, we held fast to the dream that one day we would have a global ministry and a permanent home. During the next few years, we really did grow, moving from one rented facility to another, including a school gymnasium (stale popcorn smells infinitely better than sweaty gym socks), until finally securing the theater, where our congregation eventually numbered 2,500.

We had finally reached the point where we felt comfortable making more specific plans to locate and purchase a permanent church home. Our goal was to move by the year 2001, the Living Enrichment Center's twentieth anniversary.

The only trouble was, we received our eviction notice in 1992.

It's only natural to perceive eviction negatively, to curse the landlord who is saying, "You'll have to move on." Yet when we're in an accusing or fear-filled state of mind, or feeling overwhelmed with the daily details of our lives, we have tuned out the voice for God, the very voice that will lead us to our dreams. Eventually I came to find tremendous meaning as a result of being evicted from our church home, because I was led into my dream.

Almost simultaneously, however, I reached the difficult decision to face the end of my twenty-six-year marriage.

Despite my best efforts to ignore it, my voice had persisted: "Mary, you deserve to be happy." I busied myself with the changes facing our church, but when I fell into bed exhausted each night, making mental lists of all I needed to do the following day, the voice would interrupt.

"Quiet!" I'd command.

Still, the voice persisted. I decided I needed some solid, specific advice from another human being. Maybe a good friend could help me reach some conclusions about where my life was heading. While on a speaking trip to Atlanta, I arranged to visit the Rev. Dr. Barbara King, a longtime friend. Although she and

I had never discussed my marriage, I trusted her wisdom. I decided I would present my dilemma to her logically and without emotion so that I could reach a rational decision.

I burst into tears before she even answered the door.

"I need to talk to you," I sobbed.

"It's your marriage, isn't it?" Barbara asked, inviting me into her living room.

I was stunned. "How did you know?"

"Oh, honey," she said, almost laughing at my startled expression, "anybody who knows you knows that! You two aren't on the same wavelength, never have been. I can see you aren't happy together."

"Yes, but what about our children?" I moaned.

"Your children know what's going on. Everyone who knows you does, except you," she said kindly.

"But the church . . ." was my next objection.

She was ready for that one, too. "Your church will be fine. Every Sunday you tell people in your congregation to honor their hearts, that they will grow into their greater selves by following a dream, by honoring the truth. You tell them that they bless others by growing, not by remaining cramped and resentful in a life that no longer fits them. That's what you preach, isn't it?"

I nodded.

"This is not a casual choice. You've spent years giving your marriage your best. Why do you deny yourself the hope you offer to others?"

I didn't have an answer for her.

"The best minister you can be," she finally observed, "is one who is willing to live the truth, no matter how difficult it might seem."

It was a hard truth for me to face. When I returned from that trip, I wanted to tell Haven our marriage was over. But there was something I had to do first. Ever since I was little, I had relied on my father's quiet strength and wisdom to see me through the rough spots. One afternoon I sat alone with him and poured my heart out.

"Dad," I began, "I know you know what's been going on with me. It's no secret that I'm not happy in my marriage."

"Yes, I know." He waited for me to continue.

"Well, I've talked with my friend Barbara King, and she's helped me see the situation more clearly. And I've listened to myself. I know it's my decision to make, but I want to know what you think."

Slowly my dad leaned forward, put his arm around me, and said, "You have to do what gives you life."

Do what gives you life. I wept with relief.

The two evictions—from my marriage and from our church home—happened almost simultaneously. Haven and I could no more squeeze back into the narrow confines of our marriage than our growing church could stay in a movie theater that was being divided into three screens. That bungee jump—a directive from my inner voice—had propelled me toward something bigger. When I stood upon that wobbly bungee platform high above the ground, I literally stood at the edge of an old existence. I could have remained frozen at that spot; it certainly felt safer to have something solid beneath my feet, no matter how small, no matter if it allowed me no room to maneuver. Or I could jump. After twenty-six years of marriage, Haven and I divorced.

Have you received an eviction notice in your own life? Are you standing on a platform right now? Have you reached the edge? Whatever the circumstance, that eviction notice is an invitation from the Holy Spirit into a greater experience. When the time comes to jump, you will know. You will be told. Listen to your voice.

◆ Build a Relationship with the Still, Small Voice of Inspired Insight

Often people ask how I distinguish the voice for God from less reliable chatter—my ego, my history, my doubt, or my fear. How will you know your voice? You'd like a signal that alerts you and says, "Okay, this is the real thing; listen up!"

I like to tell a story about a man who received every possible signal. The dam above his town has broken, and a flood is imminent. A Jeep comes by his house, and the driver says, "Get in. I'll drive you to higher ground."

The man refuses, saying, "No. God will save me."

When the river rises, forcing the man onto the second floor of his house, he looks out the window and sees a boat gliding toward him.

But when the oarsman calls out, "Get in and I'll row you to higher ground," the man again replies, "No, no, God will save me."

As the water rises, he climbs to the roof, and a helicopter hovers overhead and drops a line. The pilot yells, "Grab hold and I'll pull you aboard."

The man still says, "No, no, God will save me."

Finally the man drowns. When he arrives in heaven, he asks God in bewilderment, "Lord, why didn't you save me?"

God answers, "I tried. I sent you a Jeep, a boat, and a helicopter, but you turned them all down!"

Just because we have reached a point of crisis during which our inner voice can no longer be silenced does not mean we will necessarily act on its guidance. Old ways die hard. How many times, when questioning which way to go, have we heard the voice saying, "Go this way!" but we chose to head in another direction? We ignore our inner voice and later say, "I knew I should have listened. I just knew it!"

Calmly, clearly, and without judgment, our inner voice is always ready to help us move toward our highest good anytime we choose to listen. We find ourselves navigated to our dream. As we increasingly listen to and follow our inner guidance, we gradually develop a deeper relationship with God. The voice gets clearer and louder because we pay attention, because we become attuned to its vibration. We don't have to wait for a crisis. We can communicate with our still, small voice every day, if we desire. God can do for us only what God can do through us. We start finding the Jeeps, boats, and helicopters in our lives the moment we choose to listen to our voice for God.

A woman from our congregation wrote me a letter describing how listening to her voice guided her toward fulfilling a dream: "I was desperate; I'd lost my job, I was depressed, I was lonely, I didn't know what to do. I had heard about a singles potluck, and the voice inside me urged me to attend, but I didn't really feel that good, and I hadn't gotten ready.

"Still, I kept feeling this nudging to go to the singles potluck. It got later and later, until I realized that if I actually did go, I'd be an hour late. So that was it. I decided not to go. But that nudging! It said, 'Go.' And so finally I thought, 'Okay, if I'm to practice following this voice, I'd better go. If I'm late, I'm late.'"

So she raced to the store for chips and dip. Arriving at the potluck over an hour late, she found one of the few vacant seats at the dinner table. As it happened, the person sitting next to her just happened to be looking for an employee with her skills and background.

She concluded her letter: "The voice said, 'Go.' All I had to do was what I was told."

You will be told, very specifically. Listen, and you will be led. Willingly follow your voice for God, even if you would rather sit home and fret.

Perhaps you are still uncertain who's speaking. Ask yourself this question: Who is my closest earthly friend? Suppose that friend calls you on the telephone. You pick up the receiver and say hello. Your dearest friend, on the other end of the line, begins talking without identifying himself or herself. All of us recognize the voices of our dearest friends, even if we haven't heard from them in years. The intimacy built over time creates a connection such that you just *know* your friend's voice.

The voice for God is no different, really. You need only listen. Over time, as you practice listening to and following God's guidance, you develop a way of knowing. Just as you know your dear friend's voice, over time you distinguish immediately the distinctive resonance of that still, small voice.

As you grow to recognize the voice, you come to trust its wisdom. Think again of your best friend. You entrust your friend with your deepest secrets, knowing that if your friendship is solid, true, and faithful, you will never be betrayed. That voice for God already knows your secrets and would never betray you. Your voice will guide you if you tune in to its frequency, which isn't always easy to do.

Imagine all the radio stations of the universe in the same room with you right now. You are holding a little transistor radio, and depending on how you tune your dial, you can listen to K-VICTIM, you can listen to K-CRITICISM, you can listen to W-BLAME, and you can listen to the big one that many, many of us spend our time tuned in to, W-FEAR.

There's another frequency, though, and that is the station of inspired insight. The static interference of our fear may require us to keep tuning the dial, but keep trying. In the New Testament, we are told, "God is love." That is as simple as it gets. To tune in to God's voice, then, tune to the loving frequency available in your mind and heart. Practice lifting your awareness with gratitude and empathy. You will become an amplified receiver for the inspired insight available through direct communion with the still, small voice.

God's voice speaks directly to us every day. We amplify our

hearing of that voice according to our willingness to listen and follow its guidance. The voice will impart an inspired idea, and if we disregard that idea, the voice quiets. Then the voice sends the impulse again, but if we discount the message, it's as though we've turned our radio volume way down, and the voice grows faint. If we pay attention, the voice amplifies.

I've found that the best way for me to reach that voice is through prayer. We fill our minds with so much clutter, all we hear is static. Prayer clears our mind and quiets our soul so that the still, small voice comes through. My daily prayer, for instance, always begins with gratitude. I give thanks for all God's blessings. As I give thanks, I feel more peaceful. And amid that peace, I begin to hear the voice. Inspired ideas come to me as I sit quietly and listen. But unless I'm still and peaceful, I cannot hear.

Beginning prayer with gratitude works for me, but it is by no means the only way. Catholics pray with rosaries; Buddhists pray with beads; some people chant aloud. There is no right or wrong way to express your devotion, no Emily Post for prayer. You need to find a method that feels right to you. The only way to tell if your prayer has worked is in the results you achieve. Do you feel more peaceful and attuned to God? Can you hear the still, small voice? When you pray sincerely, the universe always responds. We may not instantly change our circumstances through prayer, but thoughtful, genuine prayer cannot help but alter how we perceive a situation.

My daughter, Jennifer, finds her inner voice through prayer and was once guided to make a very difficult decision. She had planned to marry on New Year's Eve in 1993. She had fallen in love with a young man, an actor from Mexico, two years earlier. They had a long-distance relationship but had been able to arrange lengthy visits. Part of me felt concerned because she was so young, only nineteen at the time. But I felt guided simply to support her. So we found a wonderful white off-the-shoulder gown embellished with roses, and a veil and slippers to match. We ordered engraved invitations.

One day in November Jenny came into my room, crying. She said, "You know, when I was leaving school and going off to Mexico, I told my friends, 'I'm going to Mexico,' and there wasn't any part of me that said I should not go. But now when I'm telling people I'm going to get married, it's like there's this little part of me that goes, 'Eh, eh, eh,' like a warning, and I can't get rid of it."

I thought, "This is good. It's not good that she's upset, but it's good that she's listening."

"Maybe it's just fear and I'll get rid of it," Jenny said finally. She decided to spend some time alone, praying. She attended a retreat, and when she returned, she told me that with her prayers, her hesitation had only grown stronger. Unwilling to deny her guidance, she called her fiancé and tearfully confessed, "It isn't that I don't love you, and it isn't that I don't want to marry eventually. It's just something about now. Now is not the right time."

The day before Jenny left Oregon to return to college, her wedding dress, now altered and nonreturnable, arrived via UPS. Late that night, all alone, she put it on and gazed at herself in the full-length mirror. Then, after carefully repacking the dress in its box, she wrote herself a poem. I share here some of my favorite lines:

Tonight I opened my wedding dress box to try it on only in my
   dreams.
From the tiny silk slippers to the glimmering veil, the dress was
   a sight to see. . . .
The dress was beautiful and so was I, but something in my heart
   said no.

I don't know if I'll ever know why, I just listen and trust and
    go. . . .
We must stay true to ourselves enough to learn and grow each
    day.
For who knows what God has in store for us, our destiny is in
    His hands.
I know my dreams come from fairy tales and my love is sweet
    and tender.
I want to always dream and risk and love, because those are the
    things to remember. . . .
When I am to open this box again, it will come from my inner
    sight.
I will see myself whole, 100% clear. Yes, I know it feels right.

She wrote at the bottom: "This poem is dedicated to your
strength and courage in listening to your inner self, even when
it was hard. I love you, from me. Jenny."

My daughter's faith in her still, small voice and willingness to
follow it touched me deeply. Over the next two years I observed
her grow, deepen, and mature from a young girl into a woman
ready for greater responsibility. There came a day when she felt
truly ready to go to the altar. The young man of her dreams had
waited for her. When they said "I do," there was not even a tiny
whimper of "No, you don't."

Sometimes when you pray, you may find yourself asking for a
sign to guide you in a particular direction. You do not have to be
in the midst of prayer for those signs to crop up, because God is
always available to you. You look around and begin to find messages of higher wisdom meant specifically for you. They may
come as an answer to a prayer or a cry for help, or as the result of
a simple request for guidance. How will you know these signs?

When circumstances and ideas come together in unlikely

ways, the universe is reaching out to help you with what some people call coincidence. You can dismiss coincidence as a peculiarity of fate, or you can learn to interpret an unlikely accord as yet another message that enables you to distinguish your still, small voice. Coincidence is a signal that the voice is speaking. We recognize harmony as distinguishable from the cacophony of noise that plays in our minds. We listen so that we can decipher the meaning. Coincidence is a powerful message in code, sometimes easy to decipher and sometimes seemingly opaque. I've learned to notice coincidences, even if they arrive with a large beak and beady eyes.

One day we were having a business meeting in my office, struggling for solutions to the church's latest financial crisis. We had been laying plans for moving out of the theater and as a result had temporarily run short of funds. We didn't have enough cash to pay the lease or the staff. I was afraid, saying, "We've got to get through the summer. Right now things are so tight, how are we going to do this?" My fear, as it often does, encouraged me to take on the burden alone. "I've got to make this happen. It's up to me. What do I need to do?"

No answers were forthcoming. With no one even noticing, I prayed silently, "God, I need help." Suddenly a hawk came and landed on the windowsill. I had been in that office three years, and no bird had ever landed outside my window. That hawk flew right up, landed there, screeched loudly, and then flew away. I felt scolded, totally scolded.

In my office is a dictionary of symbols, so I got out the book and looked up *hawk.* The hawk, it said, symbolizes "the unmistakable and ever present power for the overcoming of any obstacle." I could have dismissed the sign, saying, "Oh, look, a hawk landed." Yet I have learned that no coincidence exists without meaning if I am willing to pay attention.

The hawk reminded me to turn to my source, not my ego, for the power and guidance to overcome my challenge. I reminded myself that running short of ideas was the real issue, not a shortage of funds. If you have inspired ideas, you will find a way to get what is needed to sustain you. I recognized that my source was speaking to me through this hawk, reminding me to listen for higher help. As I listened, I heard, "It's time to enlist the help of others." Immediately I thought of a man who loved our church and might be willing to lend us funds until our own became available. Help had literally winged its way to my window.

During the difficult times of our lives, we can ask God very specifically for a sign to reassure us or offer guidance about which way to proceed. This is a cocreative process. God provides the sign, but it is up to us to be aware enough to decipher its meaning. Donna Lee, a woman from our congregation, told me a story of how her family received a powerful and healing message. Donna Lee's nephew, James, had been killed suddenly in a boating accident on a lake in Michigan. Young and vital, this twenty-six-year-old was suddenly gone. James's mother, Susan, was devastated. Donna Lee flew to be with Susan, knowing the greatest gift she could give was her faith.

Susan's birthday was several days after the funeral service. The sisters made no plans other than to spend the day at home. Susan was feeling so sad and lonely for her lost child that Donna Lee said to her, "Let's pray together and simply ask for a sign that James is all right." Following the prayer, they went into the living room to sit down. As they sat and talked about James, Susan began to get restless. She got up and began to scan the bookshelf, and then had a sudden impulse to reach for a book she hadn't looked at in years. Absentmindedly she sat back down on the couch and began thumbing through the pages. As she turned one page a piece of paper fell out. There, on her lap, lay a birthday card James had made some twenty years before, stuffed for some unknown reason into a long-forgotten book.

Here now, all these years later, presented on her birthday, was a card from her son, bright with crayon hearts and flowers and the words "Happy Birthday, Mom. I love you. James." Truly her prayer was answered; the voice for God had guided the family to an old book with a card inside. In that "coincidence" a mother found comfort in her grief.

Whatever you're facing, whether it's a challenge of the heart, the mind, your finances, or your career, the loving presence that created you is available to guide you into a greater life. As you pray you become more keenly aware of God's presence in every moment, and you build a relationship with the still, small voice of inspired insight, a voice that resonates with the familiarity of a best friend.

◆ Go to the Edge of the Light You See

Do you remember the movie character Indiana Jones? In *Indiana Jones and the Last Crusade*, when he's getting close to the Holy Grail, there's a big chasm to cross. Indiana is guided to believe that if he'll just step out, a bridge will appear. But all he can see is the deep cavern. Should he fall into it, he will surely die. He must trust that if he steps out, he'll be supported. He knows that his dream, finding the Holy Grail, requires a literal leap of faith. He hears his father's voice in his mind saying, "You must believe, son." He steps out into the void, and the bridge does appear. As he takes the next step more of the bridge appears. Step by step, his faith allows him to walk to the other side. There he finds the Holy Grail. The Holy Grail represents your dream. Your current dream will lead you to even greater dreams if you are willing to take each step as it appears. Once you listen deeply and feel your guidance, take the step, even if you feel yourself bungee-jumping off a cliff.

The Psalmist sings to God, "Your word is a lamp to my feet and a light to my path." When you carry a lantern at night, the path ahead is illuminated only a step or two at a time. Go to the edge of the light you see. Take a step, even a baby step, and only then can the light show you the next step.

Some of us want a dream, but we demand to know all the details up front. We don't want a lantern; we want a floodlight. If we can't see the end of the path from where it begins, we become paralyzed.

You know that joke about the fellow who kept praying to win the lottery but never won. He wailed to God, "Please, please let me win the lottery!" Finally one day God spoke to him and said, "Give me a break. Buy a ticket."

Guidance works only one step at a time, and only when you willingly take action. When a baby begins to walk, he or she wobbles and falls down. Imagine a baby who said, "Okay, that's it. I fell down, I'm a failure, I'll never walk!" No way. Babies learn to walk because they are willing to fall down and get up again and fall down and get up again, until they develop their sense of balance. Then they start to run! It's the same thing with learning to recognize guidance. You try it out until you begin to sense you're in guidance. Ultimately you will know without doubt when you're being guided. I'm grateful for baby steps. I'm grateful that even when we're wobbly, if we keep trying, we can take a step in the direction God is calling us. Our path may not always turn out to lead where we thought it would when we first received guidance, but over time we can begin to see the pattern. Our life is moving toward a state more awakened and beautiful than anything we could have foreseen on our own.

One of the best-known parables of Jesus is that of the seed sower. On the surface, this is a deceptively simple story about farming. Yet Jesus is teaching us that following our divine insight is no different from growing a crop. For dreams to manifest themselves, you must allow inspired ideas to take root in your mind. The great seed sower of our universe is sending us these ideas all the time, but all too often we fail to nourish them. What distinguishes great dream-builders from the ordinary person is their willingness to nourish those seeds, to follow the voice of inspired insight.

"Behold, a sower went out to sow. And as he sowed, some seed fell by the wayside; and the birds came and devoured them." Some of us possess minds so closed that the seeds of insight sown toward us never reach our minds. We don't let them in at all. They fall by the wayside.

"Some fell on stony places, where they did not have much earth; and they immediately sprang up because they had no depth of earth." Dreams come to us, and we think, "Yeah, that's a good idea." We get an excited feeling that comes up right away, but the feeling lacks depth. *"But when the sun was up they were scorched, and because they had no root they withered away."* When our dream is tested by a conflicting idea, when it's first scorched by a negative thought, we immediately tell ourselves, "It's over. My dream can't happen." "I don't have the education." "I don't have the money." "It's only a foolish fantasy," we say, and our negativity kills the dream. There's no depth to it.

"And some fell among thorns, and the thorns sprang up and choked them." Some of us have an idea, a dream. It grows in the mind. We want to plant it, but we become fearful or distracted. We say, "Yes, I want this dream," but we don't put any energy into it. We don't place our feet on the path. We just dream and think, "I'm bored to tears with my job; I've really always wanted to be an engineer, so I took a course or two, but they were too hard." These thoughts of fear are like the thorns in the parable. As we go along we start getting distracted—"I didn't think going to school would interfere with my social life so much; maybe I'll take some time off" or "I'm not smart enough, anyway"—and the weeds of fear and distraction choke out the dream because there is insufficient energy for the dream to grow.

"*But others fell on good ground and yielded a crop; some a hundredfold, some sixty, some thirty. He who has ears to hear, let him hear!*" You have a dream for your life. Let go of life-choking thoughts so that your mind can be sown with the seeds of inspired insight.

One day a six-year-old boy from our children's group planted two seeds in a little paper cup and left them in my office as a gift. After they sprouted, I took the cup home and planted the shoots in a little pot. Unfortunately, I forgot to water them, and eventually they died. Those were good seeds and healthy shoots. If only I hadn't neglected them, they would have yielded their crop. As I looked at those dead little plants, I thought, "What other seeds has God sown in me that I neglected?"

I can look back in my life and see moments of choice when an idea came and I turned away. I can also see the times when I really nurtured an inspired idea and flourished as a result. Seeing those little dead plants caused me to commit even more deeply to the seeds of good planted in my life today. I can't do anything about the ideas that are dead, but I can honor the one taking root at this moment.

God, the seed sower, never gives up: not on me, not on you.

Ed is a certified public accountant who became a consultant for our church. He recalls a time he thought the seed sower had given up on him. On the verge of bankruptcy, he figured he had planted amid thorns once too often and lost all opportunity for a crop.

Ed is an alcoholic. Many years ago, after several stays at recovery centers and a period in a mental hospital, Ed felt strong enough to at least try letting a higher power help him get sober. He found a mentor who told him, "The truth is that progress in dealing with relationships, money problems, or health problems is entirely dependent upon the maintenance of our spiritual condition. People don't like to hear that, because it places the responsibility for their happiness right where it belongs, on them."

Ed knew he was being challenged, because he had always allowed circumstances to dictate his fate.

"What's your most pressing problem?" the mentor asked. "What's causing you the most stress in your life?"

"The bank," Ed answered without hesitation. "A couple of years ago I borrowed a great deal of money, and now the bank wants to be repaid." (Odd how banks want that!) "Business is slow, and I don't have any money. I went to a loan officer at the bank to try to work something out. I told him what I was doing with my life and that I needed time. My candor impressed him, but his hands were tied. The bank needed to be repaid. So I asked to talk to his supervisor. I told the supervisor what I had told the loan officer, and I offered to pay the bank five hundred dollars a month. He said he could not accept payments of that amount in view of the large sum I owed, and he said if I did not clear up the matter, they would have to sue me. Three weeks later I got a notice that the bank had filed suit against me to collect the amount owing, plus attorneys' fees."

Ed had taken out a personal loan for $20,000. He didn't use the money to expand his business. He drank the money away. With interest, his debt now stood at $30,000.

"I guess I don't have any choice now except to declare bankruptcy," Ed said.

"Tell me," his mentor asked, "did you think they would take your offer?"

"I hoped they would," Ed responded. "I didn't know what else to do. I didn't think they would take anything less."

"So you didn't offer them what you could afford?" his confidant pressed.

"No, I offered them twice what I felt I could actually afford, and even that apparently wasn't enough."

Ed's mentor, an alcoholic who had been sober for many years

and knew all too well the workings of a diseased mind, grinned. "There were two things wrong with your offer," he told Ed. "First, you offered something you knew was not in your best interest. Offering a creditor payments that you feel you cannot make is dishonest. Dishonesty is never rewarded. Second, and most important, you did not expect your offer to be accepted, and therefore it wasn't."

"What do you mean?" Ed demanded. "I have very little ability to affect the bank's decision. I did everything I could. I even prayed!"

"I'm confused," Ed's friend answered patiently. "First you tell me that you didn't expect the bank to take your offer, and then you tell me you prayed, and then you tell me that you have no ability to affect the bank's decision. What do you think prayer does?"

"Well, I've been praying for God's will for me."

"Do you think it's God's will for you and your kids to be thrown out on the street when the bank takes your house? Do you think that by saying a prayer you will change the outcome of what God's will is for you?"

Ed thought about this for a moment. "I guess," he finally answered, "that I don't know what prayer really is, then, and I don't know what it does."

His mentor leaned forward and said softly, "The answers to every problem already exist. The rule of the universe is abundance. God doesn't take sides in a business arrangement. What you don't understand is that you are part of God. We all are. God exists in you and in me. What prayer does is eliminate the separation that exists between you and your higher power. Prayer eliminates the noise that drowns out God's voice."

This was new territory for Ed. "I don't see how that helps," he said, almost apologetically.

"It's like this. If the answer already exists, don't you think God knows the answer?"

"Yes."

"Don't you think God would tell you if you ask?"

"Well, yes."

"God will tell you if you listen. Once you hear the answer, it's up to you to follow through. The purpose of prayer is to bring you into alignment with God's will, so that when you get quiet, you hear what God is telling you. That's how you affect the outcome. You get quiet, you listen for the inspiration, and then you do the footwork. If you partner with God, the two of you will create an outcome where everyone wins. It's easy—just ask in your prayers that God's will be done for the bank as well as for you. And then expect something to happen. It may not happen right away, but it will happen."

"What will happen?" Ed asked.

"Wait and see."

Ed began to ask daily for God's will for the bank and for himself. Meanwhile, with the lawsuit looming over him, he hired a bankruptcy attorney and prepared for a court appearance. In the midst of impending disaster, Ed began to feel a sense of peace.

Until then Ed had been clinging to his last shred of ego. As an accountant, he prided himself on his ability to handle money. Filing bankruptcy would unequivocally strip him of that ego. He had hit bottom. He could finally own up that his role of money manager, at least in recent years, had been a facade. Once he got beyond his vanity, beyond defining who he was by a job title, he had cleared a channel for a higher power to work in his life.

Ed continued to ask for God's will and to listen for that voice, asking that God's will be done in the highest way for the bank and for himself. One morning, while sitting in his office, he heard the voice say, "Go to a twelve-step meeting." There was a meeting close by that he usually attended, but as he prepared to leave, the voice urged, "No, go to another meeting."

Ed found a meeting in a different part of town. While there, he noticed a man staring at him. Feeling uncomfortable, Ed bolted for the door as soon as the last speaker sat down, but the fellow who had been staring blocked his way and said, "Listen, I think I know you. Didn't we go to school together?"

Nervously Ed squinted at him and said, "No, I don't think so." After all, Ed hadn't grown up in Portland. Surely this busybody couldn't know him.

As it turned out, the two men had indeed attended the same elementary school more than twenty years earlier in a small town some two hundred miles south of Portland. The man was delighted to see Ed, and in the course of talking about their work he mentioned the bank where his father was the senior officer in charge of diversified assets—in other words, bad loans.

The blood rushed to Ed's face when he heard not only the name of the bank suing him but the very division within the bank to which he owed his debt! Not wishing to reveal his embarrassing secret, Ed simply replied, "Yeah, well, say hi to your dad," and he walked away. He was totally dumbfounded. What were the implications, he wondered, of this encounter? What a miserable coincidence, he finally decided. "Man," he said aloud to himself as he walked down the street, "I can't get away from my problems anywhere!" What Ed didn't realize is that when circumstances seem to coincide in inexplicable ways, the universe is reaching out to help you.

The next day the phone rang in Ed's office. It was his old schoolmate's father, the banker in charge of diversified assets. "My son dropped by last night," the man began, "and he mentioned running into you. At first I didn't remember you, but as he talked I began to recall your family. Then today, as I was going through the files and noticed the bank's action against you, I also noticed the notes that said you've been in to talk to the loan officer and mentioned what you're trying to do with your life. I know what that program you are following has done for my son. Listen, I want to talk to you about this. I know you probably expect me to tell you to bring your attorney, but I'd like it if you just came by yourself this afternoon. Come at four o'clock."

That was a very long day for Ed. He had some crazy hope that maybe the banker would accept his original offer. So what if he did? Ed couldn't pay that amount anyway. Maybe this big shot, as an old friend of his son's, simply wanted to say, "Yes, we are suing you and forcing bankruptcy, but hey, it's nothing personal."

When he stepped into the mahogany-paneled office that afternoon, the banker came around his massive carved desk, shook Ed's hand, and offered him a cup of coffee. Ed was surprised. He hadn't expected to be treated like a real human being.

The man went right to the heart of the matter. "I'm willing to figure out with you what we might do with this situation and what kind of payments you can make. What is it you need?"

The banker asked what Ed needed, not what he wanted. There's a difference. What Ed wanted was for the whole mess to disappear, to have his debt magically cleared or to pay $1,000 a month and pay it off quickly. But there was no way Ed could afford $1,000 a month, and there was no way the bank could make the debt magically disappear. What Ed wanted was a quick fix. Such a plan would have no space for God in it. Ed recognized that perhaps the universe was sending a message, and once again he surrendered his false pride. He answered honestly, "What I need is payments of two hundred and fifty dollars a month."

The banker thought a moment and said, "That won't even pay the interest." There was another moment of silence before he spoke again. "In view of where this loan has gotten to, I think that maybe . . . yeah, I'm going to rewrite the interest on this." He was able to adjust the interest below the prime rate, because the bank had already written off the loan as a loss. "We will accept two hundred and fifty dollars a month," he said, "and I will rely upon you to tell me when you can afford to pay more." With this new arrangement, the bank could recoup its money, and Ed would be able to continue working and clearing away his debt without filing bankruptcy.

Within four years Ed paid off his debt. There is always a way.

Before he took the first step, all Ed could see ahead of him was darkness, bankruptcy. But as he prayed for help he found guidance. He went to the edge of the light he could see, and as he did so a path appeared before him.

Even the nonbelievers among us cannot dismiss such events as fate or dumb luck. Ed listened to the inner voice that told him to attend a meeting he had never been to before, where he wound up seeing a friend from two decades past and hundreds of miles away, a friend whose father just happened to have his finger on the money Ed owed. Even luck isn't that organized. This "coincidence" demonstrated to Ed that God is always available to assist him. He learned that when you really surrender and follow the voice for your higher power, it always leads you to a greater life.

Empowered by the knowledge that his voice for God was guiding him, Ed had the courage to take action. With each step, light fell under his leading foot, illuminating the way out of his troubles. Once he received assistance, what he had once believed to be the only solution paled in comparison to the plan God had in store for him.

Growing Your Dream

As you move into your dream you may feel as if you are stepping out onto thin air. But you are not alone. The still, small voice of inspired insight is literally your best friend. The voice for God exists in each one of us, but we tend to call upon it haphazardly. Yet this is the voice that can guide us into our dreams.

1. Acknowledge the inner nudge toward outer motion. The knowing voice for God persistently nudges us in the direction of our highest good by way of a path that often confounds the logical mind. This voice will do whatever is necessary to get your attention. It may provide you with a message as seemingly mundane as "go to the singles potluck," or it may call upon you to bungee-jump out of your current existence.

2. Build a relationship with the still, small voice of inspired insight. The voice for God can become as familiar and resonant as that of our best friend. You develop a friendship by spending time with your friend, and you develop a relationship with God by listening to that still, small voice. Even so, it's not always easy to distinguish the voice amid the cacophony that plays in our minds. We can quiet our minds through prayer. And we are provided clues to the voice in the form of what seems to be coincidence. Listen for the harmony in order to decipher the higher meaning.

3. Go to the edge of the light you see. Until you take a step, you remain in the dark, where nothing but the most dire solution to any problem is visible. The light you carry may illuminate only one step at a time, but as you move forward the next step will be revealed.

Chapter Eight

INGENUITY:

Building a Bigger Believing

All things are possible to the one that believes.

—JESUS

♦ *Develop Partners in Believing*
♦ *Lift Your Thinking into the Genius Mind*
♦ *Practice Five Steps to Renew Your Faith*

On a cold January afternoon Judy struggled up three flights of stairs, a year-old baby tucked under one arm, a bag of groceries under the other, and the key to her apartment clenched between her teeth. She knew she looked ridiculous, but it sure beat putting down the groceries while she fumbled through her purse for the apartment key, making little Annie scream impatiently. When Annie wailed, the neighbors gave her dirty looks, making Judy feel as if she were a bad mother. Once inside, Judy put down her burdens and sighed, safely ensconced in what her six-year-old son had nicknamed "the shoe box." With its rectangular shape, dim light, and walls like cardboard, Judy's apartment did indeed seem a more appropriate shelter for a pair of pumps than a family of three. And in her heart, she knew that the shoe box was not where she belonged.

So she smiled, envisioning the home she had created for herself in her mind, a home without three flights of stairs and numbers on the doors. It wasn't an apartment at all, but a lovely house with a yard and flowers. The home had become so real to Judy, she had even written down the specifics of her dream, a very important step: "I want to be in the home by Thanksgiving. I can see this house with an arched door; I can see a white fence; I can see three bedrooms, one for me and each of the children; there's a fireplace; there's a window over the kitchen sink where my African violets are growing, and I can afford this place." Judy had moved in, if only in her mind. She was already eyeing a stencil kit for decorating the living room.

There was only one problem. Judy could barely make the rent on the shoe box, let alone afford the lease on a house with an arched doorway. Since her husband had left her the previous year, he sent an occasional postcard but never child support, and she'd had trouble making ends meet.

Judy frequently felt discouraged and thought about giving up. She wanted to believe she could have her house, but it seemed so distant, so unreachable, she knew she couldn't get from the shoe box to her dream home on her own faith alone. Judy recognized she needed help, people who could believe for her when she found it hard to believe in herself. Through our church, Judy joined with three other congregants who would meet weekly to assist one another in achieving their dreams. We call such a group "partners in believing."

Just as a farmer seeks help from others to improve his yield—whether it's about buying the right seed for his soil or getting the latest equipment—you can fortify your dream with support from those around you.

♦ Develop Partners in Believing

In the 1930s, when author Napoleon Hill researched the great success stories of his day—entrepreneurs such as Ford, Edison, Firestone, Du Pont—he found that every one of those men belonged to what was then called a mastermind group. They had one or two or three others with whom they joined in believing in a greater possibility than they presently experienced. They empowered one another. Jesus said: "For where two or three are gathered together in My name, I am there in the midst of them."

Do you have support systems in your life? Build a group of two or more like-minded people to meet with regularly who believe in you and can affirm you. Discuss your dream with them. Let them help you clarify your dream on paper and remind you to stay on course. The people with whom you associate can have a dramatic effect on your life. If you spend time with people who continually tear you down, your self-worth can be eventually eroded to the point where you're convinced that what they say about you is true. Conversely, when you gravitate toward those who believe in your potential, you cannot help but grow.

Select your partners in believing carefully. Although you might automatically choose your dearest friend or spouse, consider looking beyond the obvious. Those closest to you may lack the necessary objectivity to step back from your dream and examine the larger picture, and you might do them the same disservice when it comes to their dreams. Your spouse may be influenced by his or her own stake in the dream, and vice versa. And if you're always in the company of these people anyway, you may have a more difficult time setting aside a particular time each week to work on the specifics of your dream without the daily stresses and details of your lives interfering.

Consider people who have supported you in the past or whom you have supported. They may be close friends, or they may be casual acquaintances with whom you connect easily and who you feel have your best interests at heart, people whose ideas you've always respected, or even people who have succeeded in making their own dreams come true. Chances are they didn't do it alone and will gladly pass on their learning to others. They may have a new dream that needs some support as well.

Your partners in believing group can take many forms. Sometimes each person's vision is discussed during a portion of the meeting. Sometimes an entire meeting is devoted solely to one individual. Here are a few steps to help you get started:

- Make progress reports. Each person states his or her dream and the progress made since the last meeting.
- Allow time to express discouragement so that you can purge it and move on. Others may interpret what you perceive as failure as steps toward a goal. Or if you really have regressed, let the group guide you to an alternative game plan.
- Brainstorm. Together with your partners, come up with as many suggestions as possible to help your dream become reality. The rules of brainstorming prohibit evaluation until every last idea, no matter how outrageous, has been brought forward.
- Ask the "suppose" question: "Suppose your dream weren't impossible. What would be the first thing you'd do?" Ask this question again and again. It is crucial to put yourself into the mind-set that with God all things are possible.

- Follow up. It's one thing to embrace greater possibilities, quite another to take steps so that they come to fruition. Decide with your partners which action steps you will take before the next meeting, then next time review your progress with them. If you let yourself down, you'll be letting them down, too. The prospect of disappointing people we respect is often enough to get most of us moving.

- Encourage creative thinking. Your partners may want to ask you to imagine yourself moving toward the dream: "If you were getting closer, how would you know? What would be the first thing you notice? What in your life would be different?"

- Mark small victories. You don't have to wait until the dream comes true to celebrate. You will try that much harder when your partners in believing compliment your progress or even hold a mini-party to honor your overcoming a particular obstacle to your dream.

- Challenge limited thinking. We don't even know when we're trapped in limited thinking because we have come to believe that the limitation is true, so we act according to our beliefs. That results in a self-fulfilling prophecy. Your partners in believing bring a fresh perspective. They can help you see where you have closed yourself off.

Many people would have classified Judy's "limited thinking" as highly realistic. She frequently told herself, "My take-home pay is a thousand dollars a month, and my rent is five hundred dollars, which is already too much. The homes for rent in the paper are between six hundred and eleven hundred dollars a month. I really ought to stop torturing myself and just be content with the shoe box."

In fact, when she showed her group the description of her

dream home she had created, she said, "I don't know how to make this happen. It just seems impossible."

One partner said, "If you didn't believe it was impossible, what would you do?"

She paused and said, "Well, if I didn't believe it was impossible, I guess I'd start looking. I would get out there and really start looking, but I know how much houses cost. I've looked in the paper. I know the going rent."

Her partners said, "Fine. But if you didn't believe it was impossible, what would you do?"

Holding this new thought was an important shift for her. She imagined in her mind that the house she wanted, in a decent part of town, existed at a price she could afford. "I guess I'd better call a real-estate agent," Judy responded. And that's exactly what she did.

Several weeks passed, and then several months. Other members of the group seemed to be making solid progress toward their dreams. Judy started to get a little depressed. Her real-estate agent was not encouraging, telling her she was "operating outside the current market rate." Her partners in believing, however, reminded her that God was not limited by the housing index. So she practiced building a bigger believing. She envisioned herself in the house. She reminded herself that all things are possible with God, and she continued to ask for that house in her prayers. She said she came to realize that even though she had a limited income, God knew a way. God was more powerful than her take-home salary. She kept affirming the possibility of her dream and kept after the real-estate agent. There had to be a way.

Judy's dream is a metaphor for what all of us deeply desire. We are all searching for home, for that special place we rightfully belong. This belonging, this home, may be a house with an arched doorway and begonias in the garden; it may be the career that best suits us or the fulfillment of belonging in a relationship. As we journey homeward, we are buoyed by others whose support and encouragement guide us toward our desired destination.

At about this time, I too was searching for a home. In my case, I desired a permanent spiritual home for my congregation, and yes, there were many times when I did not believe it possible. Like Judy, I had sought the assistance of others in trying to bring that dream to reality. In November 1991 I asked the congregation to fill out individual vision cards defining each person's dream for the church. Once we collected the cards, I wrote a collective vision statement that read like this: "We have a global headquarters. It's a beautiful home, a campus with landscaping that reflects God's beauty: trees, flowers, meditation gardens with benches, resting places, statues of holy people. Our home is large enough to meet the needs of our community, with room for expansion. Our sanctuary is simple, yet an elegant place in which to worship. We enjoy natural light streaming in to bless all in attendance. As our church's children are of high priority, we invest in lavish youth facilities and children's play areas. We have a kitchen, large enough to meet the needs of our congregation, where we have lunches, brunches, and Wednesday night dinners. Our facilities are ecologically sound and environmentally pleasing."

Like Judy, we detailed our dream on paper, an important step. As you may recall from chapter two, writing down your dream is akin to the physical act of planting a seed. Your desires become more tangible. You can read your dream aloud daily, amending it as necessary, until you have committed the words to memory, as you would a sacred text.

We had taken the additional step of asking a consultant to assist us in our dream. The consultant, Eric, led us through a process called storyboarding—the same process that helped build Disneyland and send astronauts to the moon. He began by pointing to a wall inside an inner office, explaining that one end would represent where the church stood now, and the other end would be the realization of our dream. We would post the steps in between. As we began laying out plans along the wall, we realized we needed a symbol to mark the final dream fulfilled. But no valuable artifact emerged; no artistic hand produced a dramatic rendering. Finally one of the staff reached into a desk and pulled out a deflated green balloon. Eric held it up before us, and we all laughed. Was this the best we could do?

Then someone else inflated the balloon and tacked it to the wall. Somehow that balloon was just right, a simple expression of celebration. The mind is a tool of vision, and the church members' collective vision for a permanent home was called the Green Balloon.

A balloon doesn't remain full of air all by itself. Every now and then someone would walk by the wall and notice our little emblem starting to deflate. I'd frequently walk down the corridor to find one of our staff facing the wall, cheeks puffed out, blowing, and I would smile, knowing that all of us were doing our best to keep the dream alive.

We were taking every step possible, it seemed, yet I often found myself plagued with doubt. The late Jack Boland, then the senior minister of the Church of Today in Warren, Michigan, came to speak at our church. Jack, who believed in our ministry and believed that God had called us together as a group of people for a great purpose, asked me about our dream for the church. I outlined our plans for a permanent home, adding that our dream was millions of dollars bigger than our current pocketbook. We hoped that within a year we could make a down payment on some land and in ten years' time move into our permanent home.

Jack turned to me with a challenging look on his face and

asked, "Mary, do you believe you can have your new church this year?"

"No," I answered truthfully. "We're looking for land this year."

"Do you believe you can have your church, that the center can have its own facility?" he asked again, more intensely.

I clung to my limited thinking. "Not this year, but eventually. I'm in a place of really wanting to believe it."

Then Jack said something that shot me full of hope: "Right now, Mary, do you believe that I believe you can have this? Do you believe that I believe you can have your own church home this year?"

I knew the great faith of Jack Boland, and I could see he was serious. Jack lived far away, so our meetings were infrequent. But I had always considered him my partner in believing. "Well, yes. I believe you believe it."

"Then let my belief carry you right now. I believe that for you. Believe in my belief."

I left that lunch transformed. I had, unconsciously, closed my mind to any possibility of a greater good. Intellectually I knew it would be a huge stretch just to raise the money for bare land, let alone a whole facility. Yet in that moment, in the presence of a friend who absolutely believed in God's unlimited possibilities, a corner of my mind opened.

I said to myself, "It's certainly not probable, but it is possible." Jack opened my mind to abundance, allowing a new dimension to enter my thinking. I walked into that lunch in one mind-set and left with another.

Jack and I had lunch in January 1992. Six months later we received our eviction notice from the movie theater. We readied ourselves to move to a giant tent outside the mall until we could find a new place. We had maybe four months until Mother Nature froze us out. Now what? Our bank balance hadn't budged. Would we have to spend our few precious dollars moving to yet another temporary facility?

♦ Lift Your Thinking into the Genius Mind

Ralph Waldo Emerson said, "To believe your own thought, to believe that what is true for you in your private heart is true for all men—that is genius." The kind of genius to which Emerson is referring cannot be measured on an IQ test. He is speaking instead of a genius that lies in us all but which we only tap into in proportion to our belief.

The great genius of the universe dreamed you up. The genius of the universe placed a part of that genius in you, although you may have yet to discover it. If you do not believe in the existence of God's own genius and believe that it is available to you, then you cannot easily benefit from this inherent gift. Once we discover this genius, we come to recognize that God has a great plan for our lives, an incredible dream. God matches each dream with the dreamer. You've been already matched up for the great dream. Your pattern is already complete, although at first you don't know it.

We bring forth our genius in a number of ways. We recognize ourselves as powerful beings created in the image of the genius of creation. We listen to and follow the guidance of our still, small voice. And we willingly accept help from those we've enlisted for support. We co-create by harnessing these sources of assistance and, in doing so, bring ourselves closer to our dream. In the words of Jesus, "Ask what you desire, and it shall be done for you."

When you live in the genius mind, you reach beyond your comfort zone and dare to declare that a great dream is being dreamed through you. Pause for a moment and feel that dream, a dream that's bigger than you, a dream that will give you life, a dream that will enhance the lives of others.

As we move toward our dream, at times we may find ourselves faltering, tempted to scale back our plans. We may doubt our own abilities. Here, our partners in believing help propel us forward. They tell us that we do not have to limit ourselves to the confined world of practicality. Our greatest dreams require that we learn to practice outrageous thinking, and our partners keep us attuned to the outrageous by constantly asking, "If you didn't believe it was impossible, what would you do?"

At our church, we became outrageous thinkers. In January 1992 we had established our collective vision. By the end of October, we were moving into our permanent home. In ten months' time, we were making a move that none of us had thought could take place in anything less than ten years.

The wonderful new church home we found in Wilsonville, Oregon, just outside of Portland, had been sitting idle for years. Built as a rehabilitation center by the state, the facility had been long abandoned, apparently waiting for us to discover it. We had found the perfect home on forty-five acres with a 95,000-square-foot main building, with a kitchen, even the huge indoor swimming pool the children in our congregation had said they wanted. This facility, had we built it ourselves, would have cost $15 million, but because it had sat empty for so long, the state sold it to an investor for practically nothing. That investor turned around and offered this magnificent facility to our church for $3 million, the amount we had planned on spending just for bare land. How absolutely outrageous to think that a group of people could move from a rented movie theater into a $15 million facility in under a year, apparently without the resources!

When we sincerely pray and ask, the universe leads us step by step to our highest good. It does not always simply hand us what we ask. We co-create with God, and in the process of building our dreams, we ourselves are molded and shaped and grown. En route to our vision, we ask: "Do I trust enough to keep following even when I can't see the answers?" If it is a big dream, something beyond our present experience, we must suspend our intellect long enough to listen at a deeper level.

Norman Vincent Peale, a man who bestowed a great gift to our culture by encouraging us to strive for our highest good, wrote in *Guideposts Magazine*:

> Almighty God freely bestows the good things in this world in proportion to a person's readiness to receive. An individual coming to the divine storehouse with a teaspoon, thinking lack, will receive only a teaspoonful. Another more positive, believing person can come confidently with a gallon container and receive a gallon of life's blessings. We can only receive that which we expect according to our faith, so expand your openness.

A little girl was going through the halls of the Capitol when Borglum, the famous sculptor, was carving the bust of Abraham Lincoln. She watched him and at first couldn't quite understand what he was doing, so each day she would return. As the face began to emerge from the stone, she went up to him and said, "How did you know Lincoln was in there?" He replied, "I just took away everything that wasn't Lincoln." That is our bigger believing. It is about carving away anything that holds us back from our dream and revealing the genius that lies etched in us all.

There was a genius engraved in Judy's being, but it had been obscured by deep slashes of disappointment. She had come to trust the supportive words of her partners in believing, but a part of her felt disconnected from God. In so many ways Judy felt life had let her down. She had had so many expectations that had been followed by so many disappointments. When Judy got married, she had thought it would last forever. She and her husband had spun fantasies about the future. By now, though, she'd lost her husband, her home, her sense of belonging, and most of all her belief that a greater dream awaited her. She had reached a point where she stopped seeing greater possibilities.

This happens to all of us at times. You begin to see only what you lack instead of what you have. If you're infertile, you notice only those women with large, pregnant bellies. If you're lonely, you feel bombarded by couples holding hands. If you lack the money for material goods, everyone else's clothing appears new and elegantly stitched, and the cars that whiz by you are sleek, polished, and finely tuned. In this state of mind, we do not focus on the belief that all things are possible. There's no room for a bigger believing.

It took Judy a long time to shift from feeling denied and shortchanged to feeling grateful for all she had—for her two healthy children, even for the idiosyncrasies of the shoe box. But as she did so she began to recognize her inner genius. She began to believe in God as the great genius who orchestrates the universe, and she wanted to tap into that power. What she truly desired would manifest itself if she continued to believe—not just in the support of her group but in God as well. That gave her the power to believe in herself. Even though a farmer plants corn and cannot see anything but bare dirt for the longest time, he believes in a harvest. And so did Judy.

One day Judy's real-estate agent called and said, "I think I have found exactly the house that you want." She described a house with an arched doorway, a fireplace, and three bedrooms.

There was only one problem. The monthly rent was $775, well beyond the amount Judy could afford.

After touring the house with the agent, she went back to her partners in believing and said, "I've found the house now, but there's no way I can swing the price."

You can guess what they said: "Well, if you didn't believe it was impossible, what might you do?"

"I don't know what I'd do. I'm believing I can't afford the rent."

"What can you afford?"

"I can afford what I'm paying now. It's five hundred dollars a month."

"Why don't you offer that amount?"

Judy laughed. "Talk about operating outside the current market! They'll never accept that. I mean, they're asking seven hundred seventy-five dollars. It might as well be a million."

"Yes, that's what they're asking. But how do you know what they'll take? If you didn't believe it was impossible, what would you do?"

Judy thought about this a moment. "I guess I'd write a letter and propose paying less rent." So she wrote a letter to the owner of the house, describing her dream and how much it would mean to her and the children to live there. She wrote about what she would do to care for that home, how she would plant flower bulbs, how she would care for the yard and polish the hardwood floors and stencil the living room walls. Judy spelled out her dream in all its loving detail. Then she stated what she could afford.

Judy followed every step for dream-building. She ignited her desire to reach the place she knew she belonged in. She had an intention and wrote it down. She asked for higher guidance and followed her voice. Through the assistance of her partners, she believed not only that she was worthy of such a home but that it was possible to find a home that logic dictated was beyond her means. She believed in her own inner genius, knowing its connection to the great genius of the universe, God. She was grateful for what she already possessed and trusted the universe to respond.

♦ Practice Five Steps to Renew Your Faith

Our congregation had found a permanent home that logic dictated was well beyond our means. While we could congratulate ourselves on remaining faithful to the dream even when it looked impossible, our work was far from over. Locating a new facility had been a whirlwind, exhilarating process, but moving into our home was an entirely different matter. Just because we had managed to secure a mortgage didn't mean we could hang on to it. And the building had been abandoned for so long that it needed major repairs.

The roof leaked so badly, you would have thought we had an indoor sprinkler system. We didn't even have a furnace for this 95,000-square-foot behemoth. Permits proved troublesome, and there was no parking for our 2,500 congregants. I started feeling all kinds of fear about what would happen. What about this and what about that? Certainly we have all had this experience of formulating a dream, moving into it, and then encountering unexpected problems. Listening to my voice of fear, I was slipping into scarcity thinking rather than embracing what my heart knew to be true: Abundance is the first law of the universe. My limited thinking was telling me we couldn't possibly finance and manage such a tremendous project.

We'd been riding so high, taking such giant steps, that my bigger believing had become depleted. I found myself falling prey to panic. Instead of remembering that a long journey is accomplished one step at a time, that the inspiration we need to handle life's challenges speaks in the quiet spaciousness of an open, trusting heart, I tried to solve everything at once, on my own. My body responded in kind; my shoulders ached, a sign I was unconsciously attempting to take on this great load all at once and alone. I needed to replenish my faith with the support of all those people who were bringing such tremendous energy to the church, but all I could think about was all the obstacles before us.

There is a Zen Buddhist story about a Western man who was considered a leading thinker of his time. He had several degrees in philosophy and wanted to travel to the East for an encounter with a Zen master. He traveled thousands of miles and waited many days for a private interview with the Zen master. He approached the table to sit with the master, and tea was brought into the room. As a servant placed cups before them, the Western man began to regale the master with his accomplishments, his academic credentials, and the many books he had read. The master was silent as the other talked on and on about the knowledge he had acquired, explaining that while he wanted to be the master's student, his teacher should realize how much he already understood.

The Zen master carefully picked up the teapot and began to pour tea. Abruptly the man stopped in the middle of his monologue. The master had filled his guest's cup, but he continued to pour tea, which overflowed the lip, filled the saucer, ran across the table, and dripped off the edge, finally splashing on the visitor's feet. "You're pouring tea everywhere," the man observed incredulously.

To which the Zen master responded, "You are like this teacup. It is so full, it cannot contain anything new. You are so full of yourself, you have no room for anything else."

With my mind so full of my fear, I too had no room for anything else. I prayed for renewal: "Please, God, move in my life. Show me again how to trust, how to find the inspiration I need to meet these challenges."

Once again the answer came in an unexpected way. Our church had scheduled its annual retreat in Mexico. We took with us over two thousand prayer requests brought from home from the center's members. We intended to carry them to the great Aztec pyramids near Mexico City. The Aztecs considered these pyramids sacred ground. We would use the amplified energy field of an ancient place of prayer to magnify our requests in the universe.

Our retreat center was in a mountainous area near Cuernavaca, just outside the city. We found Mexico City a stiflingly hot metropolis for which we'd worn far too many clothes. We trekked from our tour bus to the foot of one of the pyramids, arriving sweaty, cranky, and irritated at ourselves for not having brought enough water. Nonetheless, we conducted a prayer meeting, a powerful experience that energized some of the group, who announced they wanted to climb the pyramid. Looking up at the steep stone steps, I thought, "No, not me. I'm too tired and hot; I think I'll just stay here at the base and pray."

In the meantime, several members of the group had grown worried about finding our bus. The driver had told us to meet him at gate five, but we suddenly realized that the ruin site was a complex labyrinth. Two groups of people went off in opposite directions to see if they could get their bearings. When they returned, each group had a different perception of which way to proceed.

"We're sure gate five is to the right," one group insisted.

"No, no, it's to the left!" insisted the other search party.

Either way, the next gate was far off in the distance and a wrong choice would prove disastrous in the hot sun. Tensions rose with the temperature, and soon people turned to me and asked, "Well, Mary, which way do we go?"

How should I know? I was as hot, thirsty, tired, and confused as anyone in the group. These are the times when the persistence of daily spiritual practice pays off. Taking a deep breath and closing my eyes, I tried to quiet my intellect, which was harping on the heat, being lost, and on and on and on. Then it came through to me; the voice said, "But you want the view."

The view? "I guess if I'm going to get a view," I thought, "I've got to go as high as I can." I decided to climb the pyramid. I told the group to rest until those of us climbing returned. I spoke with calm assurance, as if I knew the way, despite my not having the foggiest idea how to lead our group out of this labyrinth.

As I put one foot in front of the other up the pyramid, I was reminded of the many mountains I had already faced in my life, and I recalled that each one of them had been scaled in just this manner: one step at a time. About a third of the way up, a companion looked over and said, "Here, Mary, let me carry your purse." Yet another realization came to me; I thought about the many times when, as I climbed the mountains of my life, there were always those who were willing to love me and assist me in my journey, once I had made the choice to take action and begin the climb. They bolstered me, helped me to believe in something larger than myself. The universe delights in supporting us if we will take the steps necessary to move forward. God reaches out to us through others.

Finally reaching the top, I was rewarded with a breathtaking vista. My biggest obstacle, I realized, had been me. My limiting ideas, my fear, would stop me from getting where I really wished to go and block the dreams I desired to make manifest. As I silently vowed to get out of my own way, I took in the full scope of my vantage point, looking out over the horizon. There I made my affirmation: "God, help me remember to turn to You for the strength I need, instead of trying to do everything on my own. Let me be willing to receive Your help through both the still, small voice of insight and the assistance of others." I didn't have to solve the problems involved in moving into our church home all by myself. Others were there, had always been there, to offer support. Together we would make the move. After I completed my prayer, my eyes went to the exact spot where the buses awaited us below. My heart raced with joy, not just for having found our way back to our transportation but for once again having found my way through the labyrinth of the world by means of belief followed by action. I had reached the place where my mind could begin to experience the renewal it sought. My voice had said, "You want the view," and I had climbed to the top.

When you renew your faith, you expand your horizons. You gain a mountaintop view. You see further. You realize you are but a small point of awareness in God's universe. When you stand on the ground, the world around you, including your problems, looks really big. When you stand on top of a mountain, what appeared so huge on the ground seems so much smaller. From this higher perspective, the obstacles to your dream no longer appear so enormous. By contrast, when you become too full of yourself and your troubles, you leave no space for the wisdom of others, especially the wisdom of God. You become locked into the limitations your closed mind has conjured.

Are you living at the mountaintop, or have you enclosed yourself in a telephone booth? Your mind expands with the breadth of your view. You can alter the panorama whenever you choose.

"Be transformed by the renewing of your mind," said the Apostle Paul. Years ago, Dr. Raymond Holliwell, dean of the school of Christian philosophy where I received my ministerial degree, taught his students five steps for renewal. You can fit these five steps on a scrap of paper or count them on your fingers. I run through the steps as I sit at traffic lights, while exercising, or right before I go to sleep at night. Run through them one at a time, focusing, and your faith will be renewed.

1. God is. Remember that. We get so lost in the drama and detail. We get lost in our problems. We get lost in circumstances. Pause. Say "God is." There is a presence and a power in this universe; that power and presence is God. There is order in the universe. The planets are not colliding. The trees are growing. Your body knows how to renew itself. You are not contained or limited by this bag of bones; who you are is much grander. There is evidence everywhere of a higher power. Feel yourself expanding and relaxing. Remind yourself that God is.

2. I am. You are part of this universe. You are created by God. Your life is connected to all life. You cannot separate from this power. Right where you are, God is. The power of the universe is available to work through your life. You don't have to go looking; God is already here. Say "God is, and I am part of this power."

3. The truth is . . . When we get to number three, we direct the truth to a particular area of our lives on which we're focusing. There's a challenge you're facing? Say "God is. There's a presence and a power in this universe, and I am part of this presence and power. I cannot exist apart from it. The truth is, there's nothing I'm facing that's bigger than God." Whatever the challenge, remind yourself to lift yourself to a higher dimension of knowing. God is, you are, and the truth is that whatever you're facing, God's greater than that—greater than limited income, troubled relationships, disease, greater than all fear. The truth is, God is greater than any challenge. Put the challenge back in perspective. It's not bigger than God, and God is, and you are part of God's life, and so this can get handled. Say "God is, I am, and the truth is . . ."

4. Let go. "Because God is, and I'm part of the life of God, the truth about this situation is that God is greater than anything I'm facing, so I can let go and trust." You can let go of your fear. You can let go of your anxiety. You can let go of your resentment. You can let go of your worry. You can relax. You can trust. You can breathe. Notice your body as you say "I can let go." Breathe out. Let your shoulders drop down a bit. Unwrinkle your forehead. Unclench your jaw. Letting go opens our inner receptors so we can hear God's guidance. You let go with mind and body, finding inner peace.

5. Thank you, God. The field of gratitude provides an environment in which the seed of your potential has room to grow. Say "Thank you, God. I may not have reached my dream, but I am grateful for that which I do possess. Gratitude opens my eyes to greater possibilities." When you thank God, you can see more than what you do not have. You can appreciate what you have and make room for all that is forthcoming. You can hear the whisperings of your intuition and feel the guidance as it gently guides you.

Practice this renewal process three times a day for a month, and it will begin to change your life. You will lift yourself into a different field of awareness. You will take your mind off your problems and put it on God, where the "how" begins to emerge. You decide on the "what" and lift your awareness, and the "how" begins to speak to you as you listen. Practice this simple affirmation:

> *God is.*
> *I am.*
> *The truth is . . .*
> *Let go.*
> *Thank you, God.*

Slowly you will replace fear and doubt with faith, trust, and hope, the nutrients required to nurture your dream.

Remember Judy? She had sent her letter to the house owner in mid-October. Ten days later the owner called her. "I don't exactly know why I'm doing this," he told Judy. "I've decided that if you really do what you described in your letter, I will lease you this house for one year at a reduced rate."

Judy's new rent turned out to be $500, the exact amount she'd been paying for the shoe box.

So by Thanksgiving she and her children had literally moved into their dream, giving thanks at a turkey dinner in a house that, were it not for a bigger believing, would have remained impossible. By the following year Judy had a new job, which more than paid for her increased rent. And then she got pro-moted.

By the third year, Judy worked out a purchase plan with the owner. She bought the house she had grown to love so dearly. The home she had longed for had become her own. Judy literally moved into her dream, and so can you.

Growing Your Dream

Build your believing with the assistance God provides you through others. Buoyed by partners who believe in you, the discovery of your inner genius, and a renewed faith, you begin to step into your dream.

1. Create a partners in believing group of like-minded individuals and meet weekly to build the blueprint for your dream. Choose people who will keep believing in you even when you cannot. Your partners will ask, "Suppose the dream weren't impossible. What would be the first thing you'd do?" This will help expand your believing and keep you moving forward.

2. Lift your thinking into the genius mind. The genius of the universe dreamed you up and carved a genius inside all our beings. But many of us cannot identify our inner genius through all the slashes of disappointment. Once you discover that inner genius, you move past perceived limits into outrageous thinking, where brilliant ideas move you into your dream.

3. Practice five steps to renew your faith. If you're trapped in a phone booth, it's hard to see further than your immediate problem. When you possess a mountaintop view, however, everything that troubled you looks so much smaller. From this higher perspective, your faith can be renewed. Jot down the five steps for renewal on a piece of paper and review them regularly to elevate your thinking to a higher level: *God is. I am. The truth is . . . Let go. Thank you, God.*

Chapter Nine

FAILURE:

Finding Meaning in the Defeated Dream

> The thing we call failure is not in falling down—it's in staying down.
>
> —MARY PICKFORD

♦ *Before You Declare Defeat, Take Inventory*
♦ *Make a Stand for Better over Bitter*
♦ *Use Failure to Move Through the Levels of Awareness*

Every one of us has known failure. Writers draft technical journals while fantasizing about the Pulitzer Prize. Would-be entrepreneurs spend years toiling for others, waiting for the moment to strike out on their own; sometimes that moment never comes. Talented chefs open their own restaurants only to see them close within a year. Musicians compose jingles. Every athlete wants to play first string, run the marathon, or win the gold, but few do. Lovers pour their heart into a relationship only to watch it disintegrate. Nurturing couples go childless. Loving singles who desire partnership find that those relationships continue to elude them.

Suppose you attempt to follow all the steps in this book for building your dream; you invest time, energy, your very soul. Through faith and hard work, you overcome seemingly insurmountable obstacles and pull yourself out of every ditch along the path. You master your fears and forgive those who have wronged you, realizing that behind every unskillful behavior lies a hurting human being. And you visualize yourself in that wedding dress or receiving that trophy so often that it feels real. But suppose the reality never comes to pass. What then?

Of any step in dream-building, the most difficult one to accept and work through is failure. And yet failure is frequently an integral part of achieving a great dream. In fact, all people who spend their lives building great dreams have known great disappointment.

If what you desire cannot come into being, for whatever reason, then something greater is trying to happen in your life, regardless of how the circumstances may appear.

♦ Before You Declare Defeat, Take Inventory

In any dream, large or small, there may come a point at which you are tempted to give up. You've done the best you know how and sincerely devoted your heart and energy to create a reality that just doesn't quite materialize. This is a critical crossroads in your dream-building. If you've reached the point of diminishing returns—such as the time my former husband and I kept farming on land ill-suited to meet our needs—you may be better off pursuing another dream. On the other hand, you do not want to stop just short of the miracle. What can help your decision is a reexamination and reaffirmation of the beliefs and desires that brought you this far. This involves three challenges. Ask yourself: *Am I giving up on my dream too early? Am I seeing my situation from the greatest perspective? Do I need to retest my dream?*

Am I giving up on my dream too early? Anne, a longtime member of our congregation, decided she wanted to quit her painting business and open a small boutique. She and her partner raised money, but as the deadline for escrow approached, they remained $4,000 short. They had borrowed every penny they could, gone to every family member, every friend, every bank, and maxed out every credit card. For years they had dreamed of selling clothes, and perhaps designing them, and now, just as they expected to move into their dream, it hovered tantalizingly out of reach. Feeling tormented and fearful, they finally considered giving up. They prayed for guidance, for a sign telling them whether to deepen their resolve or find a new dream.

There are moments in all great dreamers' lives when they don't know whether to abandon or endure. When you reach that confusing point, pray this prayer: "If this dream is for my highest good, increase my passion for it and show me a way. If this dream will not benefit myself and others, redirect me. This, or something better."

The phrase "This, or something better" is my way of acknowledging my co-creation with God. As co-creators, we shape the thinking that molds our dream to the highest good we can perceive in a given moment. At the same time we recognize that our own perception of that highest good is limited. God, however, knows all. If I say, "It's what I want or nothing at all," I'm unable to access direction from my Creator's limitless knowing. If I were traveling along a winding coastal road, would I not want someone in a helicopter to radio me directions about what lies beyond the next bend?

And so as we proceed toward our dream, we pray for, believe in, and work vigorously in the direction of our dream. If it does not come to pass, then we know God has something better in store for us. God knows what we cannot. If God wills a greater good for us than the one we are pursuing, we let ourselves be redirected, open to the grace of God.

"This, or something better" are the final words to each of my prayers. When we come to really know our Creator, we recognize that God's will is for our greatest good, even if we cannot fully comprehend the meaning just yet. If what I'm pursuing conflicts with that greater good, then I really don't want it, because there is nothing greater than God's will. And I want nothing less.

One morning Anne prayed again and awaited guidance. The escrow was due to close at 5 P.M. the following day. She had committed herself to helping out at her son's school for parents' day, but now she decided to cancel. She needed to focus all her energy on the escrow.

"I told my son I couldn't come, and I saw his eyes drop and his chin quiver. My heart sank," Anne said. "I realized some things mean more than money, so I promised to show up."

Anne was, in fact, receiving her sign.

"As I was waiting for the activities to begin, I sat with another parent in the hallway, and we started talking. She said, 'How are you doing?' I told her my dream and that we hoped to end our painting business. Out of the blue, she asked, 'Are you interested in selling that business? My brother-in-law, a painter, is moving to town, and he might be interested in buying your painting business.'

"The thought of selling had never even occurred to us. We were just going to stop painting. I described our painting business in detail and even gave her a copy of our income statement, which I had among the loan papers in my car. I gave the woman my card. The next morning she called and said, 'I talked to my brother-in-law and he's interested in your business. I told him I'd loan him the money to get started. How much do you want?'

" 'Five thousand dollars,' I threw out.

"She said, 'You know, I don't have five thousand dollars, but I could come this afternoon and write you a check for four thousand.'

"Without hesitation, I said, 'It's yours,' hung up, and said, 'Thank you, God.' "

Anne learned several important lessons critical to dream-building. She had been ready to concede failure rather than sacrifice someone she valued—in this case, her son. Had her dream died as a result, her "failure" would not have been in vain. So often we are distracted by ambition and lose our true way. In the process of trying to obtain what we think is our dream, we can miss what matters most. Anne also learned that when you are tempted to give up, ask for assistance. You may be redirected, or you may be granted the stamina to persevere.

Dream-building requires persistence, the same tenacity needed to grow Chinese bamboo. If you nurture this plant in its first year, the bamboo grows a puny two-inch shoot. The second, third, and fourth years are the same—two inches a year. Yet if you persist in caring for the bamboo, in its fifth year it grows eighty feet! The challenge is that not one of us knows the exact growing season for our dream. We can never be sure if we are on the verge of the moment when our tiny, wispy shoot will burst into a mighty eighty-foot stalk. Those who succeed in building their dream keep on. Every day, continue to nourish your dream.

Am I seeing my situation from the greatest perspective?
Imagine you've sent your eighteen-year-old daughter off to college; she's been gone twelve weeks and you get this letter: "Dear Mom and Dad, I'm sorry I haven't written lately, but all my things were destroyed in the dorm fire. My eyes are almost com-

pletely healed now, and the doctor assures me there will be no permanent damage from the smoke. While the dorm is being rebuilt, I have moved in with my boyfriend. I think you met Roy when you were here for parents' weekend. I know how much you've always wanted grandchildren, so you'll be happy to know I'm expecting a baby the end of next summer."

Then the letter goes on: "Please excuse this exercise in English composition. There was no dorm fire. My eyes are not damaged. I am not living with my boyfriend. I am not pregnant. However, I did receive a D in English and an F in French. And I wanted to be sure you got this information in the proper perspective."

How would you feel if you were the parent after reading the first part of that letter? Wouldn't your anxiety level have risen about two octaves? Then you read on and breathe a sigh of relief: "Sweetheart, is that all? We can handle that!"

Sometimes perspective can mean the difference between success and failure. Perspective determines the opportunities we see and the choices we make. Perspective determines how we experience any outcome. What we perceive as failure can also be interpreted as feedback. Perhaps your perceived "failure" is simply feedback, input to guide you in altering your approach or refueling your engine. There have been so many times in the course of growing our church when I felt on the brink of failure. Yet what those near failures provided me with was feedback indicating that I needed a new strategy and should make some midcourse corrections. Carefully consider your perspective. Is there a message in what looks like failure that may be an answer to building your dream?

One of my favorite stories is about a little boy named Jimmy Taylor, who was born with physical and mental difficulties but who had a great heart and a big spirit. His father helped him learn to run, though the boy did so in a very awkward way. One day Jimmy decided he wanted to enter the Special Olympics.

As they were on their way to the event, Jimmy said to his dad, "I'm going to win the race!" His dad worried because he knew the degree of difficulty his son had in running, and so he said, "You know, Jimmy, it doesn't matter whether you win the race; what matters is that you do your best."

"No, no, no. I'm going to win the race!" Jimmy defiantly asserted.

His father tried again to convince his son. "Don't worry about winning; just do your best."

"I'm going to win the race!"

The gun went off and the kids set out, and Jimmy immediately fell behind. He was trying valiantly to catch up, when he heard a cry from behind him. The only child even slower than he was a little girl who had stumbled and fallen, scraping her knees. In a moment of decision, Jimmy turned around, went back, and took her hand to help her up. One by one the other kids saw him trying to help, and they too turned around on the track. All the children in the race came back to Jimmy and the girl, where they joined hands and ran to cross the finish line together.

On the way home, Jimmy proudly told his father: "See, I told you I was going to win!"

Jimmy had dreamed of winning a race, and even though some people might insist that he had failed, the little boy maintained an entirely different point of view. On your path as a dream-builder in this life, you will meet with what some call failure and what others label dubious accomplishment.

Some people call divorce failure. For many years I was one of them. My experience now teaches me to think of our marriage as completed rather than failed. How could a union that created four precious children and helped build a wonderful church be labeled a failure? Haven and I recognized that what our remaining together would have modeled for our children is that you should not be true to yourself. We did not want our children to live anything less than their greatest lives. Having spent years exhausting every possibility for staying together, we were finally able to release ourselves from a marriage that was no longer life-giving. Perhaps "until death do us part" can have a meaning beyond the physical death of the partners. None of us is meant to live in a limited version of our selves.

Haven and I both knew that what some people call failure often paves the way to awakening. The process of loss, grief, and acceptance that accompanies the breakup of a marriage can actually increase your capacity for love, trust, and compassion. Divorce can have a positive impact. In our case, we could both continue to parent our children compatibly. We could go through a difficult time and move into more fulfilling lives. Having public ministries, our separation was a complex process, but our decision came out of a deep respect for each other and a belief that there is no such thing as private good—that if we followed our hearts, ultimately all of us affected by the breakup would find our good as well.

Failure becomes feedback when you take the learning it offers you and use it to guide you forward in your dream-building. Continue to challenge your thinking regarding any perceived failure. Ask yourself, "What is the feedback this 'failure' has for me? Is there another way to perceive the situation that can actually support my dream, or am I truly being redirected to something greater?"

Do I need to retest my dream? When you review the five questions you asked before committing to your dream, you may find yourself less far afield than you imagine. *Does the dream still enliven me?* Carefully set aside for the moment all your feelings of fear and failure. Right now they're masking your enthusiasm. It may well be that your passion for the dream has dwindled; on the other hand, it may just have been covered over. *Will continuing to pursue this dream align with my core values?* Anne made her values a priority even when facing a difficult decision. You cannot betray those closest to you and still expect to prosper. By honoring a commitment to her son, Anne found herself in the precise environment that ultimately allowed her to fulfill her dream. Jimmy stopped to help a little girl who had fallen because he valued kindness above all. Notice that at the exact moment both Anne and Jimmy followed their hearts, placing their present dreams secondary to the needs of those around them, their dreams opened up. *Do I still need help from a higher source to make this dream come true?* As we begin to worry about failing, we often cling more tightly to our attempts to control every detail. Leave room for God to work through you. *To continue to manifest my dream, do I need to grow more into my true self?* You've made it this far. Perhaps you need only stretch a little further than you anticipated. *Will continuing to pursue this dream ultimately bless others?* If your desire to benefit others remains just as strong as when you began the dream-building process, then one way or another you will do so in time. The dream you originally envisioned may come true, or it may be replaced with another. It is in that space between the death of one dream and the dawning of the next that you face your most divine challenge.

♦ Make a Stand for Better over Bitter

When your dreams are dashed, you can choose to become bitter, or you can choose to become better. The world is full of those who choose to remain shackled to broken dreams, using failure to rationalize staying stuck. We have all known people who remain at a job they despise for twenty-five years or more, complaining bitterly each day and always reminding us, "I could have been . . . I should have been . . . but I got cheated out of my chance . . . my promotion . . . my dream." They are stuck believing life "did it" to them, missing the power they possessed all along to co-create with God.

If you know in your heart you have done everything possible

to build a particular dream, and what you have set your heart upon does not come to pass, then you can trust that something better is trying to happen.

God's will is for our greatest good. Our dream is for a particular good. Sometimes we fail because we have not been diligent enough, persistent enough, or willing enough to do what is required. Other times we have truly done all that can be done and we still fail. Then our challenge is not to stare longingly at a door that is bolted shut but to find the open window where a guiding light beckons. You have to lean into the new dream, even if you can barely glimpse its outline from where you stand. *Move toward the light and lean toward the good.* If you become bitter, your capacity to see future opportunities dies with your failed dream. When you stay feeling sorry for yourself, you cannot grow. You remain stuck, never emboldened to move into a greater dream.

Even if the path you travel brings you tremendous pain, you can trust in a greater good. Jesus did not wish to be crucified: "Take this cup away from Me," He prayed. Yet He also trusted the greater good. "Nevertheless," He continued, "not what I will, but what You will." Had Jesus not been crucified, there could have been no resurrection, the promise given to humanity for all time.

I'm not saying that you should deny your pain. Some failures can leave you so stranded that you feel you could not possibly determine which direction is forward. If, for instance, you devote your life to building a business, only to watch it crumble, how do you muster the fortitude to try again?

A man in my congregation, Bill, had built a very successful career for himself in life insurance at a young age. In fact, his sales ranked among the top two percent worldwide, and his income soared to match. He owned a five-thousand-square-foot brick home and two condominiums. "And still I wasn't at peace," he said. For a long time Bill had dreamed about becoming vice president of an insurance company. "And then when I started making more money than the vice president at my company, I said, forget it, I want to be a president."

As it happened, a prominent figure in the insurance industry offered Bill the opportunity to do just that—to develop a company that focused on selling policies as a kind of savings plan. So certain was Bill his company would flourish, he encouraged all his friends to invest. Some of them even helped him raise funds for the company's public stock offering. He spent the next few years working from 6 A.M. to midnight, building his dream. Bill's new insurance agency recruited over eighty-five agents; they would be awarded purple Mercury Cougars for outstanding performance. "It was wonderful. We went forth with such enthusiasm," Bill recalls.

Then they stalled. Bill's sales force was not exactly a veteran one. Part of his dream had been to provide opportunity to others, and he had deliberately hired promising individuals who had little or no experience. The state insurance council, concerned about the innovative elements of the policy, mandated amendments that made the plan more difficult to sell. Potential customers proved reluctant to try something new, and the salespeople lacked the experience to convince them.

Assets dwindled to the point where the board decreed only a merger would keep the company afloat. The prospective buyers treated Bill like royalty—up until the moment the merger was complete. That day, the entire staff, save Bill, was fired. But he was now required to track his activities on paper every fifteen minutes and send the reports to the new owners. "It was like working for Jaws," Bill said.

Bill quit, hopeful that the stock he owned in the company would one day be worth millions. Instead, the owners forced him to sell out immediately for next to nothing. He had borrowed heavily on his dream and now could not afford to pay up. Worse yet, all those friends who had trusted him lost their investment as well. Guilt at having betrayed their trust ate away at him. "I was broke, spiritually and financially," he said. "For the first time, I could understand why people killed themselves."

Bill went back to work selling insurance as an independent agent. Now he began to see all he had missed while pursuing his dream. While his wife had remained loving and loyal during the years Bill was gone so much, those years could not be recaptured. His children seemed to have grown up without him. He was living with a family he hardly knew. He began to realize that he had neglected the dream he once had for family at the expense of his dream for a career, and he recognized the true price he had paid. Bill set out to rebuild his family along with his finances.

At age fifty-one Bill's wife was diagnosed with Alzheimer's. Bill wanted to do nothing but remain at home and care for her, but that was impossible. Now, more than ever, he needed steady income, as his wife required full-time assistance and eventually a nursing home. Finally, as his debts and expenses mounted, Bill shed the final vestiges of a lifestyle long since gone: He sold the Mercedes and the huge house—even the house's antique furnishings.

But something had happened. As Bill told me recently, "I had a net worth of almost nothing, but I didn't feel like a failure anymore. I realized I didn't need the big house or the big car or all the possessions. I was starting on more of a spiritual path, realizing I didn't always need to *make* things happen; I could allow them to happen." Letting go of his need to acquire and hold on to things, Bill found in the midst of failure a fulfillment his former life had never provided.

Bill began writing books about his experiences and teaching seminars on coping with failure. Those enterprises have not made him rich, but they have fulfilled his desire to help others. "Because I had the failures, I have empathy and understanding and intuition for how to get people through their problems," he said. "You need to have adverse experiences in order to obtain wisdom.

"I have discovered that there hasn't been anything adverse in my life that didn't turn out to reward me in another way. Had it not been for the loss of my business, I might have remained on the treadmill and might not have gotten the level of love I received from my children." Even his late wife's illness, he said, provided him an opportunity to care for someone in a way he once could not have imagined.

At age sixty-nine, Bill says, he is still finding his way. But he doesn't mind. He enjoys life. He looks forward to writing another book and continuing his seminars. Even though he recognizes that the financial success of his youth is gone forever, he believes he is now in possession of a power money cannot buy.

"I have found the power to choose," he says. "I could choose to feel sorry for myself or choose to be thankful. I choose to feel thankful."

Professional losses can render you bitter if you let them, but it is personal losses that most challenge our fundamental belief in the goodness of God. If you have nurtured your dreams with integrity, how can you not feel horribly betrayed when those you love are taken away without reason? How can you possibly dare to dream again? When someone close dies, you lose not only the presence of that person but your sense of security—the feeling that when you awaken the next morning, the world will not have been drastically altered from the day before. You are also at risk of losing your sense of security in your relationship with God.

People whose dreams—whose entire world—have been shattered often come to me seeking some sort of explanation. I wish I had all the answers, but I do not. Some people are fond of simply saying "It's God's will." While it's true that God's will is always for our greater good, that greater good may not be understandable from our present perspective. "It's God's will" may be spiritually correct, but it can feel dismissive to anyone who has suffered a huge loss. And that loss must be grieved and cared for.

I remember going to be with a mother and father whose three-month-old baby had just died. They were deep in their grief, and they could not stop asking "why?" Why would God let this happen? Why, why, why?

"I don't know," I told them. "But I do know one thing for certain. I know that this tragedy in your life does not mean God has abandoned you. God is available to see you through your loss. God is available to guide you into a greater good. Even as you grieve, God is present."

There's an old story about a nine-year-old boy who was the Keeper of the Seal under King Louis IV. The boy was revered as having great mystical powers, and so one day the king went to him in the hope of finding out something that mattered greatly to him. "I will give you an orange," said the king, "if you can tell me where I can find God."

The Keeper of the Seal gazed at him for a moment and then responded, "I will give you two oranges if you can tell me where God is not."

As long as we stay in the why question, we stay stuck, because there are no tangible answers. But we can learn to ask another question. This other question is, "Now what?" The answer to that question will determine the path your life will take. You can choose to become embittered over a profound loss, frozen in the pain you feel. Or, if you are willing, with God's help you can find a way to go on and even use this terrible loss to grow into a larger life.

When faced with loss, you can abandon your faith or you can strengthen your faith. Believing in God and in yourself as a co-creator with God does not protect you from tragedy. It does, however, mean you do not have to endure your tragedy alone. It means that you have access to the comfort, grace, support, and guidance of the loving presence we call God. When you've experienced a tremendous loss, it is healthy to grieve deeply. But if you possess faith as a mustard seed, at some point you will surrender the lost dream to the new dream God has in store for you.

Let me tell you about a man named John. As a child, John believed that family was everything. His dream was to grow up, get married, and create a family much like the one in which he was being raised. But his faith in family was threatened as one by one, John began losing those he loved most.

When John was nine years old, his younger brother died of a brain tumor. After that, all John could think about was getting a horse. He couldn't have told you why at the time, but he knew a horse would help fill up the empty space in his heart. Sadly, his parents turned him down. A horse was beyond their means.

During John's freshman year in college, his older sister was killed in an automobile accident. For a time he found solace in church, but he didn't stick around. He tried to concentrate on his studies, but by his own admission, John was not a natural student. He went on wild, drunken sprees—almost, as he put it, "as if I was determined to kill myself."

Anxious to escape and longing for what he envisioned as a wide-open frontier, John packed his bags and headed west to complete his education in Oregon.

There John discovered engineering; he appreciated the exactness of a science built on absolutes. Everything fit nicely into a predictable formula. In this methodical, precise, black-and-white discipline, there were no nasty surprises. Some things, perhaps, he could control; he would become an engineer.

Upon graduating, John was hired by an international high-tech company. But soon after he started work, his father, like his sister, was killed in a car accident. John had adored his father. Now he was bitter and angry to a depth he had not believed possible. Yet something kept him going. Somewhere, in the midst of his grieving, he began to make a choice for better.

John's dream of a family came within reach when he fell in love with and married Nancy, a co-worker. They both wanted a traditional marriage. Soon Nancy was staying home with their son and daughter, while John's career continued to flourish. He began to feel the security and contentment that had eluded him for so long. He began to trust life.

Then, after thirteen years of marriage, Nancy was diagnosed with ovarian cancer. Two months later, she was gone.

During the year following her death, John did not know what to do with his grief. He pushed it away, but the grief only came back bigger. He tried to accept and move through the sorrow, only to feel as if he were drowning in it. At first he thought he could fill the void in his life. He went shopping for a new wife the way some people shop for a new car, trying one model and then the next, even though he recognized deep in his heart that he really wasn't ready to buy.

"I wanted to have a wife and family and to live happily ever after," he said. "Then as soon as I got a taste of that, it was taken away. I think now if I get close to anything, maybe somehow I will lose that, too."

But by the first anniversary of his wife's death, John began to find moments of greater clarity. "I've been trying to put death and grieving in perspective and see how they have affected me all my life. In some ways I've become even more of a believer in my dreams. Life is too short not to live for today and enjoy every precious moment. I am more convinced you need to build on what you have, and take strength from what has happened to you.

"It's like a tulip," he said. "When the bloom dies off, the bulb remains down in the soil so it can be nourished and grow again. And then the next season it comes back stronger for having matured. By the following season it's even stronger. That's how I choose to see myself."

John has become closer to his children. Making their breakfast every morning, helping with homework, buying their clothes—things once done only by their mother—he has come to know and appreciate his son and daughter in a way he never had before. It has also made John realize how profoundly a parent impacts a child's well-being. Had John chosen bitterness, he would have been emotionally unavailable for his children. That wonderful relationship would have been poisoned. Instead, it has been sweetened. John is finding he has the power to choose how to respond even to great loss, and you do too.

Those who are willing to take one step after another eventually cross the bridge of their grief, and over time the pain of the loss gives way to acceptance. Finally they feel ready to step into a new dream.

I was in Atlanta in 1981, when I met a mother who had found a new dream following unimaginable tragedy. Her son had been among the victims in the Atlanta child murders of that era. As I sat and listened to this woman speak during a conference for church leaders, I realized that God had helped her choose better over bitter in a most remarkable way. She told the story of her son's death, her hatred toward the killer and desire for revenge toward the killer, how she wanted him to suffer as she was suffering. Trapped by tremendous pain, she asked God to heal her. She found she couldn't be free of the pain and still hold on to the anger.

Through the grace of God, she slowly began to believe in the power of forgiveness and rehabilitation for all God's children, even the one who killed her son. She challenged every one of us in that audience to let go of every blaming thought, let go of personal power, and embrace a relationship with the one from whom all life comes. She was absolutely radiant in her faith. Not one of us could doubt her transformation from victim to victor even in the most horrendous circumstances. She was dedicating a portion of her life to working with those in prison, helping them find a new faith and purpose.

"In the midst of my greatest tragedy," she told us, "I have found God's love. This love knows no limits and is more powerful than anything."

With God, we can find the strength to go on and build anew.

♦ Use Failure to Move Through the Levels of Awareness

The fundamental question each of us must ask ourselves, said Albert Einstein, is this: "Is the universe a friendly place?" If you have been one of those people fortunate to coast through life without great misfortune or failure, you may answer yes without hesitation. You'll likely rate the universe according to your experience of it: "Let's see—I've got a good job, I'm happily married with great kids, everybody's healthy, and I'm about to fulfill my dream of running in a marathon. Friendly? I'd say the universe is downright wonderful!"

How much more difficult it is to perceive as friendly a universe that has, with seemingly deliberate cruelty, stolen from you the dreams and, especially, the people you love best. Yet in some ways, people who have undergone tremendous tragedy and still embrace the universe with love receive the greatest gift of all. They live in a sense of unshakable security. They know that no matter how tremendous their loss, no matter how great their failure, they are never alone. God is always with them. It is your failures rather than your victories that can move you most quickly into the higher levels of awakening.

Einstein also said, "The significant problems we face cannot be solved at the level of thinking that created them." We have to learn to think outside our present challenges, for only by moving into greater awareness can we move into an expanded life. Only as we awaken do we come to find that the universe is truly friendly and that life works toward a good that is greater than what our limited view allows.

If we allow ourselves to be guided, our very failure can propel us toward a state of being in which we live a growing and expanding life every single day. We grow into the capacity to find the good and recognize a greater dream. In the process of dream-building, we awaken to ourselves as co-creators with God. Every religion has its supreme messenger who encourages us to discover this truth.

For instance, when Buddha was asked, "Are you a god?" he answered, "No."

Next he was asked, "Are you an angel, then?"

Buddha again said, "No, I'm not an angel."

"Well, then, what are you?"

To this question the Buddha simply replied, "I am awake."

We are largely asleep to ourselves as co-creators with God. Yet Jesus reminds us: "If thine eye is single, thy whole body is filled with light." This means that when we fix our attention on God, the answers we truly need are provided. As we practice dream-building, we find we are not only laying the foundation for a specific dream; we are building a life.

My friend, the Rev. Marcia Sutton, introduced me to a model for the four levels of awareness that I have adapted to fit my own beliefs. I call these levels *Why Me?*, *By Me*, *Through Me*, and *As Me*. As we move through them we learn to live a greater life, realizing that failure is part of our natural co-creation with God. Let's explore the first three levels now. The highest level, wherein there is no separation between the individual and God, will be discussed in chapter ten.

Why Me? In the first state of awareness, life seems to be happening *to* you. You feel powerless, a victim of circumstance, and all you can see is how life has failed you. You remain at the hated job or refuse to risk a relationship for fear of losing again. When your boss yells, when the stock falls, or even when the dinner burns, you wonder, "Why me?" Every circumstance, every relationship, and in particular every failure is viewed through the distorted lens of victimization. Our culture often supports this *Why Me?* thinking, using the mind as a tool of fear rather than a tool of spirit. We hear such messages all around us: "If the weather is bad, I feel lousy." "If the economy is down, so too are my options." "What has happened to me has caused me to be the way I am."

The reality is that your response to circumstance or failure, not the event itself, determines the way you are. This stage of awakening is actually a state of sleep. We are asleep to ourselves as co-creators. We are asleep to the power we have, as a co-creator, to choose any possible future. The overriding feeling is one of victimization. We are sure life is happening "to us," never realizing the power of the thoughts we hold.

Now, as a minister, I'd like to think of myself as holding to a higher awareness, but it's all too easy to slip. I remember one winter when the church was struggling just to pay the rent. We had our Christmas service all planned, when a huge snowstorm hit Portland unexpectedly. We had to cancel all the services at the last minute—which meant that a Christmas offering the church badly needed was also canceled. I struggled with fear and feelings of victimization. Unable to confront Mother Nature face-to-face, I blamed the weatherman on TV. If he were any kind of responsible meteorologist, I fumed, he would have seen this thing coming sooner and not put our lease at risk.

Eventually I canceled my pity party and moved away from blame. As I remembered that my true power lay in how I chose to respond to this situation, an idea popped into my mind. Why not have Christmas a week later? The staff organized a phone tree to call all the congregation, and the following week our services drew what was for us at that time a huge crowd. Not only did all our parishioners turn out, they brought their friends from other churches whose holiday services had also been canceled. We had a great celebration of Christ's birth, and the church received plenty of funds with which to begin the new year. And I offered a silent prayer of blessing for the weatherman.

A woman named Amy whom I met in Montana during our year on the road told me how, for eight years, she kept asking, "Why me?" When Amy's husband was running for elective office, she worked tirelessly with him on the campaign. She pounded on doors, licked envelopes, put in twelve- and fifteen-hour days. Amy shared her husband's dream to enter politics and believed that the two of them would work together to bring about much-needed reform in the state. Amy's husband won the election; the couple's hard work was making the dream come true.

Then, the morning after the victory party, Amy's husband came to her and said, "I'm in love with my secretary. I want a divorce."

Amy was devastated. "I hated that man. He got his divorce, but I hated him. I filled myself with hatred for two years, until I was dying," she said.

We can't hate someone else without the venom of that hatred seeping into our own bodies. Emotions are energy. Whatever we are feeling reaches our very cells. Amy developed an entwining tumor that wrapped itself around her liver. One day, despite emergency surgery and two blood transfusions, doctors told her family, "She will not make it through the night."

As she lay dying, Amy said she saw a being of light at the edge of her bed. It was Jesus Christ with arms open wide, illuminating the room and saying to her, "You have a purpose for being. You will be healed."

Amy's doctors considered her a medical miracle. The tumor shrank and then disappeared. She left the hospital, grateful to leave the pain behind her. The illness helped reconcile Amy and her mother, who had been estranged for years. Then, six months later, the mother died. Amy felt victimized once again. This time the feeling of blaming life for her sorry state didn't go away.

By the time she attended our three-day workshop, she had been stuck eight years in the belief that the world was out to get her. At some point during our workshop, she realized that her perceptions alone had determined her feelings. Amy, who had been born and raised in bear country, told us this:

"Mother bears usually have twin cubs. They take care of them for about two years. They teach the cubs to climb and fish. Then, when the cubs are about two years old, the mother bear tells one twin to climb one tree and the second twin to scale another. The mother bear instructs her young to remain there, and then she leaves, never to return.

"The cubs stay there all day. Then all night. They stay into the next morning and through the next night. By about the third day, the cubs get really hungry. They climb down from their trees and enter life on their own."

Amy said she had finally come to recognize herself in these cubs. "I have been stuck in my tree for eight years," she said. "It's time I came down."

Some of us spend our entire lives stuck, unable to move beyond disappointment, beyond feeling victimized and abandoned. "Why me?" we ask, until we climb down out of the tree and recognize we have not yet even begun to explore the forest.

By Me. The shift in awareness from *Why Me?* to *By Me* is life-transforming. As we give up blame, as we leave the idea that life is happening "to me," we enter the realm where we perceive life as happening "by me." We now begin to see the incredible power of our thoughts and the choices we make. You cannot move into this next state of awareness and still hold on to blame. Every time you want to condemn someone or feel victimized by circumstance, you fall back into the *Why Me?* state of thinking like a victim and get stuck again. And the stuck person truly is powerless, glued firmly to a victim's point of view. In *By Me*, you take responsibility for your experience.

Here we begin to recognize and develop our creative capacities. We recognize our thinking as creative and find we can indeed influence our own destiny through our thoughts. We begin experimenting with minor outcomes. I learned, for instance, that I could send my awareness ahead of my car to help me drive directly to an open parking space at the overcrowded mall. I found I had that capacity. At the *By Me* level, you explore the power of your own thinking, tapping into capacities you didn't even realize you possessed. We learn that our experience is plastic under the power of our thought; our experience molds to the shape of the thought forms we hold. Your thoughts create your experience of reality.

The *By Me* level of awareness can be fairly ego-driven. It's typified by the force of will. It's the stage at which you tell yourself, "I want a car" or "I want a relationship, and by golly, I'm going to get what I want." At this stage you move in life more through force than faith, but you are at least beginning to take responsibility for your actions. You cannot bypass this level. It is essential that you recognize your own power before you can begin to co-create with God.

This state is largely driven by a sense of personal will and personal power. You grasp for the things you think you desire. You don't dare relax, for the only person who can make things happen is you. And you receive only partial benefit from failure; you tell yourself instead, "Next time I'll try to control things better. I failed because I was not in full control." You do not truly believe that the universe is a friendly place. And in so believing, you must maintain control.

Over the years people in our church have come to me asking about how they can better make manifest a particular dream. They want a car or a relationship, and their desire is very powerful. They may get their Mercedes or new partner or whatever, but they will not find fulfillment until they join the little "i" of the ego with the greater "I" of their Creator. When you are out to satisfy your ego, you will eventually want a bigger car or a better relationship.

I was talking to someone about his dream, the pollution-control company he had built from scratch. He had received the monthly bank statement and found his business was $44,000 in the red for that month. Immediately he went into panic, thinking "Oh, my God, how will we survive a forty-four-thousand-dollar loss?" He wanted to control the loss, and he became very frightened. This was his company, and everything that happened in it, good or bad, he told himself, was "by me."

At the *By Me* level, you come to realize your own power to bring about those things you desire, yet deep down you know that your own power is limited. Without a higher power to turn to, *By Me* is often a stressful, fearful way to live.

Through Me. As you grow more aware, you begin to sense there is another way to live. Instead of dreaming only for things, you begin to dream for meaning and values. Those who serve only their own ego can wield tremendous power, but they do not serve a greater good. We develop the power of fulfillment in *Through Me*. In this stage, control is replaced by a profound and personal relationship with your Creator. You no longer feel alone. You may be physically alone, but you know you are not without a divine support system. You know that the presence and power that created this universe is available, present, and supportive of your greatest good.

In *Through Me*, we begin to wake up sufficiently to really be guided by a higher power. We recognize that we do not know all the answers, yet we know that the one who does is right where we are. We know that God works through us according to our willingness to listen and follow the guidance we receive. We know that there is no challenge too great, no failure so big that with God there is not an answer. In *Through Me*, we give up personal control and continually ask for guidance to bring about only that which is highest and best for all concerned. We find we are not so attached to a particular outcome. Yet in this relaxed receptivity, we are more available to the guidance that builds great dreams.

My friend with the pollution-control company realized that he could not withstand the $44,000 burden if it represented nothing but loss. So he went off by himself and thought, "Now, wait a minute. This fear-thinking is not the energy that will make this business prosper. What am I doing?" He asked the universe for a fresh perspective. He said, "What's really true here? How can I see this differently?"

In a flash of insight, he realized, "I could see this differently because it's taken a lot of talent and a lot of creativity and a lot of development for us as a business even to be in a place where we could have such a big loss. That's good. We invested a large sum of money in a training experiment. We learned something, and that cost us forty-four thousand dollars. We'll see this money as an investment in learning. The same talent and ingenuity and genius that brought us to a place where we could have such a huge loss is here now to be used for a greater gain. With this new learning that we've just invested in, we can rise to a whole new level of experience."

Out of that frame of mind came some ideas. He used the loss as feedback, followed his insight, and made some changes. His business rebounded and soared to new heights. No one was laid off. In fact, several employees later mentioned to him how his attitude had inspired them to commit to their jobs with renewed vigor.

In *Through Me*, you align your thinking with a grander plan. This is a very heightened state of living, in which you reside in a field of amplified well-being. Yes, you will continue to experience some sorrow and sadness and loss, but those painful emotions do not rule your life. In this stage you learn to benefit from an otherwise negative experience. When the car breaks down, the dinner burns, or the basement floods, you don't exactly tell yourself, "Wonderful! I'm so lucky." But you know that this experience does not have the power to destroy your peace of mind without your permission. Only as you maintain a peaceful state of mind will you be able to recognize the opportunity in the experience.

When Haven and I divorced, our youngest, Mat, the only child still at home, was the most impacted of any of our children by the change in living situation. To make matters worse, his vision of family shattered at about the same time that his other most cherished dream was stalled. This kid had dreamed of being the greatest football player in the history of Hillsboro High School—specifically, the star running back. I'd watch him practice. He'd show up hurting when he would rather have stayed home nursing his injuries. The dedication, the attention, was incredible. Next to his family, football was his whole life.

I ached for my child's pain when his dreams of family and football were halted. And yet in the very process of moving through that pain, Mat evolved into a much more powerful person. He has found the unshakable security of the true dreambuilder. He wrote a paper for his senior high-school humanities project describing that process. That paper has become a treasured possession. Mat wrote:

"Having ministers for parents, I have always been taught about God, but being the youngest in the family, I never fully understood the significance of His presence in my life. Family was very important in my household when I was young. Due to my older brothers' and sister's hectic schedules, we always planned for 'family time' on Sunday afternoon. After church, the usual ritual was to go to lunch and a movie. No friends were allowed to come during 'family time,' and during this time we would all open up and tell personal significant events that were happening in our lives. We would laugh and tell jokes and become closer and grow together as a family. My family was my support system. I looked to them for everything—advice, comfort, laughs. They were always there for me. Sometimes I would talk to my friends whose parents had separated and families were split, and they would tell me how hard things were in a family like that. I would think of my family and give thanks that I was so fortunate to have such a healthy household. . . .

"Then, during the summer before my freshman year, something I would have never expected to happen, did. My parents got a divorce; I was shocked and confused. How could they do this to our family? I was sad, but most of all angry. My whole support system, which I had looked upon as invincible, had been torn to shreds. My parents were not there for me anymore. My mom was needing to do her thing, and so was my dad. My sister was wrapped up in her grief, and so I didn't know who to turn to.

"So I turned to myself. My rationale was that sooner or later everyone is going to let you down; you cannot depend on anyone but yourself. So that is what I did. Depending on yourself means that you have to be able to support yourself. I became the strongest, physically and mentally, that I possibly could. I absorbed myself in my school life so I wouldn't have to deal with my home life. I was striving to be the best in everything that I did, doing it by myself and for myself. I got straight A's all year and became the MVP of the football team and the track team. I was also awarded more awards than anyone else on freshman graduation night. I was feeling pretty good; as long as I was succeeding outside, I didn't have to deal with what was inside.

"Continuing on my familiar path, I entered high school. Still getting straight A's, I was looking to have another excellent year on the football team. Until God pulled a little trick on me. During the third game of the season I rushed in to block an extra-point try. A member of my own team had rushed in from the other side and rolled into my leg. I heard *pop, pop, pop,* and fell to the ground screaming. The pain was so great, my leg went numb. The trainers came running out onto the field and started examining it with great care. They moved it left and right, but my knee bent horribly the wrong way. They quickly sent me to the hospital. . . .

"After the doctors examined me, they told me quite bluntly that both my football season and my track season were over. These words pierced my ears as a single tear rolled down my cheek. Sadness overwhelmed me, like a fire built in the depths of my belly. I could not understand why God would do this to me. I had trained so hard and dedicated myself to succeeding. I could not understand why He would pull me off the path I had chosen for myself. Once again, the only support system that I knew, the one I thought was the most stable, the one I thought I could depend on, was taken out from underneath me. Bedridden, with a cast from my hip to my ankle, the only thing for me to do was think and cry. I tried so hard to find even the smallest amount of goodness in my situation, but I was constantly drawing a blank. So the only thing I focused on was getting better. . . . But deep down I knew that I had lost my support system, that depending on only myself would not work. I felt lost and I felt alone.

"Then, one Sunday morning, I was sitting in church and I had a revelation. I realized that God had been with me through every moment of my life, and that He was my support system. Every gift that I have been given and every accomplishment I have made, it has been through Him that I have lived. I realized that I could depend on Him instead of myself, and with Him I will be able to overcome any turmoil that I may face within my life. A weight was lifted from my shoulders, and I no longer felt alone. I knew then that God has a special plan for me, one that I cannot even comprehend. And that I must travel the path that I was meant to if I am to succeed in life. Using this knowledge, I have continued to live through God and for God. My life has been truly enriched, and I have never felt alone since."

Mat wrote that when he was seventeen years old. It is never too early and never too late to begin a new life. Mat could have shut off his relationship with God when he felt his own dreams had been canceled. The divorce and the prospect of giving up athletics initially led Mat to wonder, *Why Me?* Then he tried to do everything on his own, living *By Me*. But Mat kept himself open to guidance, and after a growing season had passed for him, he harvested a new faith, living *Through Me*. His new direction was abundantly clear. Mat, at that tender age, learned a valuable lesson about how the process of loss can ultimately yield the product of growth.

As we grow in awareness we begin to realize that our present thoughts form the mental framework of our experience. Slowly we release ourselves from seeing the "bad" things in our lives— cancer, debt, divorce—as failures. When we consciously align our will with God, which is the greatest good possible, those "failures" can help us make midcourse corrections. In this life there will be great disappointments. We cannot bury those hurts. But we can surrender our demand and control of what must be and open ourselves to even greater possibilities.

The abundant life is not about acquiring and amassing. This life is for awakening to who we are—co-creators with God. Our dreams are the stepping stones to that awakening. Whether or not your specific dream comes true or fails is terribly significant to you in that moment. But even if you do not win the prize or have a baby or marry the one you love, that does not mean fulfillment will elude you in this lifetime. Our internal destination is one of awareness and inner peace. That's the great dream. We grow the greatest dream through the practice of trying to manifest our smaller dreams. When we fall short, when we grieve our losses and trust in a higher power, we are able to endure with the sure knowledge that something greater is happening in our lives.

We find that something greater as we ask God to work through us each and every day. You will find yourself stuck at times. We all do. Write down this affirmation, or one of your own creation, and tuck it in your wallet. Then during those moments when you feel tempted to give up, when you feel beleaguered by misfortune, open the paper and read it aloud.

There is a perfect pattern in this universe
And I am a part of this design.
I believe in God; I believe in me;
I believe in my dream.
God, help me release any thoughts of blame for all my disappointments.
Help me let go of the need to control every outcome.
Teach me to take Your will and make it mine.
Help me see every "failure" as an opportunity to learn life's greater lesson.
Let my dream bring me closer to You, for this is the greatest dream of all.

Growing Your Dream

All great dream-builders experience failure. The power that failure will have in your life is determined by your response to it. You can find within every adversity the seed of a greater good.

1. Before you declare defeat, take inventory. There is a time to give up and a time to persist. When you reach a point where you do not know the proper direction, pause and ask God for a sign. Pray, "This, or something better." Pay attention, and you will be either granted renewed vigor for your dream or redirected to an even grander vision. Check your perspective. Often, how you look at your experience determines the difference between success and failure. Retest your dream to see if it still enlivens you with a passion and purpose that will help you grow and benefit others.

2. Make a stand for better over bitter. Great dream-builders refuse to become embittered even in the face of tremendous loss. If you refuse bitterness and choose to become better, you will find an inner reservoir from which to draw renewed strength and the inspiration and courage to keep going or to begin again.

3. Use your failure to move through the levels of awareness. In the initial phase, you feel like a victim who frequently is wondering, *Why Me?* As you cast off blame, you feel a new control: You are responsible for your own experience. You realize the great power you wield through your thinking and can direct that power toward a desired end. You experience life from personal power, life *By Me.* Deeper and more meaningful dreams are built as you release personal control and engage in cocreation with God. Here you align your will with God's and allow a higher power to work *Through Me.*

Part Four

GATHERING THE CROP

Chapter Ten

IMPACT:

Harvesting Your Dream

Men go abroad to wonder at the heights of mountains, at
the huge waves of the sea, at the long courses of the rivers,
at the vast compass of the ocean, at the circular motion of
the stars, and they pass themselves by without wonder.
—St. Augustine

♦ *Trust the Process: The Process Is the Product*
♦ *Savor the Fruits of Your Dream*
♦ *Reap the Infinite Harvest: You Thought You Were Building Your
  Dream, but Your Dream Was Building You*

We have built our field of dreams, and now it is time to harvest.
We planted the seeds of thought in fertile soil. We nourished
them with care. Even when the ground remained bare, when

scorching sun threatened to wither the roots, when we feared heavy rains would wash away the sprouts, we continued to tend our dream, holding tightly to our faith. And our faith has been rewarded. We marvel at what is now beginning to emerge. If we've treated the seed halfway right, we're struck by how God delights in giving us a wondrous bounty. Our dream ripens, bursting into being, filling every inch of our field with splendor; every stalk, laden with fruit, glows in the deep, harmonious colors of nature.

We experience a thrilling sense of abundance.

So much of our selves went into raising this crop. We can taste the toil, the pleasure, and the disappointment in every bite. If we buy an apple at the grocery store, it may look polished and perfect, but it lacks the distinctive tartness of one picked right off our tree. The one we grow is fresher; more important, it is our own. We fertilized the ground, pruned the branches, and protected the tree from pests. Somewhere in the process of that hard work, we came to recognize a greater meaning. Our toil and our devotion, combined with the power of God, has yielded a truly magnificent harvest. It is a harvest we could never have foreseen or obtained all on our own. It is the brilliant product of our co-creation with God.

By virtue of having built this dream, you enter what I call the field of impact. That is, the dream becomes more than a physical manifestation of your desire. Your dream can profoundly affect every aspect of your life and the lives of those around you. In truth, you can begin to experience impact at any step along the way of dream-building. But often you do not recognize the full power of this impact until you reap the harvest. Recall that the dream test required you to choose a desire that would cause you to grow into more of your true self. And now, as you stand in the midst of the matured crop of your life, you feel a pulsating energy, an enhanced aliveness. You have grown in patience, wisdom, and compassion; all of the fine qualities that humans can develop have evolved in your being and begun to radiate outward.

Remember Lisa, whose heart threatened to shut down like a broken furnace after her dream man went back to someone else? As she shivered in her cold house, awaiting the furnace repairman, Lisa vowed to keep an open heart despite the risk. That decision has impacted every relationship in her life. When she chose to become loving, she found not only more fulfillment with a future partner but a greater love with friends and family.

The dream test also required that others benefit from your undertaking. As it happens, sharing our harvest turns out to be one of our greatest joys. As we gather our crop we inevitably discover that we have produced far more than we can possibly use ourselves. We load up basket after basket of zucchini or tomatoes and haul them off to feed the neighbors.

My daughter, Jenny, in overcoming her fear of the water, impacted first her own life; then her story impacted others. The little girl who stopped clinging to the edge of the pool became the woman who had the courage to listen to and follow her heart, to postpone her marriage, even if it meant losing the man she loved. Janice, the forty-two-year-old woman who wanted to go to college but was afraid, told me that she began to master her fear after hearing me share Jenny's swimming story in church one Sunday.

People who impact others willingly share their largess and their light. Impact is so vital that my son Rich, an actor, dramatizes the concept in a humorous skit he occasionally performs during our church services. He has created a superhero character he calls Impact Person, who, as Rich puts it, "becomes faster than a negative thought, stronger than a bad mood, able to leap his greatest fear in a single bound." Impact people possess a secret weapon: They have the power to let the hand of God move through them and touch the lives of other people with their light and their love.

Judy, the single mother who wanted a home that logic dictated was beyond her means, became such an impact person. She stepped outside of ordinary thinking to achieve her dream, and in so doing was forever changed. Judy now has a reservoir of knowing. When another dream comes along that seems impossible, her faith will carry her into that new dream. She knows nothing is impossible.

The impact of Judy's dream is that anyone who has heard her story is inspired to step out and believe, "Maybe this could happen to me." I know several people who moved beyond their conventional thinking after hearing what Judy accomplished. One of those people was Randy, an auto mechanic who dreamed of having his own shop—specifically, one that specialized in Formula One racing cars. No bank would loan Randy money to finance his dream. Fighting discouragement, Randy lifted his thinking. It did something he hadn't considered before: he wrote a business plan and found four backers for the initial phase of his dream. After three months he had repaid his backers and hired two assistants. Judy's harvest did not disappear after a single growing season. The seed of faith that brought her crop to life continues to take root in the lives of others.

◆ Trust the Process: The Process Is the Product

A teacher who had gone to Africa with the Peace Corps received a beautiful seashell from a man whom she had been trying to assist. Knowing that the ocean was thirty miles away from where he lived and that there were no cars in his remote village, she was a little confused. "Where did you find this?" she asked him. "Did a trader bring it to your village?"

"No, no," he said, and told her that he had walked to a town along the coast.

She said, "You walked thirty miles to bring me a seashell? That would be sixty miles round trip! Thank you!"

"Yes," the man acknowledged. "Long walk part of gift."

When you make a present by hand, or devote time and energy to shopping for just the right thing, your efforts become part of the gift. Dream-building is a long walk for most of us. It wasn't always easy to reach this point. Sometimes you wanted to give up. You became tired or afraid, or you took a wrong turn. That you kept going produces benefits beyond what you can physically identify as a dream come true. Ultimately the long walk was worth it. The long walk—the process—is part of your gift.

Trust the process. If you are headed in a particular direction, confident of your purpose, you cannot help but bump into people proceeding along the same path. I have taken that long walk not once but many times. Looking back on the choices I have made with God's help fills me with awe and gratitude. As a young woman with a failed kidney, I remember thinking it didn't matter all that much if I died. From my limited view, I could not possibly see beyond my own suffering. But in a moment of co-creating with God, I decided to live. In choosing life, I was present to parent my child, and I went on to give birth to three more. My children have turned out to be one of my greatest blessings. Their field of impact radiates far beyond me.

When I made the decision to begin a new life after my marriage ended, its particulars were unknown to me. I dreamed of a truly compatible, spiritual partnership and opened myself to the possibility. I trusted that when the time came, I would willingly step forward in faith. I would risk my heart. When you're lonely, it's tempting to seek partnership by devoting all your energy to finding someone. Yet these frantic searches are not part of a process of trusting. You are more likely to attract a person with whom you will find spiritual kinship when you pursue that which makes you feel most fully alive. In my case, that was our new church home. The months of transition following our move to a permanent home were exciting but highly precarious. I plowed into the daily details with a vigor I had not known I possessed. And so it happened that when I was least looking for it, the universe rushed in to answer another dream.

Our church needed someone with financial acumen, a person with the skills and temperament to guide us through the mortgage loans, permit fees, and seemingly endless negotiations. Ed Morrissey not only had a background as a CPA but also had experience assisting church organizations with their finances. Little did Ed or I realize during those first two years of working together on the church's finances, when our conversations centered primarily on ledgers and fluctuating interest rates, that we would find a greater meaning together.

One day Ed called the church to ask about an irksome bill, and instead of greeting the church's CPA with my usual businesslike hello, I found myself hearing his voice on the other end of the line as if for the first time. In that instant something sparked between us, even though we could not physically see each other, and there has been no turning back.

I began seeing Ed as someone who wanted to do more than just add up numbers at the end of the month. This was a man of mission. He was helping to build our church. While in the army he ran a home for Korean orphans. He had helped start a charity to provide medical treatment to Portland's homeless. Ed and I found we had a great deal in common: Both of us shared a deep and abiding faith in God and had learned to trust the wisdom of our still, small voice. Ed had found his power to impact after he nearly lost everything to bankruptcy, as mentioned in chapter seven. As I got to know Ed better, I looked at the way he was living his life and recognized someone with whom I could find true spiritual partnership.

Once, impatient and unsure if Ed felt the same way about me, I asked him, "So, where do you have me parked in your mind? Are we just friends, or what?"

He looked right at me. "Friendship," he said, "is no small thing."

Having already mentally decided on chocolate for our wedding cake, I felt let down. "A friend?" I said to myself.

But he was right. Friendship is the basis for any lasting relationship. I needed to be patient and trust the process. Eight months after that conversation, he proposed.

Our love for each other has become the realization of our mutual lifelong dream to find partnership that would reach through every level of our being.

Over time we find that our process of dream-building leads us to service, and service has a tremendous impact. I was eating lunch with my son Mat at an outdoor market in Portland, when a member of our congregation walked by. It was a beautiful sunny day, and we invited Michael to join us. As we sat eating, Michael shared his story. He said, "You know, I was running on these very streets fourteen years ago." He looked at Mat and said, "If you don't believe there's a God, just look at me. Next week I'll have been in recovery fourteen years. These are the streets where I was lying, cheating, stealing three hundred dollars a day to feed my heroin habit, until I finally learned to surrender. It took the most horrible moment of my life, literally going into the gutter, before I was willing to let go. But I did let go, and God moved in."

As he was telling us his story, I marveled at how, out there in the sunshine, we were being treated to this wonderful, impromptu sermon. "There I was, twenty-eight days in the treatment program, and then I came to live in a halfway house, and they gave me a job washing windows. I thought, 'I can't wash windows. Somebody might see me.' I was quite an arrogant drug addict."

Michael went on, "One day I was washing windows, and all of a sudden I got it. 'This is my job. Washing windows. That's my job right now. To wash the windows of my perception. To wash the windows of my soul. To wash the windows of myself so that the true essence can shine forth.' "

Michael said he began to love those windows and really enjoy the cleaning of each one, recognizing that as he wiped each pane with renewed purpose, his own pain was coming clean. He moved into his dream of a sober, stable life, using the simple tools before him.

His "long walk" was in learning to wash windows enthusiastically. Those who become fully themselves in the process of fulfilling their dreams embrace enthusiasm, the magic sparkle that begins to bring forth the extraordinary.

My son Rich has also evolved for having trusted the process. He came to realize one of his greatest dreams by literally serving others. When Rich took off for Los Angeles to pursue his dream of being an actor, he had almost no money. He didn't have a job. He had nothing except his dream. But he moved confidently in the direction of that dream. He endeavored to live the life that he was imagining. He found a little room to rent and then he got a job working in a hotel doing room service.

After six months, the life Rich had imagined for himself had not come into being. He started questioning his dream; his belief in his dream began to contract instead of expand. He began to resent his job; if that was all he had, he felt, he didn't have very much. Rich called me one day, really depressed. "This isn't what I came down here for," he said, "to bring people chicken sandwiches at midnight." He feared his dream would not manifest itself, and he wondered if he should just give up and head home.

I said, "Rich, just keep holding the idea. Take the step that's in front of you and God will steer you into an opportunity. Just hang in there."

He called me about three days later and said, "You won't believe what happened. A couple of nights ago I decided that

God must have a plan for me. I was doing room service again and I decided I shouldn't be afraid. I needed to trust God's timing and learn more about serving. Up until then I was doing my job, but I wasn't really giving it my best. So I made a fresh start. I was doing the room service with a new attitude, and this guy I was serving asked me what I was doing in L.A. I told him about my dream of acting. He said that he knew the owner of a restaurant where the waiters dress up as characters, and they get a chance to practice their acting skills while they're waiting on people. He gave me the owner's name, and I called the guy. I went down for an interview yesterday. I tried out as three different characters, and they hired me! They'll even let me go for auditions when I have them. Now I get to play a character and practice my profession, and I'm even making more money!"

Rich had changed his mind about his job. He wasn't just delivering chicken sandwiches anymore; he renewed his mind so that God would have room to work through him in manifesting a portion of his dream. If you believe, "No, it's not possible to be an actor when all you're doing is room service," then you'll never make it out of the hotel. You'll live your life trapped in a place designed only for temporary stays, and you'll curse fate for refusing to allow you to reach the destination where you belong. Rich found his way out by performing the same tasks he had all along, only with a new attitude. I have seen again and again that when people focus on helping others from their present position—not waiting for that elusive day when they believe they can afford generosity or a big heart, but when they serve from where they stand—doors open. Rich's commitment to give his best at room service radiated a loving energy. God is love, the world is our mirror, and that energy is beamed right back at us. You attract to yourself whatever you radiate.

One of my favorite Buddhist sayings is: "Before enlightenment, chop wood and carry water. After enlightenment, chop wood and carry water." You can do your job and make it drudgery, or you can treat it as service. As you serve you become more aware of the presence of God and the wonder of simply being alive. Your task may not change, but how you experience that work is transformed. In the process of building the tangible portion of your dream, the intangible deeper qualities—an increased awareness and increased sense of aliveness—grow. This is the real product.

♦ Savor the Fruits of Your Dream

You need not wait for the harvest to savor these fruits. No matter where you are in your dream-building, you have grown in a way worthy of celebration. We can stay so focused on the future that we miss the beauty available in the present moment. The first shoot that springs from the earth and the first bloom on the zucchini are miracles of growth not to be dismissed or overlooked. And if the plant has been slow to bud, there's all the more reason to rejoice. People who savor the fruits of their dream do not lack for problems. In fact, their fruits taste all the sweeter because it took so much to ripen them.

There are many ways for you to savor the fruits of your dreams. You can enjoy the bounty of what you have grown, feast on the spiritual fruits, and share those fruits with others. You can become a mentor to help others plant their own dreams.

Something in every one of us wants to contribute, to make a difference in this world. Something in you knows you were born to influence, not just to accumulate. Today you can make a difference. You can bring a word of inspiration. Today you can extend God's love and shine your light in your corner of the world. There is so much darkness in our world, yet we can choose to shine the light of faith, hope, and love right where we are. Honor your heart. God has an outrageous offer for you, an outrageous offer for a life that will absolutely awaken and empower you, contribute to all, and bless our very planet.

My life has been blessed with an abundance of dreambuilders. I have watched them savor the fruits their lives have produced. I know a mail carrier who carries mail in such a way that any of us would be honored to receive our mail, because he first blesses epistle and junk mail alike before he places it in a mailbox. This is the act of carrying mail with the hands of Christ, the hands of Buddha, the hands of Krishna. I know a physician who sees more than a diseased kidney in bed 3A or a liver problem in bed 4C; he sees a whole person who may be experiencing kidney challenges or liver challenges but who nevertheless is a whole person. He treats the whole person to heal not only a disease but a life. I know a hair stylist who does more than just style the hair on people's heads; she helps people, knowing that they come for a soul styling in her presence. A man who is a member of our congregation told me, "Before I came here, if someone asked me where I worked, I would have told them I work at the city dump. Now I say I work at a healing center called the City Elimination Clinic, where we release our old junk."

Ed and I chose to savor the fruits of our dream by holding a blending ceremony prior to our wedding. This ceremony symbolized not only our union as man and wife, but the joining of our families: our parents, our children, and our children's children to come.

The children were an especially important concern for me. All too often I have seen men and women balk at building a relationship with their new partner's children. "Gee, she's the perfect woman for me, but she's got this kid, this baggage. . . ."

People who perceive their bounty as baggage are not savoring the fruits of their union. At best, they're tolerating them. Children know the difference.

I realized that the union between Ed and me would impact my daily life profoundly because his two children are so much younger than my own. At the time we decided to marry, my four children were twenty-seven, twenty-five, nineteen, and sixteen. Ed's two sons were eleven and six. I had been a parent since I was seventeen years old. At first I was tempted to turn away: "Oh, my gosh, do I want to raise kids again? I'm almost free of that."

One day, while praying, I asked God to either open my heart to these children or redirect my life. I asked: "Dear God, my youngest one is sixteen. Now you want me to take on helping to raise a six-year-old? You want me to go back ten years?"

I heard the voice gently respond: "Mary, I'm not sending you back ten years. I'm sending you forward."

My heart opened in a most remarkable way as I embraced these young boys in my life. God's grace moved in my heart, and I fell in love not only with Ed but with his sons.

For our blending ceremony, Ed and I chose the symbol of a family treasure chest. Two days before our wedding, Ed and his boys, along with my children and their partners, gathered for a special dinner. I asked all the children to bring something they considered symbolic of the family treasure we were committing to create. We set a hand-carved treasure chest in the center of the table and, one by one, each of us put in an item with special meaning. Ricardo, my two-year-old grandson, went first. He donated his pacifier, which we agreed symbolized the comfort we would bring to one another.

Ed's younger son, Matthew, then seven, brought a nine-volt battery, which he said represented energy for the family. Twelve-year-old Michael brought his favorite watch as a symbol of the importance of the time we would spend together.

My son Mathew was still recovering from his football injury. He had kept a football with him for months to remind him that dedication would eventually return him to the game he loved. Mat brought to the treasure box the laces he had cut from his football, a symbol of lacing together our family through dedication.

Then my older children and their partners each placed an item in the box. After Ed and I made our contributions, we prayed and closed our treasure box, knowing that its contents will always remain available to us all.

Rituals like these help us place a framework around the changes taking place in our evolution. That ceremony was the culmination of a dream, but it was also the beginning of another one. Our blending ceremony symbolized our commitment to build not just a good family but a great one. Building our lives together is building a new dream.

Do you recall Thoreau's lesson in the art of dream-building? He spent his life studying spirituality and concluded his major treatise with the wisdom gained from his sojourn at Walden Pond. As we look again at his message, we find opportunities to savor the fruits of our devotion and labor at each step along the way.

"*I learned this, at least, by my experiment: that if one advances confidently in the direction of his dreams . . .*" You cannot move toward anything fulfilling if you're not dreaming. Honor the discontent stirring deep in your soul. Your longings are calling you to a greater good. We listen to our desires and willingly take risks in order to bring those desires into form. Respect the feeling that's nudging you toward a greater experience. This is your life speaking to you, saying, "I'm glad you're restless. Your restlessness is a call to a greater life. Don't settle for a little life." You may not believe your heart's desire is possible, but as you come to understand and experience co-creation with God, you begin to believe in the impossible.

"*. . . and endeavors to live the life which he has imagined . . .*" God has given you the power to imagine. You can create the same life with different pictures to it over and over, year after year, or you can imagine a life carefully and vividly and distinctly. Set your intention for the dream you desire and put it to the highest spiritual test: Does the dream enliven me? Does it align with my core values? Will pursuing this dream cause me to grow into my greater self? Does the dream require God's help? Will the dream benefit others?

"*. . . he will meet with a success unexpected in common hours. He will put some things behind. . . .*" This is a success you cannot plan. This success is your birthright. You deserve to experience a wonderful life, to have your deepest dream come true. Focus on the good to discover your own core of innocence. Stop dragging Harry; leave behind the deadweight of your past, and practice gratitude. Savor the success that is already yours.

"*. . . pass an invisible boundary . . .*" As you proceed in your dream, you will be distracted and thrown off course by your fear, which gussies itself up in some pretty alluring disguises. You need to recognize fear as a companion in your journey, but you, not the fear, are the master. Do not let your fear keep you trapped behind some invisible boundary. As you feed your faith and starve your fear, you step confidently over the line and keep heading toward your destination.

"*New, universal, and more liberal laws will begin to establish themselves around and within him; or the old laws be expanded, and interpreted in his favor in a more liberal sense. . . .*" Infuse the universe with your treasure. Many people put off giving until they think they can afford it. If you truly desire an abundant life, you have to take the good you possess, bless it, and multiply it by circulating a portion to the universe. As you replenish the world around you with your time, talent, and treasure, you move forward. What you circulate comes back to you tenfold. As you circulate your good and move toward your dream with a giving heart, you feel as if new universal laws are at work for you. You step into the freely given abundance of the universe.

"He will live with the license of a higher order of beings. . . ." Forgiving others frees you to build the dreams close to your heart. Without forgiveness, your negative emotions leak toxic energy into every area of your life, stunting or entirely choking out your dreams. It is very easy to condemn the person who has wronged us, but if we can sense the being separate from the un-skillful behavior, we can begin to heal. Practice seeing the other person as someone who has forgotten his true self. You can forgive someone who has amnesia and acts in gross confusion. As you release yourself from blame and condemnation, you begin to live in an amplified field of freedom: the license of a higher order of beings.

"In proportion as he simplifies his life, the laws of the universe will appear less complex. . . ." As you move into your dream, you may feel as if you are stepping out onto thin air. But you are not alone. The still, small voice of inspired insight, the voice for God, exists in each one of us. You simplify your life by distinguishing that voice from all the chatter in your mind, all the doubts, fears, and voices of insecurity. Acknowledge the inner nudge toward outer motion. The knowing voice for God persistently nudges us in the direction of our highest good, providing us with signposts in the form of coincidence and inspired ideas. As you heed these signs and follow your guidance, the laws of the universe no longer seem so confounding. Everything that happens becomes part of a pattern. And as you align with this pattern of the universe, you feel empowered to take the next step.

". . . and solitude will not be solitude, nor poverty poverty, nor

weakness weakness. . . ." If you tell yourself, "I'm poor," then you will take no steps to move into your dream home. If you define yourself as unlovable, you increase the distance between yourself and the relationship you desire. It's time to redefine. Build a bigger believing by considering ideas outside conventional thinking. The genius of God inside you has no limits. Fortify yourself by developing partners in believing, people who can believe for you when you begin to doubt yourself.

"If you have built castles in the air, your work need not be lost: that is where they should be. . . ." All great dream-builders experience failure. They spend a portion of their lives building castles that they can never touch. If what you desire can never come to pass, take heart. In each adversity lies the seed of a greater good. God has not abandoned you. As you make a stand for better over bitter, you find that it is your very failures that can propel you toward a higher level of awareness.

"Now put the foundations under them." We put foundations under our dreams and make them real one day at a time, one step at a time, until we find that we too have joined the ranks of the great dream-builders. I encourage you to say in your prayers, "This, or something better," because that gives room for God to grow in you a greater dream, one that you cannot see from where you stand now. Keep moving vigorously in the direction of your dream. As each new dream comes to pass or falls by the wayside, you can continue to grow. Reserve a miracle zone in your mind, a place where no disbelief can taint or color or destroy your faith, a little reserve that says, "I don't know how my dream will happen, but I believe it can happen. I believe that the power of this universe is greater than any problem I face. I'm going to challenge the maps that I've held: the map that says I'm limited, the map that says my bank account drives my possibilities, the one telling me my education drives my possibilities, the one that says my family of origin drives my possibilities. I'm going to challenge those maps because there's a part

of me that is eternal. And I'm willing to give that part more attention. I'm going to reserve a corner of my mind for pure possibility and savor every moment, embracing it as a new possibility."

That space in our mind expands until we believe unconditionally in our dream. Your real self is so much grander and more majestic than anything you've imagined, and you and I are living out of only a portion of our real selves. You have the capacity for all kinds of miracles. Should we falter or even fail, that does not mean the miracle has eluded us. We can learn and grow even through suffering. We can move into a higher dimension of being as we begin to recognize ourselves as co-creators with God.

♦ Reap the Infinite Harvest: You Thought You Were Building Your Dream, but Your Dream Was Building You

In the movie *Mr. Holland's Opus*, a high-school music teacher dreams of writing a symphony. He has the passion to create a world-class symphony, and he hopes his music will one day earn him a great deal of money. He never realizes his dream, and finally he retires from teaching. Feeling dejected and lamenting his lost dream, he prepares to leave the building for the last time and walks into the school gymnasium. He stumbles upon a surprise party in his honor, where hundreds of his former students have gathered. The master of ceremonies is a woman who once lacked self-confidence and considered herself a failure. But through the encouragement of her former teacher, she found value in herself and went on to become governor of the state. She speaks before all those gathered: "We are your symphony, Mr. Holland. We are the notes of your opus. We are the notes of your life."

The great composition of Mr. Holland's life was helping others build their dreams; in so doing, he built himself. The eternal harvest of your dream is that which lives on beyond whatever outcome may occur. You thought you were building your dream; instead, your dream was building you.

You are not the same person as the one who began building the dream. You have reached the edge of who you knew yourself to be and stepped beyond to find that you contained so much more than you ever knew. Now you gather your crop at harvest and, in so doing, marvel not only at the bounty of the corn or deep red color of the tomatoes but at the miracle of growth. The greatest impact comes not from achieving your dream but from awakening to the person you become as you step into it. As you listen to the still, small voice of insight and pursue your dream for a higher good, spiritual gifts unfold like surprise presents. These gifts allow you to find pleasure and joy in all that surrounds you, gifts that far exceed any relationship, career, or award you had originally desired. The person you evolve into as you build your dream through the struggles, victories, and disappointments—this is the true harvest. Your evolution can begin at any age and knows no bounds.

You will be rewarded with something far greater than the car, the career, or the relationship that was the original object of your desire. You, living in this grander scheme, are then able to take on an even more magnificent dream. Your vision has expanded. You now see a dream that never even touched your mind at an earlier stage. Then you vigorously pursue the new dream, and once more you grow into a greater version of your real self. As this pattern repeats itself again and again, you finally discover that there is no separation between yourself and what you dream. You become your dream.

People whose dream has built them know something that the embittered and unhappy among us do not. They know that their dreams are not separate from the rest of their lives. They do not yearn for a prosperous business or a loving relationship one minute and shortchange the baby-sitter or spurn their best friend the next. They realize that the person they become as a result of this often arduous journey is itself the fulfillment of a dream. The perfect job or relationship isn't most important. What's important is that through attempting to obtain a particular dream, you can grow your whole life more fully. If, through the process of building your dream, you give yourself the opportunity to let that God seed in you grow and develop, you become more of the real you. True dream-builders develop conscious contact with their Creator while finding a more personal relationship with

The philoso⸍   ⸍s said this almost two thousand years ago: "Yc⸍   ⸍on of the essence of God; and contain par⸍   ⸍hen, are you ignorant of your nobl⸍   ⸍ whence you came? Why dc⸍   ⸍ting, who you are who e⸍   ⸍know that it is the Div⸍   ⸍ You carry God about wi⸍   ⸍ng of it."

⸍ght her dream was complete ⸍oved. She was no longer alone. ⸍d be sweet, she thought, and it ⸍d her husband had shared with his ⸍ildren from his first marriage. Then ⸍decided to sue for full custody, and a tria⸍   ⸍denly life was overflowing with lawyers, bills, sha⸍   ⸍d resentments. Cheryl and I talked a great deal, and she ⸍   ⸍to see that the problem was not "out there," that the problem was not her husband's former wife. Without even knowing it, Cheryl had been nourishing the seeds that produced a fruit she did not now want to eat. She came to see an opportunity to clear the field and to begin to sow new seeds.

She realized how many times over the last two years she had created dissension through her own jealousy. Cheryl had resented her husband's first wife, envious that this woman still called her former in-laws Mom and Dad. She paused and looked honestly at her part in the present conflict. She stopped feeling like a victim. She knew she couldn't control the outcome of the trial, but she could influence the process. She asked God to move through her.

If it is true that all our experiences mirror ourselves, then we must look honestly at the troubling reflection and say, "What part of me has created this conflict? The problem is not out there. The crop I harvest comes from the seeds I have sown." Since Cheryl wanted to reap a harvest of love, she decided to sow the seeds of greater loving. She wrote her husband's ex-wife a letter that said she was truly sorry for her part in causing conflict.

The day before the scheduled trial Cheryl came to a prayer meeting where she expressed her terror. She was afraid of losing partial custody. More than that, she was afraid of the anguish this trial could cause her stepchildren. No longer did she want to fight with their mother, but what more could she do? In her mind she envisioned going into court. Someone would win. Someone would lose. The greatest good she could do was in simply refusing to throw any more mud.

One member of the prayer group suggested that in the presence of God's love the problem could just dissolve. The idea that there could really be a peaceful solution had never occurred to her. Cheryl asked us to join with her in prayer that God would lead the three parents in finding a harmonious and healthy resolution for all involved.

Late that afternoon she returned home to find a message on her answering machine. Her husband's first wife had called to say she had come to a decision. She said, "Thank you for your letter. I have decided this should not be a legal issue. I think it's a therapy issue. Let's all go into counseling so that together we can find a way to co-parent our children."

Cheryl thought her harvest lay exclusively in building a life with her husband and his children. In accepting the children's mother, she grew in her own capacity to give and receive love.

When you live your dream each day, you have reached the highest state of awakening. Recall the earlier stages: In the initial level of awareness, you are a victim: This is the *Why Me?* level. You exaggerate, flagellate, and aggravate your problems, forever cemented to your perception of powerlessness. In the second level, *By Me*, you begin to discover your personal capacity for accomplishment. The danger here is in trying to force results purely with your own will. You can wield tremendous power but still remain shy of true fulfillment. In *Through Me*, you co-create your experience with God, aligning your limited perspective with a grander plan.

Ordinary people experience flashes of the extraordinary as they take the final step of faith. As you practice dream-building you will experience moments of pure grace when you realize God is working *As Me*. The dream you thought you were building indeed has built you. As the Apostle Paul says, "Behold, I tell you a mystery: We shall not all sleep, but we shall all be changed in a moment, in the twinkling of an eye."

In that twinkling comes a burst of clarity that forever changes our lives. We say, "Aha!" We thought we were building a dream. In a flash, we glimpse whom we have become or whom we might become as the product of our dream-building. Goody Cable felt that flash as she sat in the library of her completed hotel with the coffee almost gone, rain pounding against the windows, and people around her cozily sharing their deepest thoughts. Scott, the contractor who felt shame over not having served in the Vietnam War, felt that flash when a roomful of veterans greeted his confession not with disdain but with acceptance.

We can all experience a glimmer of what it feels like to live

As Me. Think of mothers and fathers as they set a lovingly prepared meal before their family, or builders who step back to gaze at their completed project. The writer who may be composing jingles all at once feels the creativity flow through his fingers onto the page; the words are beyond anything he ever dreamed of composing. The actor in a community theater becomes Macbeth, and just for a moment the audience knows it, too. A woman with whom I exercise felt such a flash when she realized she had been holding back from every relationship in her life, just as she had held back from a father who was never available for her. The wall she had built to protect herself had actually been a barrier to what she wanted most. "In this moment, I literally felt something crumbling inside, and my heart expanded," she told me. Since that time she has been walking around in love—not with a particular person, but with life.

This state of pure grace, this fountain of inspiration, cannot be forced. You can allow it to happen only by living a pure and compassionate life. When Jesus says, "Follow me," He models a pattern of a life fully in harmony with the greatest good possible.

We live at the *As Me* level when we experience no separation from God. The dreams we build on the earth are temporary, but the transformation in our soul is eternal. Building our life as a co-creator with God is the most important thing we will ever do.

As you move through each step of building your dream, you grow not only closer to achieving a harvest you can smell, taste, and feel, but into the eternal harvest of awakening.

> *The field is ready.*
> *The seed is good.*
> *Your life is willing.*
> *Plant, my friend.*
> *Your harvest is assured.*

tated was beyond her means, became such an impact person. She stepped outside of ordinary thinking to achieve her dream, and in so doing was forever changed. Judy now has a reservoir of knowing. When another dream comes along that seems impossible, her faith will carry her into that new dream. She knows nothing is impossible.

The impact of Judy's dream is that anyone who has heard her story is inspired to step out and believe, "Maybe this could happen to me." I know several people who moved beyond their conventional thinking after hearing what Judy accomplished. One of those people was Randy, an auto mechanic who dreamed of having his own shop—specifically, one that specialized in Formula One racing cars. No bank would loan Randy money to finance his dream. Fighting discouragement, Randy lifted his thinking. It did something he hadn't considered before: he wrote a business plan and found four backers for the initial phase of his dream. After three months he had repaid his backers and hired two assistants. Judy's harvest did not disappear after a single growing season. The seed of faith that brought her crop to life continues to take root in the lives of others.

♦ Trust the Process: The Process Is the Product

A teacher who had gone to Africa with the Peace Corps received a beautiful seashell from a man whom she had been trying to assist. Knowing that the ocean was thirty miles away from where he lived and that there were no cars in his remote village, she was a little confused. "Where did you find this?" she asked him. "Did a trader bring it to your village?"

"No, no," he said, and told her that he had walked to a town along the coast.

She said, "You walked thirty miles to bring me a seashell? That would be sixty miles round trip! Thank you!"

"Yes," the man acknowledged. "Long walk part of gift."

Remember Lisa, whose heart threatened to shut down like a broken furnace after her dream man went back to someone else? As she shivered in her cold house, awaiting the furnace repairman, Lisa vowed to keep an open heart despite the risk. That decision has impacted every relationship in her life. When she chose to become loving, she found not only more fulfillment with a future partner but a greater love with friends and family.

The dream test also required that others benefit from your undertaking. As it happens, sharing our harvest turns out to be one of our greatest joys. As we gather our crop we inevitably discover that we have produced far more than we can possibly use ourselves. We load up basket after basket of zucchini or tomatoes and haul them off to feed the neighbors.

My daughter, Jenny, in overcoming her fear of the water, impacted first her own life; then her story impacted others. The little girl who stopped clinging to the edge of the pool became the woman who had the courage to listen to and follow her heart, to postpone her marriage, even if it meant losing the man she loved. Janice, the forty-two-year-old woman who wanted to go to college but was afraid, told me that she began to master her fear after hearing me share Jenny's swimming story in church one Sunday.

People who impact others willingly share their largess and their light. Impact is so vital that my son Rich, an actor, dramatizes the concept in a humorous skit he occasionally performs during our church services. He has created a superhero character he calls Impact Person, who, as Rich puts it, "becomes faster than a negative thought, stronger than a bad mood, able to leap his greatest fear in a single bound." Impact people possess a secret weapon: They have the power to let the hand of God move through them and touch the lives of other people with their light and their love.

Judy, the single mother who wanted a home that logic dic-

Gratitudes

A HEARTFELT THANK YOU—

To Christy Scattarella, who helped me translate stories, principles, and practices into the written word. You are wonderful.

To Melody Englund and Ginger Hendricks for your assistance in research, editing, and overall support.

To my editor, Toni Burbank, for your belief in this project and your endless attention and help in making the message clearer and stronger.

To everyone who generously shared their story so others might be inspired and blessed.

To the congregation of Living Enrichment Center for showing me again and again the power of practicing these principles. Your lives are living examples.

To Haven Boggs for your care and support in this project and many others.

To my dear friends Joan and Scott Benge, Rick and Mary Ellen Brandeburg, Colleen Schuerlein and David and Linda Swanson. Your friendship is one of my life's great blessings.

To my parents, Jack and Dorothy Manin, and my sister, Jackie Henry. Your belief in and encouragement of me has been more support than you can ever know.

To my wonderful children for being truly who you are and for your graciousness in support and sharing of yourselves.

To these dear and courageous souls spreading the good news through the gospel of their own lives and who personally take precious time to encourage and support me: Leo Booth, Joan Borysenko, Howard Caesar, Alan Cohen, Wayne Dyer, Gay and Kathlyn Hendricks, Jean Houston, Barbara Marx Hubbard, Marianne Williamson, and Gary Zukav.

To Ed, my husband, my love, my partner, and my best friend. You see, support, coach, and call forth the great dreams of my heart. Without you this book would never have been written. Because of you, I am eternally grateful. Thank you, my love.